BRITISH WOMEN FICTION WRITERS

of the 19th Century

BRITISH WOMEN FICTION WRITERS
of the 19th Century

Edited and with an Introduction by

Harold Bloom

CHELSEA HOUSE PUBLISHERS

Philadelphia

ON THE COVER: Emily Mary Osborn, *The Flower Seller*. Gavin Graham Gallery, London, Great Britain. Photo Credit: Bridgeman/Art Resource, New York.

CHELSEA HOUSE PUBLISHERS

EDITOR-IN-CHIEF   Stephen Reginald
MANAGING EDITOR   James D. Gallagher
PRODUCTION MANAGER   Pamela Loos
PICTURE EDITOR   Judy Hasday
ART DIRECTOR   Sara Davis
SENIOR PRODUCTION EDITOR   Lisa Chippendale

WOMEN WRITERS OF ENGLISH AND THEIR WORKS:
  British Women Fiction Writers of the 19th Century

PROJECT EDITOR   Robert Green
CONTRIBUTING EDITOR   Anne Horn
SENIOR EDITOR   Therese De Angelis
INTERIOR AND COVER DESIGNER   Alison Burnside
EDITORIAL ASSISTANT   Anne Hill

Introduction © 1998 by Harold Bloom

First Printing
1 3 5 7 9 8 6 4 2

Library of Congress Cataloging-in-Publication Data

British women fiction writers of the 19th century / edited and with an introduction
  by Harold Bloom.
    p.   cm. — (Women writers of English and their works)
  Includes bibliographical references.
  ISBN 0-7910-4482-3. — ISBN 0-7910-4498-X (pbk.)
    1. English fiction—Women authors—Bio-bibliography—Dictionaries. 2. Women and
literature—Great Britain—History—19th century—Dictionaries. 3. Women novelists,
English—19th century—Biography—Dictionaries. 4. English fiction—19th century—Bio-
bibliography—Dictionaries. 5. English fiction—Women authors—Dictionaries. 6. English
fiction—19th century—Dictionaries. I. Bloom, Harold. II. Series.
PR868.W6B75   1998   97-50561
823.8099287'09034—dc21   CIP

CONTENTS

Elizabeth Gaskell 138

Harriet Martineau 160

BRITISH WOMEN FICTION WRITERS

of the 19th Century

THE ANALYSIS OF WOMEN WRITERS

HAROLD BLOOM

I APPROACH THIS SERIES with a certain wariness, since so much of classical feminist literary criticism has founded itself upon arguments with that phase of my own work that began with *The Anxiety of Influence* (first published in January 1973). Someone who has been raised to that bad eminence—*The Patriarchal Critic*—is well advised that he trespasses upon sacred ground when he ventures to inquire whether indeed there are indisputable differences, imaginative and cognitive, between the literary works of women and those of men. If these differences are so substantial as pragmatically to make an authentic difference, does that in turn make necessary different aesthetic standards for judging the achievements of men and of women writers? Is Emily Dickinson to be read as though she has more in common with Elizabeth Barrett Browning than with Ralph Waldo Emerson?

Is Elizabeth Bishop a great poet because she triumphantly meets the same aesthetic criteria satisfied by Wallace Stevens, or should we evaluate her by criteria she shares with Marianne Moore, but not with Stevens? Are there crucial gender-based differences in the representations of Esther Summerson by Charles Dickens in *Bleak House*, and of Dorothea Brooke by George Eliot in *Middlemarch*? Does Samuel Richardson's Clarissa Harlowe convince us that her author was a male when we contrast her with Jane Austen's Elizabeth Bennet? Do women poets have a less agonistic relationship to female precursors than male poets have to their forerunners? Two eminent pioneers of feminist criticism, Sandra Gilbert and Susan Gubar, have suggested that women writers suffer more from an anxiety of authorship than they do from influence anxieties, while another important feminist critic, Elaine Showalter, has suggested that women writers, early and late, work together in a kind of quiltmaking, each doing her share while avoiding any contamination of creative envy in regard to other writers, provided that they be women. Can it be true that, in the aesthetic sphere, women do not beware women and do not suffer from the competitiveness and jealousy that alas do exist in the professional and sexual domains? Is there something in the area of literature, when practiced by women, that changes and purifies mere human nature?

I cannot answer any of these questions, yet I do think it is vital and clarifying to raise them. There is a current fashion, in many of our institutions of higher education, to insist that English Romantic poetry cannot be studied in the old way, with an exclusive emphasis upon the works of William Blake, William Wordsworth, Samuel Taylor Coleridge, Lord Byron, Percy Bysshe Shelley, John Keats, and John Clare. Instead, the Romantic poets are taken to include Felicia Hemans, Laetitia Landon, Charlotte Smith, and Mary Tighe, among others. It would be heartening if we could believe that these are unjustly neglected poets, but their current revival will be brief. Similarly, anthologies of 17th-century English literature now tend to include the Duchess of Newcastle as well as Aphra Behn, Lady Mary Chudleigh, Anne Killigrew, Anne Finch, Countess of Winchilsea, and others. Some of these—Anne Finch in particular—wrote well, but a situation in which they are more read and studied than John Milton is not one that is likely to endure forever. The consequences of making gender a criterion for aesthetic choice must finally destroy all serious study of imaginative literature as such.

In their *Norton Anthology of Literature by Women*, Sandra Gilbert and Susan Gubar conclude their introduction to Elizabeth Barrett Browning by saying that "she constantly tested herself against the highest standards of male-defined poetic genres," a true if ambiguous observation. They then print her famous "The Cry of the Children," an admirably passionate ode that protests the cruel employment of little children in British Victorian mines and factories. Unfortunately, this well-meant prophetic affirmation ends with this, doubtless its finest stanza:

XIII

They look up with their pale and sunken faces,
　　And their look is dread to see,
For they mind you of their angels in high places,
　　With eyes turned on Deity.
"How long," they say, "how long, O cruel nation,
　　Will you stand, to move the world, on a child's heart,—
Stifle down with a mailèd heel its palpitation,
　　And tread onward to your throne amid the mart?
Our blood splashes upward, O goldheaper,
　　And your purple shows your path!
But the child's sob in the silence curses deeper
　　Than the strong man in his wrath."

If you read this aloud, then you may find yourself uncomfortable, on a strictly aesthetic basis, which would not vary if you were told that this had been composed by a male Victorian poet. In their selections from Elizabeth Bishop, Gilbert and Gubar courageously reprint Bishop's superb statement explaining her refusal to permit her poems to be included in anthologies of women's writing:

> Undoubtedly gender does play an important part in the making of any art, but art is art and to separate writings, paintings, musical compositions, etc., into sexes is to emphasize values in them that are *not* art.

That credo of Elizabeth Bishop's is to me the Alpha and Omega of critical wisdom in regard to all feminist literary criticism. Gender studies are precisely that: they study gender, and not aesthetic value. If your priorities are historical, social, political, and ideological, then gender studies clearly are more than justified. Perhaps they are a way to justice, or at least to more justice than women have received throughout thousands of years of male domination and aggression. Yet that is a very different matter from the now vexed issue of aesthetic value. Biographical criticism, like the different modes of historicist and psychological criticism, always has relied upon a kind of implicit gender studies and doubtless will benefit, as other modes will, by a making explicit of such considerations, particularly in regard to women writers.

Each volume in this series contains copious refutations of, and replies to, the traditionally aesthetic stance that I have advocated here. These introductory remarks aspire only to a questioning, and not a challenging, of feminist literary criticism. There are no longer any Patriarchal Critics; they are all dinosaurs, fabulous beasts fit for revival only in horror films. Sometimes I sadly think of myself as Bloom Brontosaurus, amiably left behind by the fire and the flood. But more often I go on reading the great women writers, searching for the aesthetic difference that yet may prove to be there, but which has not yet been found.

I N T R O D U C T I O N

FOUR OF THE GREATEST British novelists were women writing in the nineteenth century: Jane Austen, George Eliot, Charlotte and Emily Brontë. In all of the century now ending, only Virginia Woolf among British fiction writers approached their eminence. Elizabeth Bowen and Iris Murdoch, though considerable artists, were of another order, comparable say to Elizabeth Gaskell of the earlier period. It seems to me an enigma worth pondering that an era in which women have been freer than ever before to fully develop their gifts has not shown an aesthetic achievement dwarfing the previous century. Virginia Woolf made the prophecy that "Shakespeare's sister," stifled in the earlier time, would emerge in a more enlightened age. Perhaps she yet will come, to astonish those who follow us in the twenty-first century, but her appearance will have little to do with feminist ideology. Austen, George Eliot, and the Brontës demonstrate that enormous literary genius is a very rare endowment, essentially independent of social determinations.

It is accurate to say that among nineteenth-century British writers, only Charles Dickens ranks with the four great women novelists. Sir Walter Scott, Anthony Trollope, William Makepeace Thackeray, even Thomas Hardy, cannot match Austen, the Brontës, and George Eliot in the art of fiction. Yet in the twentieth century, the panoply of male novelists in Great Britain is extraordinary: Joseph Conrad, E. M. Forster, D. H. Lawrence, James Joyce, and Samuel Beckett among them. The conclusion again seems inevitable: novelists are like poets, composers, painters, and sculptors in that they manifest, at their most sublime, by accident (or nature) rather than by historical or social conditioning. You can encourage competence, perhaps even talent, by enlarging and democratizing the public sphere, but genius will not be engendered by social engineering or by ideological revolution. No British woman poet of our century is worthy of critical comparison with Christina Rossetti or Emily Brontë. Even the best American women poets of our time—Marianne Moore, Elizabeth Bishop, May Swenson—will not sustain the sublime company of Emily Dickinson.

No critic, of whatever persuasion, would commit the error of regarding Jane Austen, George Eliot, and the Brontë sisters as a continuous tradition. Austen's deepest affinities were with Dr. Samuel Johnson and with Samuel Richardson, very different indeed from George Eliot's Wordsworthianism and the Brontës' fierce attachment to Byron. All that truly allies these four great novelists is their astonishing mastery. We have lived, since the later 1960s, in a critical climate for which historicism is everything and individuality nothing. We have had most peculiar dogmas imposed upon us: "the death of the author" and "the unreality of the self." Professors of Literature now frequently profess everything except imaginative literature: cultural history, politics, consciousness-raising, and a considerable intensity of racial, gender, ethnic, and sexually-oriented cheerleading. The highest values of reading Jane Austen, George Eliot, and the Brontë sisters remain aesthetic: all of them served the interest of art. They reward us with heightened perceptions, ghostlier demarcations, more profound cognitions, keener sounds. But I suggest that now they have a particular usefulness in our confused time. Their genius was their own, emanating from personal endowment. Each, an original moralist, valued imaginative sympathy and the integrity of the self over any creed or societal persuasion. We honor them most by emulating their independence of all cant and rant.

JANE AUSTEN
1775-1817

JANE AUSTEN was born on December 16, 1775, in Hampshire, England. She was the seventh of eight children born to the Reverend George Austen and Cassandra Leigh Austen. Although Jane briefly attended two schools (one run by a Mrs. Cawley and the Abbey School in Reading), she received most of her education at home, where she began to write plays and stories at around twelve years of age. These works are now collected in *The Juvenilia of Jane Austen and Charlotte Brontë*.

Very little is known about Austen's life, which appears to have been uneventful and centered around her family. Her appearance, according to family and friends, was attractive. Her art, according to herself, was rather slight. Indeed, she appeared to equate her literary endeavors with such ladylike accomplishments as needlework or singing, finding it "rather too light and bright and sparkling." Austen began her first novel, "Marianne and Elinor," in 1794. Like many of her novels, it would wait years for publication; when it appeared as *Sense and Sensibility* in 1811, it had been extensively revised. Similarly, *Northanger Abbey*, Austen's spoof of the "Gothic novel," would wait even longer. Written in 1798 as "Susan," it was not published until after the author's death.

Although most of Austen's plots center around courtship and marriage, she never married. She is believed to have had one love affair, however, and to have received—and rejected—a proposal from a Harris Bigg-Wither. Austen moved with her mother and sister to Bath in 1801, to Southhampton in 1805, and to Chawton Cottage, in Hampshire, in 1809. These moves reflected the the three Austen women's continuing economic struggles, but evidence suggests that Austen's quiet life at Chawton Cottage—located on the estate of Jane's brother, Edward, who had been adoped by Thomas Knight—was not unhappy.

In 1811, Austen began to publish her work. She brought out *Sense and Sensibilty* first, in 1811, anonymously and at her own expense. It was followed by *Pride and Prejudice* in 1813. The novel was a revision of her earlier work, *First Impressions*, and was advertised as the work of the anonymous author of *Sense and Sensibility*. *Mansfield Park* was published anonymously in 1814, and sold out before the year was done. Austen found a new publisher for *Emma*, which appeared in 1815. The next year, a second edition of *Mansfield Park* came out, and in 1817, Austen wrote *Persuasion*, which many scholars believe is a reworking of *The Watsons*, a novel she had left unfinished a decade earlier. During that year, however, she was suffering from Addison's disease. Although her family sought treatment for her at Winchester in May, she died two months later, on July 18, 1817. Austen was buried in Winchester Cathedral. After her death, her family destroyed her letters in an effort to protect her reputation. Posthumous publication of her writings continued: *Northanger Abbey and Persuasion* appeared in 1818; in 1820, her juvenilia and a fragment of an earlier novel were published. Today she is considered a classic of the English canon.

CRITICAL EXTRACTS

SIR WALTER SCOTT

Accordingly a style of novel has arisen, within the last fifteen or twenty years, differing from the former in the points upon which the interest hinges; neither alarming our credulity nor amusing our imagination by wild variety of incident, or by those pictures of romantic affection and sensibility, which were formerly as certain attributes of fictitious characters as they are of rare occurrence among those who actually live and die. The substitute for these excitements, which had lost much of their poignancy by the repeated and injudicious use of them, was the art of copying from nature as she really exists in the common walks of life, and presenting to the reader, instead of the splendid scenes of an imaginary world, a correct and striking representation of that which is daily taking place around him.

In adventuring upon this task, the author makes obvious sacrifices, and encounters peculiar difficulty. He who paints from *le beau idéal*, if his scenes and sentiments are striking and interesting, is in a great measure exempted from the difficult task of reconciling them with the ordinary probabilities of life: but he who paints a scene of common occurrence, places his composition within that extensive range of criticism which general experience offers to every reader. The resemblance of a statue of Hercules we must take on the artist's judgment; but every one can criticize that which is presented as the portrait of a friend, or neighbour. Something more than a mere sign-post likeness is also demanded. The portrait must have spirit and character, as well as resemblance; and being deprived of all that, according to Bayes, goes 'to elevate and surprise,' it must make amends by displaying depth of knowledge and dexterity of execution. We, therefore, bestow no mean compliment upon the author of *Emma*, when we say that, keeping close to common incidents, and to such characters as occupy the ordinary walks of life, she has produced sketches of such spirit and originality, that we never miss the excitation which depends upon a narrative of uncommon events, arising from the consideration of minds, manners, and sentiments, greatly above our own. In this class she stands almost alone; for the scenes of Miss Edgeworth are laid in higher life, varied by more romantic incident, and by her remarkable power of embodying and illustrating national character. But the author of *Emma* confines herself chiefly to the middling classes of society; her most distinguished characters do not rise greatly above well-bred country gentlemen and ladies; and those which are sketched with most originality and precision, belong to a class rather below that standard. The narrative of all her novels is composed of such common occurrences as may have fallen under the observation of most folks; and her dramatis personæ conduct themselves upon the motives and principles which the readers may recognize as ruling their own and that of most of their acquaintances. ⟨. . .⟩

The author's knowledge of the world, and the peculiar tact with which she presents characters that the reader cannot fail to recognize, reminds us something of the merits of the Flemish school of painting. The subjects are not often elegant, and certainly never grand; but they are finished up to nature, and with a precision which delights the reader. This is a merit which it is very difficult to illustrate by extracts, because it pervades the whole work, and is not to be comprehended from a single passage.

⟨. . . Her merit⟩ consists much in the force of a narrative conducted with much neatness and point, and a quiet yet comic dialogue, in which the characters of the speakers evolve themselves with dramatic effect. The faults, on the contrary, arise from the minute detail which the author's plan comprehends. Characters of folly or simplicity, such as those of old Woodhouse and Miss Bates, are ridiculous when first presented, but if too often brought forward or too long dwelt upon, their prosing is apt to become as tiresome in fiction as in real society. Upon the whole, the turn of this author's novels bears the same relation to that of the sentimental and romantic cast, that cornfields and cottages and meadows bear to the highly adorned grounds of a show mansion, or the rugged sublimities of a mountain landscape. It is neither so captivating as the one, nor so grand as the other, but it affords to those who frequent it a pleasure nearly allied with the experience of their own social habits; and what is of some importance, the youthful wanderer may return from his promenade to the ordinary business of life, without any chance of having his head turned by the recollection of the scene through which he has been wandering.

—Sir Walter Scott, "Emma," *Quarterly Review* (October 1815), excerpted in *The New Moulton's Library of Literary Criticism*, Vol. 6, ed. Harold Bloom (New York: Chelsea House Publishers, 1987), 3457–59

T. E. KEBBEL

No doubt Miss Austen belongs essentially to the eighteenth-century school of literature. There is little we should now call romance in any one of her five novels. They are good genteel-comedies. They play the surface of life, and represent its phenomena with the most finished elegance. But they do not stir the deeper passions, or more tumultuous emotions of our nature. We should question if a single page that Miss Austen has written has ever moistened the eyelid of the most impressionable man, woman, or child who has lived since she first began to write. On the other hand, the quiet fun, the inexhaustible sly humour, the cheerful healthy tone, the exquisite purity, and the genuine goodness which are reflected in every line she wrote, carry us down the sluggish stream of her stories without either weariness or excitement, and with a constant sense of being amused, refreshed, and benefited. In these respects she has been compared to Addison. And we think the comparison a just one. ⟨. . .⟩

To those critics who would ask us what moral purpose Miss Austen proposed to herself in these delineations of common-place society, it is perhaps enough to reply that every picture of human life, however trite or conventional, must have a moral of its own if we have only eyes to see it. Without plunging into any such profound question as the ethics of art in general, we may affirm that nearly all Miss Austen's novels have a very plain moral, and one that admits of easy application. All of them have a family likeness, and a general tendency to bring out into prominent relief the peril of being guided by appearances. The danger to which a young lady is exposed by imagining too readily that a polite gentleman is in love with her; and the danger to which a young gentleman is exposed by imagining too readily that a good-natured girl is in love with him; the misunderstandings that arise from careless conversation, from exaggerated reserve, from overrated pretensions, from all the little mistakes which create the common embarrassments of ordinary society; these are the minor mischiefs which her pen is devoted to setting in their proper light, and no man or woman turned forty will deny that such work may be of great utility, or that anybody who chooses to read her novels with a view to practical instruction may learn a great deal from them. Our space will not allow us to illustrate these remarks by examples. But we refer our readers more particularly to *Emma* and *Persuasion* in confirmation of the truth of them.

We have yet to mention two of Miss Austen's most characteristic excellencies—her dialogue and her style. In regard to the former we must of course remember what a vast change in this respect has passed over society since she wrote. For all that, the dialogues in Miss Austen's novels strike us as much more natural than the dialogues in Richardson's, upon whom she had apparently endeavored to form her own. But her genius was too strong for her. She wrote, moreover, only upon those scenes of life with which she was perfectly familiar; whereas Richardson was in total ignorance of the habits and conversation of that society which it was his ambition to describe. There is something very quaint about the conversations in Miss Austen's novels, but we cannot help feeling certain that it was exactly what people of that class in those days would have said. When Anne Elliott, a young lady of the period, advises Captain Bennick, a young officer in the navy, who is given to quoting Byron, to go through a course of our best English moralists, she does so in perfect good faith, and without a suspicion of wrong. But how charming is the art that can make us accept this as the perfectly natural thing for her to have said on the occasion. The conversation between Henry Tilney and Catherine Morland, on the first night of their meeting in the Bath ball-rooms, is another instance of the same kind, though not so striking perhaps at the first. There is, of course, always a difficulty in placing one's self entirely *en rapport* with any writer who describes the living manners of his or her own age, which is at a long distance from his own. Do what we can, we feel solitary in their company. When we read a writer of our own day who describes the manner of a hundred years ago, we feel that we have a companion in our enjoyment. That cannot be felt by any one who reads Miss Austen.

Her style deserves the highest commendation. It has all the form and finish of the eighteenth century, without being in the least degree stilted or unnatural. It has all the tone of good society without being in the least degree insipid. For a specimen of crisp, rich English, combining all the vigour of the masculine with all the delicacy of the feminine style, we suggest the opening chapter of *Northanger Abbey* as a model for any young lady writer of the present age.

—T. E. Kebbel, "Jane Austen," *Fortnightly Review* (February 1870), excerpted in *The New Moulton's Library of Literary Criticism*, Vol. 6, ed. Harold Bloom (New York: Chelsea House Publishers, 1987), 3450–51

JANE NARDIN

In *Pride and Prejudice*, Jane Austen makes the basic assumption that a person's outward manners mirror his moral character. If, in this novel, a man or woman always displays good manners, it is perfectly safe for the reader to assume that his character is truly good. The characters in the novel continually try to evaluate one another's manners and the moral worth to which they are a clue. Often these evaluations are wrong, but it is important to note that they are never wrong because the manners of the individual in question have lied about his character. If an attempt to judge character from manners backfires in the world of *Pride and Prejudice*, it is invariably either because the judging individual has misperceived the nature of the manners of the individual he is judging, or because the standard of propriety according to which the judgment is being made is a mistaken one. The problem of judgment in *Pride and Prejudice* is not, as it is in *Persuasion*, for example, primarily a question of penetrating behind the facade of the manners to the reality of moral character; rather it is a question of perceiving and estimating the nature of an individual's manners with a reasonable degree of accuracy.

In a novel where a person's public manners are assumed to be an accurate clue to his private character, the definition of what truly proper manners actually are has an extraordinary importance. The reader must be convinced that the standard of propriety in question is one to which intelligent people of good feeling can give their wholehearted adherence. Jane Austen, it seems to me, achieves this aim in *Pride and Prejudice*. Elizabeth Bennet's standards of decorous behavior do not grate upon the reader's sensibilities as, for example, Elinor Dashwood's excessively rigid and stoical conception of propriety sometimes does. Yet Elizabeth's standards of propriety, at least at the close of the novel, are being presented as identical to the best standards of proper behavior held by her society, as well as identical to the standards of the novel as a whole—and so conformist an ethic might be expected to offend modern readers. ⟨. . .⟩

By failing to live up to the novel's ideal of propriety—a respect for the conventions of propriety modified by an understanding that those conventions are not ends in themselves—or by revealing the fact that their concept of proper behavior differs from that suggested by the novel as a whole, the characters in *Pride and Prejudice* reveal their own moral shortcomings. And it is not merely that something vaguely wrong with the manners is a clue to something vaguely wrong with the character, for in fact the flaw in the manners usually turns out to be a very precise counterpart to the moral flaw in question. ⟨. . .⟩

Many other examples could be given of the way in which manners mirror the moral character in the world of *Pride and Prejudice*, for this is true of nearly every character in the novel. And this is an important difference between *Sense and Sensibility* and *Pride and Prejudice*. In *Sense and Sensibility*, the rules of propriety are ultimately justified by their connection with the concept of duty—and true propriety consists in following them to the letter, even when they oppose personal judgment and feeling. This is a very exacting and theoretical standard of propriety and perhaps that is why Jane Austen does not assume that to fall below this high standard is invariably evidence of real immorality. Thus, Mrs. Jennings's frequent improprieties are signs that she has not always lived in good society and that her friendly interest in others is sometimes carried to an uncomfortable pitch—but not that she is in any sense a bad person. Mrs.

Jennings does not have Elinor's sophisticated understanding of the function of a code of propriety in the social system, but she can still be a good woman in her less stoical and intellectual way. Also, since the external manifestation of *Sense and Sensibility's* code of true propriety consists simply of obeying all the major and minor rules of propriety to the letter, it can easily be followed by those unfeeling, unintelligent people, like Lady Middleton, who have few personal desires or judgments urging them to disobey. But *Pride and Prejudice's* standard of propriety suggests that the truly proper individual must disobey the rules whenever sound common sense and good morality approve—so that only people possessing these two important attributes *can* live up the novel's ideal of propriety, even in a purely external sense. That is why improper characters must be either immoral or stupid in *Pride and Prejudice*, but not in *Sense and Sensibility.* ⟨. . .⟩

It seems paradoxical that *Pride and Prejudice*, probably Jane Austen's most popular novel and certainly the one that gives readers the greatest sense of the individual's right to be different, is the only one of Jane Austen's books, except for *Northanger Abbey*, that assumes a simple, direct relationship between conventional good manners and good moral character. It is precisely because Jane Austen manages to convince her readers, in this novel, that the laws of morality manifest themselves socially in terms of the laws of propriety—an association that is made linguistically again and again in the course of *Pride and Prejudice*: "folly and indecorum," "decency and virtue," and so forth—that we can accept the idea that her most attractive characters choose socially conventional modes of behavior freely, as a means of realizing their best potentialities. Perhaps part of the charm of *Pride and Prejudice* is to be found in the way it subtly convinces readers that what the intelligent individual wants for himself and what society wants him to be are virtually one and the same, that Elizabeth Bennet is free to be Elizabeth in the best sense, and, in addition, to be the ideal mistress of Pemberley.

—Jane Nardin, "Propriety as a Test of Character: *Pride and Prejudice*," *Those Elegant Decorums: The Concept of Propriety in Jane Austen's Novels* (1973), excerpted in *Jane Austen's Pride and Prejudice*, ed. Harold Bloom (New York: Chelsea House Publishers, 1987), 7–8, 10, 12–13, 19

BARBARA HARDY

Jane Austen took a very long time to attract technical analysis, though she has always been praised, in somewhat general terms, for her artistry. Throughout the nineteenth century she was applauded for craft, finish and neatness. These were features that even her detractors could patronize. Even if she lacked passion, soul, elevation and social range, she was neat, elegant, and tasteful. One of her best Victorian critics, Richard Simpson, wrote in 1870 that 'She is neat, epigrammatic and incisive, but always a lady', and 'art will make up for want of force', adding that her art has 'all the minute attention to detail of the most accomplished miniature-painter'. Her femininity and ladylike elegance, partly inferred from her biographers, partly from her novels, tended to be associated with her finished craft. Her accomplishments as a novelist sometimes even seem to be assimilated to her excellence as a needlewoman. Whether her novels impressed readers or left them feeling that something was missing, her artistry provoked admiration rather than elucidation. ⟨. . .⟩

Her revolution was indeed a modest one. Its modesty was more genuine and more important than any other aspect of her so-called quiet life, unobtrusive writing habits, and restrained subject-matter. One of her nieces, writing to tell her about someone's admiration of her novels, said that it was sufficiently whole-hearted to please even Cassandra, 'nothing ever like them before or since'. But to say that there was nothing like them before and nothing like them since obscures her impact. Jane Austen created a new and flexible medium in which the individual and society could be revealed together. The achievement is striking when we approach it from earlier novels, much less so when we approach her novels—as is common—after an acquaintance with the novels of the twentieth century and the novels of the Victorian period.

There are moments in the history of art when we find ourselves face to face with new clearings, heights or depths, after which nothing is quite the same again. I want to look closely at some of the ways in which Jane Austen creates such an epoch in the history of fiction. It is not altogether reckless to suggest that her most singular contribution was what I shall call her flexible medium, a capacity to glide easily from sympathy to detachment, from one mind to many minds, from solitary scenes to social gatherings. It was this medium which she conveyed to her successors and what was for her a triumph won over difficulties, became the novel's stock in trade.

The flexible medium is the dominant gift of her genius. It seems to rely on many powers, dramatic, psychological and stylistic, all of which solve her individual imaginative needs. Her art succeeds in moving in and out of the minds of her people, and in and out of crowds and communities. The combination of such social notation with such analysis of consciousness transforms our sense of what the novel can do. The achievement would be more obvious if we were not so accustomed to taking such a medium for granted in the novels that came after her. We expect the novelist to be profoundly concerned with the human mind and the society. We expect the novel to move fluently from the extreme of inner analysis to that of public life. Moreover, we expect these extremes to meet not simply in the unity of art, but in a pattern of cause and effect which relates the turmoils in the psyche to the portrait of society. The novel accumulates its impressions of society by noting the behaviour of people in social groups, playing social roles, placed in social environments. But such behaviour is made plain by contrasts with private lives.

It may also be hard to think of a picture or a drama of the individual and society, and the individual in society, as a solution to an artistic problem, since we all take it for granted that we have private and public lives. We will probably be so sophisticatedly aware of the varied functions of our roles and registers of action, relationship and speech, that some of Jane Austen's most original analyses may pass without notice. Only when we go back to Scott, to Fanny Burney, and to the great eighteenth-century novelists, Smollett, Sterne, Fielding, Richardson and Defoe, do we come to realize that the fusion of private and public worlds is a superb achievement. The novelists writing before Jane Austen tend to tilt the balance toward either the private world or the public world. The one may be made implicit in the other, even subordinate to it. If conjunction is attempted, it is made abruptly and jerkily. Characters tend to have *either* public *or* private lives.

Occasionally, we meet a more modern novelist who fails to create a balance. Virginia Woolf complained sharply that in their different ways, and for their different reasons, the novels of Arnold Bennett, John Galsworthy and H. G. Wells failed to give a sense of the individual life, losing it in their preoccupation with the surface or the problems of public life. She was probably unfair to Arnold Bennett, whose ways of implying the individual life were less subtle and less subtly fugitive than her ways; nothing is so difficult for the innovator to appreciate as an old-fashioned version of the innovation being attempted. She was right about Galsworthy's specifications and surfaces, but Wells affords a more useful instance, since his social surveys and arguments need to sacrifice, sentimentalize, or simplify the life of the individual. Like Wells, George Orwell may strike us as brilliant but bizarre in his very generalization of the public world. Novelists who fail to join the individual life with their analysis of society may collapse in imaginative failure, like so many best-sellers, but they may deliberately create an art of social surfaces because their concern, like that of Wells and Orwell, is essentially polemic, using the arts of fiction for political tracts, social studies, ideological fable and documentaries. But what we are chiefly accustomed to in the great novelists who come after Jane Austen is a controlled and profound imaginative grasp of the individual life and the collective life. ⟨. . .⟩

The subtexts of social occasion were not invented by Jane Austen, but she makes a fuller and more subtle use of them than anyone since Shakespeare. ⟨. . .⟩

After Jane Austen, George Eliot was to develop a dramatized version of such irony for similar purposes of generalizing and rebuking a social response. Jane Austen criticizes society through the drama of complex and particular types and groups, and the shy or sly irony of her rare authorial comments helps her to state a viewpoint without occupying too much space. Her moral comments are weighty, but never heavy. In her narrative voice, in the free indirect style in which she shares commentary with the characters, and in her habit of quick, vivid summary, she moves lightly and unobtrusively from character to group, close-up to distance. Like all the threads that join her private and public worlds, that of her commentary is so fine that its stitches scarcely show. But the fineness is the product of great and delicate skill.

    —Barbara Hardy, "The Flexible Medium": *A Reading of Jane Austen* (1975), excerpted in *The Critical Perspective*, Vol. 6, ed. Harold Bloom (New York: Chelsea House Publishers, 1988), 3338–39, 3345–46

ALICE CHANDLER

Although we cannot have the same degree of certainty that Jane Austen's use of what the twentieth century calls sex symbolism was as deliberate as her use of allusions, puns, and riddles, her referents are so obvious at times that it is hard to believe they are unconscious. *Mansfield Park*, Marvin Mudrick's shrine of the sexual taboo and Kingsley Amis's palace of prudery, is curiously rich in sex symbols—perhaps because it is more a hothouse than a refrigerator. It nurtures not only the blooming Bertram girls and the sexually dynamic Mary Crawford but also the nubile Fanny Price, whose growth to womanhood, in both the moral and physical sense, forms the mainspring of the novel. It is an interesting comment on nineteenth-century social values that nobody really notices Fanny until she reaches puberty. In a recent article, Ann Banfield rightly points out that the "notice others begin to take of Fanny is a measure of their increasing (or decreasing) vision and judgment." But, like other critics, she has not observed that Fanny's importance also depends on her being "in" or "out"—ripe for the marriage market or not yet sufficiently matured to warrant interest. ⟨. . .⟩

Nowhere is the combination of realism and metaphor more clearly shown than in her use of the dance. It is possible to reconstruct many of the social customs of the age simply by studying the descriptions of balls and dances in *Emma*, in *Mansfield Park*, in *Pride and Prejudice*, and even in *Northanger Abbey*; but it is also possible to see the ritualized encounters of the ballrooms as indicators of social and sexual definition. What partners *may* dance with one another, what partners *do* dance with one another—what woman the man chooses, what man the woman entices or resists—the pairings and nonpairings involved all provide dramatizations of the mating process that are seldom as visible elsewhere. Given the inhibitions of early nineteenth-century customs, the dance is one of the few places where choosing is apparent and touching is allowed. Jane Austen knew precisely what she meant when she says that "to be fond of dancing [is] the first step toward falling in love." ⟨. . .⟩

Dancing as a courtship metaphor occurs for a third, though not a final time, in one of the drawing-room scenes at Netherfield. Anxious to attract Mr. Darcy to herself, Miss Bingley is playing a lively Scotch air on the piano. The result, however, is the opposite of what she intends. It leads Darcy to draw near to Elizabeth and ask if she does not "feel a great inclination . . . to seize such an opportunity of dancing a reel." Any kind of dancing would, of course, be inappropriate with Jane lying sick upstairs, but the lively reel seems totally unconventional and suggests Darcy's inner desires. Far more than his measured request for her hand under Sir William's tutelage, this approach to Elizabeth suggests strong attraction. Darcy is implying that they can cast off the measured forms of their society and unite in a lively dance. Elizabeth's pointed rejection of his request indicates her feelings perfectly. Although she smiles when she says it (as she invariably does when Darcy is by), she "does not want to dance a reel at all." Her resistance is inspired. That Miss Bingley reads the second volume to his first, wishes for a library like that at Pemberley, is enraptured by his sister's drawings, and is willing to sing to him, play for him, dance with him, walk with him, "mend his pen" for him, provokes only his driest wit. But Elizabeth's refusal to dance with him—like his earlier unwillingness to dance with her—heightens the tension between them.

Still another semimetaphoric measure of Darcy's attraction to Elizabeth can be found in the references to her eyes. For a man like Darcy, Elizabeth Bennet is both an attraction and a threat. She is free and lively, with the easy playfulness he lacks. His eye is satiric. It takes notice, but it does not react. Elizabeth's "pair of fine eyes," dark, sparkling, and expressive, are not only quick to perceive but to communicate. "The faculty of vision," Richard Chase reminds us in another context, "is often identified in the unconscious with the energy of sex." Darcy cannot quite say, because he does not really know, what attracts him to Elizabeth. But part of the attraction is surely a sense of her vitality, of a freedom and ultimately of a sexual energy unknown in his formal and insipid circles that entices him against his judgment. It is for this reason that Elizabeth's eyes become an issue between him and Miss Bingley, who realizes, though she too is unconscious of its real origins, the source of her rival's power. ⟨. . .⟩

To say that Jane Austen's novels are essentially sexless—intellectual exercises devoid of sex or defensive about it—seems to me wrong. Her use of allusions, puns, riddles, and sex symbols points to a specific knowledge about the manifestations of sexuality, if nothing else. Far from wondering, as one critic does, if she "knew anything of the part played by the flesh and the fleshly passions," we can only register surprise at her sophisticated devices for indicating them.

But more significant than her knowledge of physical sex is the fully human way in which she implies the broad range of feelings that man and woman have for each other. All of her books underscore both the social and sexual meaning of marriage. A good marriage for Jane Austen is always supportive of the organization of society. It involves an appropriate mixing of classes and value systems that sustains the traditional qualities of English life while allowing for change and renewal. But marriage is also a sexual act in her novels— usually a reconciliation between a man and a woman whose inner feelings and conscious knowledge have been at odds throughout the story. As I have tried to show in my analysis of *Pride and Prejudice*, the signs of such attraction may only be covert. But they ring true to the complexities of human emotion and to its intensities as well.

—Alice Chandler, "'A Pair of Fine Eyes': Jane Austen's Treatment of Sex," *Studies in the Novel*, 7, no. 1 (Spring 1975), excerpted in *Jane Austen*, ed. Harold Bloom (New York: Chelsea House Publishers, 1986), 32–35, 41

THOMAS LOCKWOOD

The title of *Persuasion* (which may not be the title Jane Austen meant it to have) makes an impression of abstract thematic interest, like the titles of *Sense and Sensibility* and *Pride and Prejudice*. But the impression is oddly misleading. Jane Austen is distinctly unwilling to connect Anne's happiness with Anne's persuadable character, even though Anne herself very much wants to make out just such a connection. Certainly the idea of "persuasion" is wrought upon in the novel, and we are repeatedly teased with the word itself; there is persuasion anticipated, persuasion regretted, persuasion availing and unavailing. Characters are tested by their resistance to persuasion, though again it is less Jane Austen than Anne herself who conducts these rather obvious and not very illuminating tests.

Anne considers that she once yielded to persuasion and suffered as a result; she cannot rid herself of an uneasy consciousness about possible connections between her unhappiness and her supposedly persuadable character. But when the highly unpersuadable Louisa Musgrove dashes her head on the Cobb, Anne gratefully discovers room for another idea about persuadability: "She thought it could scarcely escape him to feel, that a persuadable temper might sometimes be as much in favour of happiness, as a very resolute character" (116). This too has the look of a moral, especially for the hopeful Anne, but really the only conclusion that can be drawn from the comparison of Anne and Louisa is that overpersuadable and underpersuadable people alike may suffer, or may be in favor of happiness. Anne may think she has found a moral here, and has in fact found something a little newer and happier—not a moral truth, despite her inveterate inclination to give it that form, but an emotional one: "'You will stay, I am sure; you will stay and nurse her,' cried he, turning to her and speaking with a glow, and yet a gentleness, which seemed almost restoring the past.—She coloured deeply; and he recollected himself, and moved away" (114). This, and not some notion about persuadability, is the truth Jane Austen by contrast is determined to catch. And so what Anne will not catch at, Jane Austen will; what Anne will put second, Jane Austen will put first; when Anne will consider what it means to be persuadable, Jane Austen will consider what it means to blush.

Anne wants a moral rationale for her suffering—a way of giving it meaning. The truth is that it has no meaning and that she suffers for no reason other than that she once lost a chance for happiness (never mind why). Neither she nor Lady Russell is actually to be blamed for what happened, of course; Jane Austen too will allow that, though Anne does more than merely allow it. For Jane Austen this unwillingness to blame comes from a feeling of irrelevance about the question—even indifference to it—a feeling again that we are trading in two different orders of truth when we ask who ought to get the blame for Anne's life of "desolate tranquillity" (36). For Anne, however, the question is always relevant, always first in her mind when she reconsiders the event, and always answered alike, as it must be if her suffering is to provide the kind of moral self-definition by which she has learned to achieve the tranquillity of all she has amid the desolation of all she does not have. ⟨. . .⟩

The story Jane Austen concludes with Anne's "Would I!" is the same story Anne herself would conclude, would feel had been best concluded, by saying she has now nothing to reproach herself with. They are not the same conclusions at all, though not exactly incompatible either: they reflect that slight but perpetual division of interest and focus, within the same story, between a moral and an emotional self-consciousness. Even within Anne herself there is a delicate and rather comical war going on between one half of herself—Jane Austen identifies it ironically as her "wiser" half—and the other. "She hoped to be wise and reasonable in time; but alas! alas! she must confess to herself that she was not wise yet" (178). Or, "one half of her should not be always so much wiser than the other half, or always suspecting the other of being worse than it was" (175). "Wise" means prudent but also implies a certain settled, ungirlish perspective on runaway feeling, her own (especially) as well as that of others, like the Musgrove girls whom Anne can regard as "some of the happiest creatures of her acquaintance" without also wishing for the exchange; it is that perspective, "her own more elegant and cultivated mind," Anne would not trade for "all their enjoyments" (41), as it is rather distantly termed. Such animal happiness is for others; she is to be twenty-seven and wisely miserable. ⟨. . .⟩

Dr. Johnson said of Clarissa Harlowe that there was always something she preferred to the truth. There is hardly anything Anne Elliot prefers to the truth, except once, during the only months of her life that Jane Austen cares to write about, when truth has become the truth of feeling. Not that Jane Austen depreciates moral truth, or depreciates Anne for her anxious habituated attachment to that order of truth, or shows even the faintest impatience with her about it. Nevertheless, with no sacrifice of sympathy for Anne—for it is sympathy also with her own best-remembered and longest-lived self— Jane Austen does make the controlling truth of Anne's story, and of *Persuasion*, an emotional truth; and if Anne is never quite prepared with Jane Austen to tell this truth, at any rate she is allowed to live it.

—Thomas Lockwood, "Divided Attention in *Persuasion*," *Nineteenth-Century Fiction* (December 1978), excerpted in *The Critical Perspective*, Vol. 6, ed. Harold Bloom (New York: Chelsea House Publishers, 1988), 3359, 3361

JULIA PREWITT BROWN

The pleasure of reading *Emma*, the very great pleasure, has little to do with the kinds of linear meaning that may be found in most novels; the pleasure comes from our willing immersion in the everyday concerns and relationships of this world, and from a glow of suggestion in the narrative that tells us: this is enough. The novel's very self-absorption makes it acceptable and wonderful. It is a world that believes in itself entirely, and hypnotized, we too believe. ⟨. . .⟩

Just as the structure of *Emma* is not causal, it is also not hierarchical. Were we to draw a picture of the novel, it would not, I believe, bring before the reader the ladder of social and moral being that Graham Hough assigns. It would look more like a road map in which the cities and towns, joined together by countless highways and byroads, stood for people. Some of the roads are curved and smooth, like those between Emma and her father or Emma and Mrs. Weston; some are so full of obstacles that their destinations (Jane Fairfax, for example) are almost inaccessible. Mr. Weston and Miss Bates are like great indiscriminate towns from which radiate roads that join almost everyone.

As the image of a road map suggests, Highbury is a system of interdependence, a community of people all talking to one another, affecting, and changing one another: a collection of relationships. Miss Bates is emblematic of Highbury in this respect. In the words of E. M. Forster, "Miss Bates is bound by a hundred threads to Highbury. We cannot tear her away without bringing her mother too, and Jane Fairfax and Frank Churchill, and the whole of Box Hill." Emma herself is as firmly connected to her world as Miss Bates.

Perceived in her many relationships with others, Emma is seen as daughter, sister, sister-in-law, aunt, companion, intimate friend, new acquaintance, patroness, and bride. And each connection lets us see something new in her.

The interaction of characters in the novel is extensive and dynamic. All characters intersect in some way. In addition to all the major combinations, we witness sufficiently realized contact between Jane Fairfax and Mr. John Knightley, Mr. Weston and Mrs. Elton, Mr. Elton and Mr. John Knightley; we learn what Mr. Woodhouse thinks of Frank Churchill, what Mr. John Knightley thinks of Mr. Weston, and what Isabella thinks of Harriet. These represent brief encounters and the almost spur-of-the-moment judgments that arise from them. For example, Mr. John Knightley has only to see Mr. Elton once during his holiday visit to know that Mr. Elton is interested in Emma. As always in Jane Austen, the smallest detail of behavior can justify the most definitive judgment.

Even the more sustained relationships seem to be composed of many individual encounters and the individual judgments that arise from them. For example, the relationships between Mrs. Elton and Jane Fairfax, Frank Churchill and his foster parents, Jane Fairfax and Emma, and Harriet and Robert Martin's sister are discussed several times by different persons, and on the basis of brief incidents. When compared to the pattern of dialogue in *Pride and Prejudice*, these dialogues and judgments seem random and self-absorbed—indeed, like "real" conversations—yet not the less reliable for being so. Mr. Woodhouse's judgment upon Frank Churchill—that the young man is "not quite the thing"—is unreasonably and uncharitably founded, yet correct; and it is acknowledged with dismay by those who hear it.

The novel is like Highbury itself; there is no limit to the combinations within it, or to the combinations speculated upon. Marriage, always the first and last relationship in Jane Austen, is confirmed in six couples in the novel and predicted in many more. (Harriet and Mr. Elton, Emma and Mr. Elton, Emma and Frank Churchill, Harriet and Frank Churchill, Jane Fairfax and Mr. Dixon, Mr. Knightley and Jane Fairfax, Harriet and Mr. Knightley.) Indeed, speculation about love relationships is the basis of the novel's plot, because the heroine is herself a relentless matchmaker. Yet to catalogue all of these real or imagined connections is misleading. In its unlikely and changing combinations, the catalogue gives an impression of social irrationality, overworked variety, and exhaustive socialization. Yet no other novel has more the opposite effect: of rich, unbroken continuity, of uncluttered awareness, routine contentment, cooperation, and harmony. This effect is achieved not only because of the interdependence of Highbury, its commune-like nature, but because events and characters are likened to one another in subtle ways, like so many hues of one color. This too helps to explain the magic and magnetic appeal of *Emma*; we are transfixed by the kaleidoscopic patterning of its relationships. ⟨. . .⟩

Because *Emma* is a novel about relationships and their natures, the "action" of the work is a dialectic. Every relationship in the novel has its unique dialectical rhythm; even the smoothest relationships encounter snags, such as the near-argument between Mr. Woodhouse and Emma about the treatment of brides. The novel's humor is almost always centered on the surprise creation of a dialectic through the sudden juxtaposition of unlikely personalities. The conversation between Mr. Knightley and Mrs. Elton about the picnic at Donwell Abbey, one of the most amusing exchanges in English fiction, does not perform at all; the humor lies in the contrast of character and is available to those who see it. Such moments border on farce because of the deadly seriousness of the characters themselves. And Mr. Knightley, the most serious of all, is not exempted from the farce of the situation; the contrast is not available to his subjective standpoint.

Three major dialectics in the novel involve Emma herself: the interior dialectic, of which only Emma is aware; the dialectic between Emma and Mr. Knightley; and the dialectic between Emma and Highbury. By the close of the novel they all seem to become the same dialectic. They are never resolved, only validated, in marriage; the only truth is the dialectic itself. Part of the novel's greatness is that it never moves to the death of total resolution.

—Julia Prewitt Brown, "Civilization and the Contentment of *Emma*," *Jane Austen's Novels: Social Change and Literary Form* (1979), excerpted in *Jane Austen's Emma*, ed. Harold Bloom (New York: Chelsea House Publishers, 1987), 45–49

IRVIN EHRENPREIS

The mark of Austen's stories is the inwardness of the action—the novelist's preoccupation with self-knowledge. If one reflects on the history of narrative, including epic, drama, romance, and the novel, two features will distinguish Austen from the bulk of her predecessors. For them the problems to be studied were those of attracting and holding people one loves, of winning and keeping power or wealth, or else of destroying enemies. In this literature the protagonist normally was sure of his own desires but not of the motives of those around him. He often felt divided between opposing impulses, but he knew what the impulses really were. It was the darkness of other people's characters that troubled him; it was the obstacles they put in his way that complicated the action.

But for Austen the obstacles lie within, and the story is one of self-discovery. ⟨. . .⟩

Though Austen's predominant method is contrast, that method receives peculiar complications. For instance, the contrast is often incomplete and waits to be filled out by the reader. ⟨. . .⟩

Not only are Austen's contrasts systematically incomplete. They are also moral. In *Pride and Prejudice*, Darcy and Bingley are not opposed to one another as fat and thin or dark and fair but as reserved and sociable, deliberate and impulsive. In Austen's system of implicit contrasts, if Bingley is open and active in his attentions to Jane Bennet, we may assume that Darcy will be cautious in advancing toward her sister's heart.

Thanks to the use of moral contrast, Austen can infuse subtle implications into devices that do not essentially involve them. For example, in her narrative tradition, speeches and gestures are normally completed. If they are broken off, the storyteller implies that a strong emotion is the cause, and the emotion as such is in general obvious. In the *Aeneid* when Neptune is angry with the winds for causing a storm he has not asked for, he breaks off a sentence starting *Quos ego*—and the listener knows he is angry (*Aeneid* I, 135).

Austen always implies hidden motives with moral overtones when she interrupts an action. In *Emma*, when Jane Fairfax refuses to continue a game of anagrams, Austen implies not only that she is embarrassed but that Frank Churchill has been indelicate and shown himself unworthy of her (pp. 347–49). Our inference depends of course on the steady contrast drawn between his assurance and her refinement. A more subtle and economical example is Eleanor Tilney's interruption of herself in *Northanger Abbey*. At the end of a friendly conversation Catherine Morland asks her whether she will be at the ball the next day. "Perhaps we—yes, I think we certainly shall," says Miss Tilney (p. 73). The reader should understand that she has just recognized Catherine's fondness for her brother, and that she wisely wishes to encourage it. The reason for her feeling is that both girls are simple, truthful, and modest, a congruity that sets them off against Isabella Thorpe.

How far Austen could carry such didactic art, we may judge from the elaborate episode, in *Emma*, of Knightley's almost kissing the heroine's hand. He takes her hand, presses it, and is certainly on the point of carrying it to his lips when he suddenly lets go (pp. 385–86). The reason, we may infer, is that he feels he has no right to seem so affectionate because Emma is (he mistakenly believes) attached to Frank Churchill. Again, we can make the judgment—and admire his delicacy—because of a contrast regularly drawn between Knightley and Churchill.

Yet the most striking and pervasive feature of Austen's contrasts is that they are metonymic. When a person is connected with a visible element, that element takes on the character of the person. For example, in *Pride and Prejudice*, when Jane Bennet and Charles Bingley exchange views on card games, they find they both like vingt-un better than the game of commerce (p. 23). Now it happens that in commerce the players barter for cards, while in vingt-un they keep their own. Jane and Bingley are people whose attachment is deep and enduring; their dislike of barter reflects the trait. ⟨. . .⟩

Austen avoids metaphor or symbolism in her art. In Scott's *Waverley* when the hero dresses himself in the tartan, he takes on its associations; it does not reflect his; for Scott uses the tartan as a metaphor for Jacobitism. But in Austen's stories, a thing, a gesture, an occupation seldom has moral significance or general meaning apart from the individual to whom it belongs. Austen can transform all the circumstances of common life into implicit moral comment: space, time, landscape, architecture, furniture. What she will not do is to attribute independent symbolic meaning to these circumstances. Darcy's attention to books indicates the depth of his moral and intellectual culture. Wentworth's indifference to books, in *Persuasion*, makes a contrast to the reading habits of his shallow friend Benwick, who replaces true feeling with literary sentiment. Games, books, articles of clothing, are in themselves neither good nor bad for Austen; they stand for no general principle until connected with a particular character. When Mary Bennet or Anne Elliot plays the piano, the performance takes on the color of her nature. With Mary it suggests self-absorption (*Pride and Prejudice*, p. 100); with Anne it suggests self-sacrifice (*Persuasion*, p. 47). ⟨. . .⟩

Austen, who does not work with conventional symbols, must play down the issues that fascinate Scott if she is to liberate her genius. So it is that her clergymen, whether heroes or fools, never discuss doctrine. If they did so, by her scheme of moral, metonymic contrasts, she would have to treat one sect as superior to another, and the religious distinction would bury the individual traits. So also, as Gilbert Ryle has observed, the protagonists of Austen's novels face their moral crises without visible recourse to religious faith; nor do they ever seek the advice of a clergyman.

For Austen, religion is a universal but indiscriminate context. She is not concerned to rank types of Christians any more than she ranks types of Englishmen. She chooses families that share the same region, the same church, the same social order—the same opportunities to strengthen their moral natures; and then she sees what the individuals make of themselves under these conditions.

—Irvin Ehrenpreis, "Austen: The Heroism of the Quotidian," *Acts of Implication* (1980), excerpted in *The Critical Perspective*, Vol. 6, ed. Harold Bloom (New York: Chelsea House Publishers, 1988), 3362, 3364, 3366, 3369–70

Susan Morgan

Most readers have agreed that Catherine Morland's experiences cannot be adequately described as a progress from "visions of romance" to realities; that, as Andrew Wright put it, "good sense, ironically, is limited too." Indeed, neither Catherine's experience nor her author's new literary principles can be described as a move toward realism. Instead we need to recognize the question which the portrayal of an unheroic heroine invokes. If fiction does not offer models to emulate, what then can be taught—by Tilneys or by novelists? At the center of *Northanger Abbey*, at the center of Austen's new idea of fiction, is the problem of education. Austen's constant subject, the relations between ourselves and other people, appears here as teaching and learning, as a novel of education.

The *bildungsroman* form reflects the more serious question—serious aesthetically as well as morally—of how to balance possibilities for character change with the continuing integrity of self. Education, then, is Austen's metaphor for exploring the extent to which we can become better or worse, the extent to which we can be affected by our experiences, and still remain ourselves. It is the metaphor for the relation between character and plot. Trilling reminds us that Austen writes of "the idea of love based in pedagogy." This idea includes not only education but the limits of education. And it is taught to us by Catherine, that "occasionally stupid" character who "never could learn or understand any thing before she was taught; and sometimes not even then." ⟨. . .⟩

The problem of understanding others, of accounting for the unaccountable, is what Catherine is in the novel to learn. She needs to for the very reason that life is unaccountable, people are not logical, words not literal, and meanings seldom accessible and clear. Catherine is beginning to recognize (to borrow Virginia Woolf's phrase) that the world is larger and more mysterious than she had supposed. Expressing this idea as moral education is a convention through which Austen explores the more essential question of how one is to see and act when the truth does not lie before us as we move. This problem connects *Northanger Abbey* with *Emma* and with all her other novels. And her study of this problem, as Austen declares in *Northanger Abbey*, separates her from her predecessors in fiction. ⟨. . .⟩

Catherine learns that truth is not a settled or a general thing, and that there is a relation between creativity and perception, between what she makes up and what she sees. When she tells Henry and Eleanor on the walk around Beechen Cliff that "invention is what delights me," Catherine has yet to recognize that invention can be a power which provides access to reality. That is why she only likes novels, why she doesn't like invention in history. Yet it is on these same grounds that Eleanor defends history. For history blends information "which may be as much depended on, I conclude, as any thing that does not actually pass under one's own observation" with all those "little embellishments." Historians, in short, "display imagination." *Northanger Abbey* is not a lesson in relinquishing the false world of the imagination for the true world of clear vision. It is a lesson in the imaginative nature of vision. ⟨. . .⟩

Catherine's attempt to understand is limited. She often makes mistakes. But Austen isn't interested in teaching her characters how to be right. Instead, she insists that they recognize and value the possibility of being wrong. The problem with heroines is that they are never wrong. And since by definition they are good, they are also complete and predictable. The only change possible for them is to decline and fall. That is why their most essential experience is to be threatened by seduction. It is also why some variation of attempted rape is such a common event in the plots of eighteenth-century novels. For a "true quality heroine," character change is character violation.

Austen transforms the notion of character, and thereby the notion of plot, by creating Catherine Morland. Experience is no longer a landscape heroines pass through, arriving at the finish either fallen or unscathed. Limits free characters for experiences undreamt of by either perfect or fallen heroines. In presenting Catherine, Austen connects moral imperfection to openness, to the possibility for change. For limits are also capacities. Because Catherine has "the common feelings of common life," she can be special, in the sense of being a particular person rather than a paradigm. And in her common and limited life Catherine needs imagination, which overleaps the borders of self. ⟨. . .⟩

Right seeing, far from being a conclusion, is to be continually achieved. The proper use of imagination is continuous, a creative process of perception and judgment. This idea has affinities with what may be "the single morality of romanticism," the belief that "formulation itself must never be allowed to settle into dogma, but must emerge anew every day out of experience. It must be lived, which is to say that it must carry within it its subjective origin, its origin in experience and self-realization." Imagining goes on as long as a person can see and think and feel, because truth in *Northanger Abbey* is never complete.

—Susan Morgan, "Guessing for Ourselves in *Northanger Abbey*," *In the Meantime: Character and Perception in Jane Austen's Fiction* (1980), reprinted in *Jane Austen*, ed. Harold Bloom (New York: Chelsea House Publishers, 1986), 110–11, 114–15, 117–19

IAN WATT

As regards the comic tradition, one of the central arguments is that when Jane Austen began to write there was no established narrative tradition that would serve her turn. More specifically, earlier writers of English comic novels, such as Fielding, Smollett, and Fanny Burney, had in different ways adopted the polar opposition between good and bad characters which is typical of stage comedy from the Greeks on. Through the finer and more detailed psychological calibration of her narrative, Jane Austen made the hero and heroine psychologically complex, and therefore capable of internal and external development. By this means the traditional conflict of "good" and "bad" characters in comedy was internalised as a conflict within and between the "good" characters; and this enabled Jane Austen to discover the answer to Horatio Bottomley's prayer—"I pray that the bad be made good, and the good nice, and the nice, interesting."

The prayer is very rarely answered—alas!—either in life or in art; but one can surely say about Elizabeth Bennet and Emma Woodhouse that they are not only good and nice, but interesting. They are made interesting because they are idiosyncratic mixtures of character traits, mixtures by no means limited to the good and unexceptionable qualities. For the purposes of comedy there remained a further task—the protagonists had to take over many of the aggressive functions which stage comedy has traditionally allotted to other actors—to the witty helpers, blocking characters, and villains. It is this, I think, that constitutes Jane Austen's greatest originality as an artist; and I would add that this literary originality is based on her psychological and moral realism, which gave the aggressive impulses a role which went far beyond the thought of her time, and, in some ways, of ours. ⟨. . .⟩

Jane Austen's novels contain three main types of comic aggression, and all of them involve the "good" characters as well as the others. The first category—which I will call the social—is concerned with how people have different ways of hitting back at the restraints which social life exacts. ⟨. . .⟩

The most intransigent and socially-destructive manifestation of aggression occurs when some challenge arises to the imperative need of individual ego to maintain its own image of itself in the face of the outside the world. This need produces the cruellest deliberate act in *Emma*, when Mr. Elton refuses to dance with Harriet Smith at the ball in the Crown; his pride has been offended, and seeks revenge. In Jane Austen, however, unconscious cruelty is much commoner, and most often arises from a mere refusal or inability to understand other people. Mr. Woodhouse, for instance, is genuinely kind in his way; but, lacking the controls of intelligence or awareness, his phobias often lead him into the milder forms of cruelty, invective and lying. Thus his tyrannical valetudinarianism leads him to disappoint Mrs. Bates's eager anticipation of a "delicate fricassée of sweetbread and asparagus," on the grounds that the latter were not "quite boiled enough"; the same phobia emerges in a more rancorous verbal form when the arrival of gruel in his family circle becomes the occasion for "pretty severe Philippics upon the many houses where it was never met with tolerable."

It would certainly be wrong, I must observe, to infer that Jane Austen condemns all social forms of aggression. For one thing, it is manifested by every character in *Emma* about whom we can make a judgment, except for two, and they are the exceptions which prove the rule: I mean Mrs. Bates and Harriet Smith—good people no doubt, but intellectually null, with one of them—Harriet—not yet arrived at maturity, and the other—Mrs. Bates—long past it.

I come now to the other two kinds of comic aggression—the interpersonal and the internal—as they are manifested in *Pride and Prejudice*. The personal relations between Elizabeth and Darcy are dominated by the aggressive elements in their characters; these alone replace the roles of the villains, the blocking characters, and the mistaken identities in traditional comedy. This replacement depends on two narrative techniques: first, the aggressive impulses at play in the comic arena are psychologised in the "courtship" of the protagonists; and they are also psychologised as conflicts inside the egos of both the lovers.

These conflicts in the personalities of Elizabeth and Darcy provide the mechanism of the main plot. At first the aggressive aspects of their characters block their separation even before they are actually acquaintances. Darcy's pride leads him to reject Bingley's suggestion that he dance with her—"She is tolerable; but not handsome enough to tempt *me*; and I am in no humour at present to give consequence to young ladies who are slighted by other men." Elizabeth overhears him, and her offended pride, exacerbated by Meryton gossip and Wickham's lies, insulates her from Darcy's rapidly changing feelings. The whole of their relationship is thus presented as an adaptation and recombination of one of the most standard modes of comic aggression, invective, to the purposes of psychological and moral realism. Elizabeth and Darcy begin by insulting the other to third parties; later their acquaintance develops almost exclusively through bouts of contemptuous raillery which are as close to the verbal combats of Greek comedy as the manners of Regency England allowed.

The reason for the tradition of invective in comedy is presumably that it offers a symbolic release from the constraints on which civilisation depends; as Freud put it, "The man who first flung a word of abuse at his enemy instead of a spear was the founder of civilisation." But in the kind of novel which Jane Austen wrote the invective and the wit-combats cannot be treated as they usually are in stage comedy, in Aristophanes, for example; they cannot merely stop, and be succeeded by a quick change to feasting, song, dance, and marriage. For in *Pride and Prejudice* the substance of the debate between the two lovers is very real—it expresses the deepest divisions in the way the protagonists see the world and experience the circumstances of their place in it. Jane Austen's moral solution to these divisions is exactly what the solution, if any, would be in real life: the pains of self-education—the realisation of the errors, the delusions, and the prejudices of the self. In narrative terms Jane Austen brings the pattern of invective to a climax by a dual psychological transformation: interpersonal aggression internalised in both hero and heroine.

—Ian Watt, "Jane Austen and the Traditions of Comic Aggression," *Persuasions: Journals of the Jane Austen Society of North America*, no. 3 (December 16, 1981), reprinted in *Jane Austen*, ed. Harold Bloom (New York: Chelsea House Publishers, 1986), 191–94

NINA AUERBACH

The silent, stubborn Fanny Price appeals less than any of Austen's heroines. Perhaps because of this, she captivates more critics than they. "Nobody, I believe, has ever found it possible to like the heroine of *Mansfield Park*," Lionel Trilling intoned in 1955, and few would contradict this epitaph today. Yet Trilling goes on to apotheosize this literary wallflower, transfiguring her into a culturally fraught emblem who bears on her scant shoulders all the aches of modern secularism. Such later interpreters as Avrom Fleishman similarly embrace Fanny as emblem if not woman, wan transmitter of intricate cultural ideals. It seems that once a heroine is divested of the power to please, she is granted an import beyond her apparently modest sphere, for, unlike Jane Austen's other, more immediately appealing heroines, Fanny has been said to possess our entire spiritual history as it shapes itself through her in historical time. Elizabeth and Emma live for readers as personal presences, but never as the Romantic, the Victorian, or the modern zeitgeist. Failing to charm, Fanny is allowed in compensation to embody worlds. ⟨. . .⟩

In adopting the role of traditional literary villains, Fanny infects our imaginations in a way that no merely virtuous heroine could do. Her hungry exclusion seems unappeasable and triumphant. Insofar as she draws sustenance from her role as omniscient outsider at family, excursion, wedding, play, or feast, she stands with some venerable monsters in the English canon. Not only does she share the role of Mary Shelley's creature, that gloomy exile from family whose vocation is to control families and destroy them, but there is a shadow on her even of the melancholy Grendel in the Anglo-Saxon epic *Beowulf*. An exile from common feasting, Grendel peers jealously through the window of a lighted banquet hall. He defines his identity as outsider by appropriating the interior; he invades the lighted hall and begins to eat the eaters. At the end of *Mansfield Park*, Fanny too has won a somewhat predatory victory, moving from outsider into guiding spirit of the humbled Bertram family. Fanny's cannibalistic invasion of the lighted, spacious estate of Mansfield is genteel and purely symbolic, but, like the primitive Grendel, she replaces common and convivial feasting with a solitary and subtler hunger that possesses its object. In this evocation of an earlier literary tradition, Fanny is Jane Austen's most Romantic heroine, for she is part of a literature newly awakened to ancient forms and fascinated by the monstrous and marginal. In the subtle streak of perversity that still disturbs readers today, she shows us the monsters within Jane Austen's realism, ineffable presences who allow the novels to participate in the darker moods of their age. ⟨. . .⟩

Fanny as Romantic monster does not dispel our discomfort in reading *Mansfield Park*, but may explain some of it. Until recently, critics have limited their recognition of the monsters that underlie Jane Austen's realism to the peripheral figures whose unreason threatens the heroine, while the heroine herself remains solidly human. Yet Fanny excites the same mixture of sympathy and aversion as does Frankenstein's loveless, homeless creature, and the pattern of her adventures is similar to his. Frankenstein's monster begins as a jealous outcast, peering in at family and civic joys. His rage for inclusion makes him the hunted prey of those he envies, and he ends as the conqueror of families. Fanny too is a jealous outcast in the first volume. In the second, she is besieged by the family that excluded her in the form of Henry Crawford's lethal marriage proposal; finally her lair, the chilly East room, is hunted down like Grendel's and invaded by Sir Thomas himself. In the third volume, Fanny, like Mary Shelley's monster, becomes the solitary conqueror of a gutted family. This movement from outcast within a charmed circle to one who is hunted by it and then conqueror of it aligns Jane Austen's most Romantic, least loved heroine with the kin she so wretchedly seeks. ⟨. . .⟩

In Mary Shelley's *Frankenstein* as well, family, nature, and even the Alps pall before the monster who is capable of being made. The monstrosity of *Mansfield Park* as a whole is one manifestation of its repelled fascination with acting, with education, and with landscape and estate improvements: the novel imagines a fluid world, one with no fixed principles, capable of awesome, endless, and dangerous manipulation. The unconvivial stiffness of its hero and heroine is their triumph: by the end, they are so successfully "made" by each other that he is her creature as completely as she has always been his. The mobility and malleability of *Mansfield Park* is a dark realization of an essentially Romantic vision, of which Fanny Price represents both the horror and the best hope. Only in *Mansfield Park* does Jane Austen force us to experience the discomfort of a Romantic universe presided over by the potent charm of a charmless heroine who was not made to be loved.

—Nina Auerbach, "Jane Austen's Dangerous Charm: Feeling as One Ought about Fanny Price" (1983), *Romantic Imprisonment: Women and Other Glorified Outcasts* (1986), excerpted in *The Critical Perspective*, Vol. 6, ed. Harold Bloom (New York: Chelsea House Publishers, 1988), 3378, 3380, 3382–83

DEBORAH KAPLAN

We will probably never know what gave Austen the desire to publish, but we can learn from *Sense and Sensibility* her justification for doing so. The novel which resulted from this period of preparation displays her contemplation and adjustment of the concept of authority. *Sense and Sensibility* expresses authority with the metaphor of paternity, and the novel does so in two modes: first, its characters render the metaphor dramatically. Indeed, the novel depicts not simply fathers who control their children but patrilineages which regulate the social identities and inheritances of subsequent generations. Though their members may be male or female, these lineages are, nonetheless, masculine institutions. They focus on and control eldest sons, who inherit and transmit in their turn their families' status and fortune. Second, the novel's narrative structure expresses the metaphor. *Sense and Sensibility* provides, really, two narratives. The narrator's account is prefigured, "fathered" by the story which Colonel Brandon tells of his cousin Eliza.

While *Sense and Sensibility* expresses metaphors of masculine authority, it also presents, through character representations, the possibility of a feminine authority. Austen draws on a social and literary code of the second half of the eighteenth century—Sensibility—in order to explore female assertiveness in a world already organized by the institution of patrilineage. Though sensibility was by no means espoused only by women, Austen attributes it in this novel primarily to female characters as a way of establishing a gender-specific opposition to conventional authority. The one exception is Colonel Brandon, a character intermittently shown to be a man of sensibility. But he is a younger son within a patrilineage which places him structurally in the same position as a daughter. *Sense and Sensibility* suggests, however, that the results of maintaining the code of sensibility are devastating to women. Like so many of her contemporaries, Austen insists that its effects are antisocial. Exponents of sensibility in the novel bear children out of wedlock, and thus identify feminine authority as illicit and immoral. As an indication of Austen's attitudes towards authority, such dramatic renderings suggest only the dangers of novel-writing. Female assertiveness constitutes a transgression.

But while Austen's novel shows metaphors of masculine authority to be socially sanctioned and metaphors of feminine authority to be illegitimate, it also subjects both kinds of tropes to a moral critique and, in the process, shows them to bear common characteristics. In both, reproduction creates resemblance—parents beget children in their own image—and such resemblances are evidence of narcissism. The novel, then, ultimately registers disapproval not just of feminine authority but of all its human forms however conventional. But as it expresses this position, *Sense and Sensibility* also reveals a way to avoid not simply female assertiveness but all self-preoccupied versions of authority. Using the resources of her own culture, Austen ⟨. . .⟩ creates a new metaphor to express authority for the self-effacing. She provides a trope not of reproduction and resemblance but of revision and difference. The trope is rendered by experiences or narratives, conveying self-preoccupied illusions, which authorize opposite and morally improved ways of life or story versions. Austen was able to achieve authority not in assertions but in the modification, the correction of such assertions. She did so literally in sitting down to rework *Sense and Sensibility* and metaphorically in formulating the aesthetic patterns the text now bears. ⟨. . .⟩

For Austen, authority belongs to the self-consciously powerless. It is achieved by recognizing the fallacy of personal power in the material world. The ability to do or determine is shown to be the ability to err. And authority is achieved by counteracting in revisions the mistaken efforts which such "doing" constitutes. Not only *Sense and Sensibility* but several of Austen's early drafts ("First Impressions" and "Susan" are only two of the most famous) were corrected by later versions. So too, "first impressions," false steps, and fanciful and distorting narratives are revised in the careers of characters like Marianne Dashwood, Elizabeth Bennet, and Catherine Morland, as well as Sir Thomas Bertram, Emma Woodhouse, and Frederick Wentworth. Perceptiveness, humility, a willingness to alter—these traits ultimately replace "power" among Austen's characters and are also necessary to reflexive, not other-directed or pioneering activity. The particular moral scope of Austen's authority is revealed by the trope which represents it. In *Sense and Sensibility*, and in Austen's other novels, characters who gain authority are able to modify themselves.

—Deborah Kaplan, "Achieving Authority: Jane Austen's First Published Novel," *Nineteenth-Century Fiction* 37, no. 4 (March 1983), reprinted in *Jane Austen*, ed. Harold Bloom (New York: Chelsea House Publishers, 1986), 206–208, 216

BIBLIOGRAPHY

Sense and Sensibility (3 vols.). 1811.
Pride and Prejudice (3 vols.). 1813.
Mansfield Park (3 vols.). 1814.
Emma (3 vols.). 1816.
Northanger Abbey and Persuasion (4 vols.). 1818.
Novels (5 vols.). 1833.
Lady Susan and the Watsons. 1882.
Letters (2 vols.). 1884.

Novels (10 vols.). 1892.

Charades & c., Written a Hundred Years Ago by Jane Austen and her Family. 1895.

Love and Freindship. 1922.

The Watsons. 1923.

Five Letters to Her Niece Fanny Knight. 1924.

Lady Susan. 1925.

Fragment of a Novel Written by Jane Austen, January–March 1817. 1925.

Plan of a Novel. 1926.

Letters to Her Sister Cassandra and Others. 1932.

⟨*Juvenilia.*⟩ *Volume the First.* 1933.

Three Evening Prayers. 1940.

⟨*Juvenilia.*⟩ *Volume the Second.* 1951.

Minor Works. 1954.

⟨*Juvenilia.*⟩ *Volume the Third.* 1963.

Jane Austen's "Sir Charles Grandison." 1980.

The Juvenilia of Jane Austen and Charlotte Bronte. 1986.

Jane Austen's Manuscript Letters in Facsimile. 1990.

Catherine and Other Writings. 1993.

The History of England: From the Reign of Henry the 4th to the Death of Charles the 1st. 1993.

ANNE BRONTE
1820-1849

ANNE BRONTË, the youngest of the three Brontë sisters, was born at Thornton, near Bradford, Yorkshire, on January 17, 1820. In the year of her birth, her father, Reverend Patrick Brontë, moved his family to Haworth, a small mill town in Yorkshire, where he had a perpetual curacy. Brontë's mother, Maria Branwell Brontë, died in 1821. Mrs. Brontë's sister, Elizabeth Branwell, took charge of the household until her death in 1842. It has been rumored that she was not particularly kind to her sister's children. Unlike Charlotte and Emily, Anne escaped being sent to the now infamous Cowan Bridge Clergy Daughter's School, where her two eldest sisters, Maria and Elizabeth, contracted tuberculosis and died. Anne was educated by her father at home with Charlotte and Emily, who left Cowan Bridge, and her brother, Branwell. The four siblings roamed the Yorkshire moors, read in their father's library, borrowed books from the local Mechanics' Institute, and wrote their own stories. Inspired by their father's gift of some toy soldiers for Branwell in 1826, Anne and Emily began work on their Gondal saga, a serial about a fantastic kingdom in an an imaginary world. Branwell and Charlotte wrote their own series about a realm called Angria. Emily and Anne would continue to write about Gondal for the next twenty years, although Charlotte would give up Angria in 1839. Anne attended school at Roe Head with Charlotte and Emily, and in 1839 became a governess to the Ingham family at Blake Hall.

Of the three sisters, Anne had the most placid temperament, and perhaps for this reason she was the most successful governess. After leaving Blake Hall, she worked for the Robinson family at Thorp Green from 1840 to 1845, gaining the trust and respect of her young charges. In 1845 the sisters, all living at Haworth, attempted to publish their writing. *Poems by Currer, Ellis, and Acton Bell*—the last being Anne's pseudonym—was published in 1846. In 1847 Anne's novel *Agnes Grey*, based on her experiences as a governess, was published together with Emily's *Wuthering Heights* by Thomas Newby, a disreputable London firm. Anne's next novel, *The Tenant of Wildfell Hall*, is often seen as a companion to Emily's *Wuthering Heights*. While this suggests a continuation of the close emotional bond that characterized the relationship between the two youngest Brontë sisters, there is also evidence that Anne wanted to assert her differences from Emily at this point in her life. She was certainly more interested in giving her readers a brutally realistic picture of life than was Emily, whose work retained the wild romance of Gondal.

Charlotte was offended by *The Tenant of Wildfell Hall*'s unsavory depiction of alchoholism, much of which was based on Branwell's drinking problems. Thus, when Newby published the novel in 1848, but implied that it had been written by Currer Bell, the successful author of *Jane Eyre*, both Anne and Charlotte were understandably angry. To dispel this rumor, Anne and Charlotte went to London to prove that they were indeed two separate people. They met the publisher John Smith of Smith, Elder and Co. and other people who were influential in the world of letters. This was to be Anne's only trip to the metropolis. After her return, Emily died of consumption. Branwell's alchoholism had already brought about his death that same year. Anne died of consumption the next year on May 28, 1849. She was 29 years old. Her poems, including those discovered after her death, were published in 1920.

CRITICAL EXTRACTS

CHARLES KINGSLEY

It ⟨*The Tenant of Wildfell Hall*⟩ is, taken altogether, a powerful and an interesting book. Not that it is a pleasant book to read, nor, as we fancy, has it been a pleasant book to write; still less has it been a pleasant training which could teach an author such awful facts, or give courage to write them. The fault of the book is coarseness—not merely that coarseness of subject which will be the stumbling-block of most readers, and which makes it utterly unfit to be put into the hands of girls; of that we do not complain. There are foul and accursed undercurrents in plenty, in this same smug, respectable, whitewashed English society, which must be exposed now and then; and Society owes thanks, not sneers, to those who dare to shew her the image of her own ugly, hypocritical visage. We must not lay Juvenal's coarseness at Juvenal's door, but at that of the Roman world which he stereotyped in his fearful verses. But the world does not think so. It will revile Acton Bell for telling us, with painful circumstantiality, what the house of a profligate, uneducated country squire is like, perfectly careless whether or not the picture be true, only angry at having been disturbed from its own self-complacent doze—just as it has reviled gallant 'S. G. O.' for nasty-mindedness, and what not, because, having unluckily for himself a human heart and eyes, he dared to see what was under his nose in the bedrooms of Dorsetshire labourers.

It is true, satirists are apt to be unnecessarily coarse. Granted; but are they half as coarse, though, as the men whom they satirise? That gnat-straining, camel-swallowing Pharisee, the world, might, if it chose, recollect that a certain degree of coarse-naturedness, while men continue the one-sided beings which they are at present, may be necessary for all reformers, in order to enable them to look steadily and continuously at the very evils which they are removing. Shall we despise the surgeon because he does not faint in the dissecting-room? Our Chadwicks and Southwood Smiths would make but poor sanitary reformers if their senses could not bid defiance to sulphuretted hydrogen and ammonia. Whether their nostrils suffer or not, ours are saved by them: we have no cause to grumble. And even so with 'Acton Bell.'

But taking this book as a satire, and an exposure of evils, still all unnecessary coarseness is a defect,—a defect which injures the real usefulness and real worth of the book. The author introduces, for instance, a long diary, kept by the noble and unhappy wife of a profligate squire; and would that every man in England might read and lay to heart that horrible record. But what greater mistake, to use the mildest term, can there be than to fill such a diary with written oaths and curses, with details of drunken scenes which no wife, such as poor Helen is represented, would have the heart, not to say the common decency, to write down as they occurred? Dramatic probability and good feeling are equally outraged by such a method. The author, tempted naturally to indulge her full powers of artistic detail, seems to have forgotten that there are silences more pathetic than all words. ⟨. . .⟩

The puffs inform us that the book is very like *Jane Eyre*. To us it seems to have exaggerated all the faults of that remarkable book, and retained very few of its good points. The superior *religious* tone in which alone it surpasses *Jane Eyre* is, in our eyes, quite neutralised by the low *moral* tone which reigns throughout.

Altogether, as we said before, the book is painful. The dark side of every body and every thing is dilated on; we had almost said, revelled in. There are a very few quite perfect people in the book, but they are kept as far out of sight as possible; they are the 'accidentals,' the disagreeable people, the 'necessary' notes of the melody; and the 'timbre' of the notes themselves is harsh and rough. The author has not had the tact which enabled Mr. Thackeray, in *Vanity Fair*, to construct a pleasing whole out of most unpleasing materials, by a harmonious unity of parts, and, above all, by a tone of tender grace and solemn ironic indignation, in the midst of all his humour, spreading over and softening down the whole;—that true poetic instinct, which gives to even the coarsest of Fielding's novels and Shakspeare's comedies, considered as wholes, a really pure and lofty beauty. The author has not seen that though it is quite fair to write in a melancholy, or even harsh key, and to introduce accidental discords, or even sounds in themselves disagreeable, yet that this last must be done only to set off by contrast the background of harmony and melody, and that the key of the whole must be a correct and a palpable one; it must not be buried beneath innumerable occasional flats and sharps; above all, we must not, as in *The Tenant of Wildfell Hall*, with its snappish fierceness, be tortured by a defective chord, in which one false note is perpetually recurring; or provoked by a certain flippant, rough staccato movement throughout, without softness, without repose, and, therefore, without dignity. We advise the author, before the next novel is taken in hand, to study Shakspeare somewhat more carefully, and see if she cannot discover the secret of the wonderful harmony with which he, like Raphael, transfigures the most painful, and, apparently, chaotic subjects.

—Charles Kingsley, from "Recent Novels," *Fraser's Magazine* (April 1849), excerpted in *The New Moulton's Library of Literary Criticsim*, Vol. 8, ed. Harold Bloom (New York: Chelsea House Publishers, 1989), 4286–88

CHARLOTTE BRONTË

The Tenant of Wildfell Hall, by Acton Bell, had ⟨. . .⟩ an unfavourable reception. At this I cannot wonder. The choice of subject was an entire mistake. Nothing less congruous with the writer's nature could be conceived. The motives which dictated this choice were pure, but, I think, slightly morbid. She had, in the course of her life, been called on to contemplate, near at hand, and for a long time, the terrible effects of talents misused and faculties abused: hers was naturally a sensitive, reserved, and dejected nature; what she saw sank very deeply into her mind; it did her harm. She brooded over it till she believed it to be a duty to reproduce every detail (of course with fictitious characters, incidents, and situations,) as a warning to others. She hated her work, but would pursue it. When reasoned with on the subject, she regarded such reasonings as a temptation to self-indulgence. She must be honest; she must not varnish, soften, nor conceal. This well-meant resolution brought on her misconstruction, and some abuse, which she bore, as it was her custom to bear whatever was unpleasant, with mild, steady patience. She was a very sincere and practical Christian, but the tinge of religious melancholy communicated a sad shade to her brief, blameless life.

⟨. . .⟩ I have said that she was religious, and it was by leaning on those Christian doctrines in which she firmly believed, that she found support through her most painful journey. I witnessed their efficacy in her latest hour and greatest trial, and must bear my testimony to the calm triumph with which they brought her through. She died May 28, 1849. ⟨. . .⟩

Anne's character was milder and more subdued ⟨than Emily's⟩; she wanted the power, the fire, the originality of her sister, but was well endowed with quiet virtues of her own. Long-suffering, self-denying, reflective, and intelligent, a constitutional reserve and taciturnity placed and kept her in the shade, and covered her mind, and especially her feelings, with a sort of nun-like veil, which was rarely lifted. Neither Emily nor Anne was learned; they had no thought of filling their pitchers at the well-spring of other minds; they always wrote from the impulse of nature, the dictates of intuition, and from such stores of observation as their limited experience had enabled them to amass. I may sum up all by saying, that for strangers they were nothing, for superficial observers less than nothing; but for those who had known them all their lives in the intimacy of close relationship, they were genuinely good and truly great.

> —Charlotte Brontë, "Biographical Notice of Ellis and Acton Bell," *Wuthering Heights and Agnes Grey* (1850), excerpted in *The New Moulton's Library of Literary Criticism*, Vol. 8, ed. Harold Bloom (New York: Chelsea House Publishers, 1989), 4283–84

Mary A. Ward

Anne Brontë serves a twofold purpose in the study of what the Brontës wrote and were. In the first place, her gentle and delicate presence, her sad, short story, her hard life and early death, enter deeply into the poetry and tragedy that have always been entwined with the memory of the Brontës, as women and as writers; in the second, the books and poems that she wrote serve as matter of comparison by which to test the greatness of her two sisters. She is the measure of their genius—like them, yet not with them. ⟨. . .⟩

'Hers was naturally a sensitive, reserved, and dejected nature. She hated her work, but would pursue it. It was written as a warning,'—so said Charlotte when, in the pathetic Preface of 1850, she was endeavouring to explain to the public how a creature so gentle and so good as Acton Bell should have written such a book as *Wildfell Hall*. And in the second edition of *Wildfell Hall* which appeared in 1848 Anne Brontë herself justified her novel in a Preface which is reprinted in this volume for the first time. The little preface is a curious document. It has the same determined didactic tone which pervades the book itself, the same narrowness of view, and inflation of expression, an inflation which is really due not to any personal egotism in the writer, but rather to that very gentleness and inexperience which must yet nerve itself under the stimulus of religion to its disagreeable and repulsive task. 'I knew that such characters'—as Huntingdon and his companions—'do exist, and if I have warned one rash youth from following in their steps the book has not been written in vain.' If the story has given more pain than pleasure to 'any honest reader,' the writer 'craves his pardon, for such was far from my intention.' But at the same time she cannot promise to limit her ambition to the giving of innocent pleasure, or to the production of 'a perfect work of art.' 'Time and talent so spent I should consider wasted and misapplied.' God has given her unpalatable truths to speak and she must speak them.

The measure of misconstruction and abuse therefore which her book brought upon her she bore, says her sister, 'as it was her custom to bear whatever was unpleasant, with mild, steady patience. She was a very sincere and practical Christian, but the tinge of religious melancholy communicated a sad shade to her brief, blameless life.'

In spite of misconstruction and abuse, however, *Wildfell Hall* seems to have attained more immediate success than anything else written by the sisters before 1848, except *Jane Eyre*. It went into a second edition within a very short time of its publication, and Messrs. Newby informed the American publishers with whom they were negotiating that it was the work of the same hand which had produced *Jane Eyre*, and superior to either *Jane Eyre* or *Wuthering Heights!* It was, indeed, the sharp practice connected with this astonishing judgment which led to the sisters' hurried journey to London in 1848—the famous journey when the two little ladies in black revealed themselves to Mr. Smith, and proved to him that they were not one Currer Bell, but two Miss Brontës. It was Anne's sole journey to London—her only contact with a world that was not Haworth, except that supplied by her school-life at Roehead and her two teaching engagements.

And there was and is a considerable narrative ability, a sheer moral energy in *Wildfell Hall*, which would not be enough, indeed, to keep it alive if it were not the work of a Brontë, but still betray it kinship and source. The scenes of Huntingdon's wickedness are less interesting but less improbable than the country-house scenes of *Jane Eyre*; the story of his death has many true and touching passages; the last lovescene is well, even in parts admirably written. But the book's truth, so far as it is true, is scarcely the truth of imagination; it is rather the truth of a tract or a report. There can be little doubt that many of the pages are close transcripts from Branwell's conduct and language,—so far as Anne's slighter personality enabled her to render her brother's temperament, which was more akin to Emily's than to her own. The same material might have been used by Emily or Charlotte; Emily, as we know, did make use of it in *Wuthering Heights*; but only after it had passed through that ineffable transformation, that mysterious, incommunicable heightening which makes and gives rank in literature. Some subtle, innate correspondence between eye and brain, between brain and hand, was present in Emily and Charlotte, and absent in Anne. There is no other account to be given of this or any other case of difference between serviceable talent and the high gifts of 'Delos' and Patara's own 'Apollo.'

—Mary A. Ward, "Introduction," *The Tenant of Wildfell Hall* (1900), excerpted in *The New Moulton's Library of Literary Criticism*, Vol. 8, ed. Harold Bloom (New York: Chelsea House Publishers, 1989), 4288–89

ADA HARRISON AND DEREK STANFORD

One of those errors of literary judgement, which criticism appears to have honoured for something like a hundred years, is to have regarded Anne as an artistic adjunct to the elder Brontës; a sort of humble footnote to her sisters' pages. It is true that George Moore did not consider her later novel a complete success; but whether or no one agrees with him as to the merits of *The Tenant of Wildfell Hall*, it is he who has struck the most resounding blow for the restitution of the youngest Brontë in her capacity as novelist. Anne, he claimed, 'had all the qualities of Jane Austen and other qualities', and again, 'If Anne Brontë had lived ten years longer she would have taken a place beside Jane Austen, perhaps even a higher place.' The judgement is unusual but not extravagant, and of a kind that is fertile in the comparisons to which it prompts us. ⟨. . .⟩

For all his ardent partisanship, it is probable that Moore's high-spirited defence was received by many minds with a small pinch of salt, his eloquence possibly smacking too much of paradox and special pleading to persuade the average sober-tempered critic. The result of this is that even today Anne has not been seriously considered as an artist. She has not so much as been weighed and found wanting, as rather unthinkingly put to one side.

A factor, doubtless, in this misconstruction is the habit of looking to find in her novels qualities present in Emily's and Charlotte's: their headlong poetry and fiery rhetoric, their highly-coloured palette and air of storm-and-stress. Of this fallacy of false approach, the critic Saintsbury is representative, for in his book *The English Novel* (1913), he writes that the 'third Brontë sister is but a pale reflection of her elders', and merely leaves the matter at that without further comment on her work. Anne, whose art participates so little in the family characteristic—the Brontë inclination towards the dramatic—is misjudged when placed side by side with her sisters. Her properties, her merits, are of another order: she is not their weak reflection, their sedulous echo, but a writer of an almost completely different-sort.

Any man, Robert Louis Stevenson observed, who was truly able to remember his childhood could write an incomparable book. What Anne remembers to perfection are the incidents and state of late adolescence and early womanhood under certain forms of stress. In the story of the governess in *Agnes Grey*, we meet with all those moments of hope and fear, those happenings, productive of keen joy or pain, which a young susceptibility and lack of experience inevitably guarantee to their possessor. But the two things mainly remarkable about this record of early impressions is the accurate, sober, unmisted fashion with which each detail is presented; and the stoic and un-self-pitying manner in which these griefs and hardships are described. With Thackeray or with Dickens, for example, the narration of such sad situations would be the occasion for some purple passage, some lachrymose lament, or some indignant sermon. With Anne, the elegy is largely implicit. She holds on always to the thread of her tale; her style never registers hysterics; and even through tears her eye is on the object. ⟨. . .⟩

Nor was Anne slow to seek the application of her psychological insight— a species of knowledge which, when transferred to the drawing-room levels of Victorian fiction—assumed a quite devastating air. What English novelist of that time, prior to the advent of Thomas Hardy, would have dared—well mindful of the unwritten law concerning conjugal obedience—to have shown the heroine bolting the door against her rightful but vicious husband, determined that a man so false and debauched should enjoy intimacy with her no longer. In a similar way, for sheer and simple frankness—a purposive outspokenness in no manner brazen—we shall find no Victorian, again before Hardy, capable of treating so unsavoury a scene as that in *The Tenant of Wildfell Hall* where the drunken husbands break in upon their wives after a much-protracted session with the bottle. Their brutalities, stupor, and acts of violation are described in a fashion which Zola might have admired. ⟨. . .⟩

As for sermonizing—her age's stock response—we find it present here in no degree at all. Instead, we witness the situation through the eyes of one who saw things neither with cynical distortion nor in sentimental terms. Anne, we may say, possessed the power of looking facts fully in the face; of keeping her gaze steadfastly upon them, however the sight might offend her. She refused to bury her head in the sand; refused even so much as to look the other way; and though she had few illusions about life, she would not permit her disenchantment to find an easy outlet in romantic grief. ⟨. . .⟩

Of the serious way she regarded her own writing, especially the writing of her second novel, we know from what Charlotte has to impart. 'She wrote it,' we are told by her, with reference to *The Tenant of Wildfell Hall*, 'under a strange, conscientious, half-ascetic notion of accomplishing a painful penance and a severe duty'; and indeed of Anne—as of few Victorian authors—we feel she never wrote for the sake of writing. Her words are always a token of good-will—of the knowledge of something she has to tell us; a something observed or experienced by her, through which she desires to instruct us for our good.

—Ada Harrison and Derek Stanford, "Anne Bronte as Novelist," *Anne Bronte: Her Life and Work* (1959), excerpted in *The Critical Perspective*, Vol. 7, ed. Harold Bloom (New York: Chelsea House Publishers, 1988), 4050–54

W. A. CRAIK

Anne Brontë clears from under her a great many difficulties that find their way into the fabric of her sisters' work, leaving herself free to handle more simply what is nearest her heart. She is wise to do so, as she is always an unsophisticated writer, a primitive in the art of the novel, gaining her results by very simple methods, which owe little to the techniques she might have learned from others. She assumes from the beginning that the reader acknowledges and agrees with her standards of right and wrong, and her view of man's duty to society, without having to share the emotional position of the narrator. ⟨. . .⟩

Characterization for Anne Brontë is far from being what is seems so often in the Victorian novel, the overriding impulse. Events, situations, and actions take priority. As any competent novelist must, she reconciles the claims of both plot and personality; but basically *The Tenant of Wildfell Hall* is a story of what happens as a result of drunkenness and dissoluteness (the qualities Helen sums up as self-indulgence.) The characters are conceived as, at the centre, those who would either create, or get into, events such as Anne Brontë is committed to depicting; and at the periphery, those who exemplify all the possible consequences. The author's hand is very strong on her characters, who are, much more even than Thackeray's, puppets on the strings of a superb puppet-master. There is never any chance that one of them may win the kind of independent life that Trollope and Thackeray both admitted theirs did, which let them alter or dictate their fate, according to the nature they had assumed. Anne Brontë ensures that what happens and those who make it happen shall fulfil her purposes; nor does she ever suggest that she herself can be influenced by them, or identify herself with her creations. ⟨. . .⟩

Anne Brontë's ways of constructing and presenting what she has to say, use, like her characterization, very simple and unobtrusive means, for results that are effective and original, and more elaborate than they seem. She continues to rely, as in *Agnes Grey*, on a candid literal narrative, without any but the very simplest and commonplace imagery, and still relies also on dialogue to produce an effect of reality, distinguishing her speakers by the content of what they say, rather than by idiom. *The Tenant of Wildfell Hall* represents an advance on *Agnes Grey* however, by its very much more complicated structure. ⟨. . .⟩

Anne Brontë is like her sisters in being unique, in being apparently very little influenced by any writer before her, and in writing for ends which the novel had not previously been made to serve. While she is not as great as either of them, she is never a bad or second-rate artist. She seems to do all that is possible by taking pains, by being fully conscious of the end to which she is working, and by directing all her powers towards it. She is not a great novelist, because she has no passion to express, nor any new or original view of human nature to expound. But she is never meretricious or showy, having always a purpose in writing worthy in itself, and fit for a novel. Her two novels are original, because both use new material to illuminate old truths about man in his society, and because both work out their own personal methods. She is not derivative—although she does not hesitate to admit influences where an earlier novelist's effects are similar to her own—since no novelist offers her a model in a similar field; and she has no successors, partly because her achievement is so modest (despite the popular success of *The Tenant of Wildfell Hall*), and partly because her effects are so closely the result of her purpose that they cannot be used for any other. The contemporary who comes closest to *The Tenant of Wildfell Hall*—as Mark Rutherford to *Agnes Grey*—is not a novelist, but a writer, Harriet Martineau, who also found that fiction was at some points the fit and proper medium for a theory, even though the theories of Harriet Martineau were more coherent, philosophical, and practical. Both women write robustly and plainly, with the startling truth that comes from the apparently self-evident and unremarkable; though neither can make the claim to the single masterpiece that Emily Brontë makes with *Wuthering Heights*, or the claim to be a major novelist with a corpus of professional writing that Charlotte Brontë's four novels make for her. Few people now dispute Emily's claim. Charlotte's, admitted in her lifetime, later suspect and disallowed, is vindicated by close critical scrutiny. Anne has rarely been thought worth the trial, but yet sustains it with a success that, though modest, is complete.

—W. A. Craik, "The Tenant of Wildfell Hall," *The Brontë Novels* (1968), excerpted in *The Brontës*, ed. Harold Bloom (New York: Chelsea House Publishers, 1987), 38–39, 43–44, 53, 56

TOM WINNIFRITH

We see ⟨. . .⟩ in the poems a gradual change in mood between the anxiety of 1841 and the confidence of 1845 on the subject of salvation. Originally Anne had her doubts about her own salvation; soon she began to feel that other far greater sinners might be saved. A similar change can be seen in *Agnes Grey*, if we assume, as seems possible, that this was written over a period of some years. In the early part of the novel there is a straightforward statement by Agnes Grey herself about the place where wicked people go when they die; in the part written later Mr Weston is more hopeful about people who may enter in at the strait gate, and Mr Hatfield's views are by implication condemned. *Agnes Grey* is however surprisingly free from religion in view of the fact that the narrator is the daughter of a clergyman who marries a clergyman; apart from the rather naïve message that good girls like Agnes Grey prosper while bad girls like Rosalie Murray do not, there is little of a specifically religious nature except in the chapters, 'The Church' and 'The Cottagers', and here, as we have shown, the confused account of Mr Hatfield's religious proclivities does not enable us to form any clear picture of what Anne is trying to attack.

This is far from being the case in *The Tenant of Wildfell Hall*, although here apart from slight portraits of the gluttonous Mr Millward and the studious Richard Wilson there are no clergymen to discuss. References to salvation are, however, numerous, and Anne's unorthodox views attracted unfavourable comment in *Sharpes' London Magazine*. The most important passage occurs in the conversation between Helen and her aunt, where there are embarassingly direct references to thirty Biblical passages which suggest universal salvation and to the meaning of the Greek word αἰώνιοϛ for which 'long-enduring' is suggested as an alternative translation in place of 'eternal'. ⟨. . .⟩

The whole passage is more like a page from a tract than a novel, though perhaps Anne is fortunate that she is writing a novel; this saves her from quoting chapter and verse for her thirty Bible references or Liddell and Scott for her Greek scholarship, since she would have a difficult case to prove. ⟨. . .⟩

'I'm sorry papa's wicked', says little Arthur Huntingdon, 'for I don't want him to go to hell.' Anne may not have realised the apparent contradiction between this point of view and her strenuous plea for universal salvation, or she may have thought that she had covered herself by the references to purging fires in the passages denying eternal punishment. But a belief in purging fires as a fitting punishment is almost as bad as a contradiction, since if Anne really believed that we go through a vale of tears now in order to avoid the torments of purgatory hereafter, she believed a doctrine that makes the virtuous seem selfish and gives the vicious an incentive to sin. As in any doctrine where a heavenly crown may be worn by virtuous self-restraint, there is a temptation to regard those aspiring to a heavenly crown as practising a form of selfishness only slightly more refined than that practised by those who restrain their lusts on earth for a little time in order to enjoy them more fully later. If one is like Huntingdon and does not restrain oneself, then one may be punished later but, as this punishment is not eternal and only hypothetical, it may seem worth the risk.

To escape this danger we can imagine somebody working out a doctrine like that suggested in *Jane Eyre*, whereby men are virtuous, not to save their own souls but to save the souls of the wicked. This theory deals with the objection of selfishness, and keeps the deterrent power of purgatory, since the wicked will be released from their torture only if enough people are virtuous. It also removes the injustice of condemning people to hell who are only marginally more wicked than those who get to heaven, since the mildly wicked will be saved by the mildly virtuous, while the very wicked will have to wait longer for the very virtuous to save them. In addition the doctrine is a natural extension of the doctrine of Redemption, much favoured by Mr Brontë, and it provides some rationale for the Last Judgement; normally it would seem an unnecessary refinement on the part of the Almighty, who has already judged most people on their deathbeds. If we follow this doctrine however the Last Judgement does serve a purpose, since it refers to the time when sufficient virtue had been accumulated to make further judgement unnecessary.

In the light of this doctrine the apparent contradictions in *The Tenant of Wildfell Hall* disappear. The sufferings of Helen Huntingdon, of Lord Lowborough, sufferings made worse by his apparent salvation, and even of Mr Hargrave, are all necessary to save Huntingdon's soul. Huntingdon himself suffers, but not sufficiently to earn salvation straightaway. The conventional happy ending with wedding bells for Helen Huntingdon and Gilbert Markham and, for that matter, for Frederick Lawrence and Esther Hargrave, is not important in itself; indeed it would be a weakness of the novel if it were so, since it appears to be largely a matter of chance that the novel does not end with Helen still tied to her husband while her lover is in gaol for the murder of her brother. The happy ending is important in that it reflects the heavenly crown that the good characters were soon to enjoy and that by their privations they had won even for the bad. Additional confirmation for this interpretation of *The Tenant of Wildfell Hall* is to be found in the close connection between Emily and Anne Brontë. Almost all the first-hand biographical information we have about them shows them working together. Acton and Ellis Bell were naturally confused, and perhaps in reaction to this some have been at pains to stress the differences between *The Tenant of Wildfell Hall* and *Wuthering Heights*. But there are also obvious resemblances, such as the similarity in initials of the houses and the main characters, the arrival of a new tenant at the beginning of each book, the gambling, drinking and swearing so surprising in books written by a clergyman's daughters, and perhaps the most important resemblance from the formal point of view, the double switch of narrators. These similarities, far greater than any suggested by a comparison of *Jane Eyre* and *Wuthering Heights*, have been noted, but less attention has been paid to the close resemblance of theme, which is also similar to that of *Jane Eyre*. The violence of language and behavior in the centre of both novels is perhaps a little overdone, but it reflects the unhappiness of the characters, as they work their way to the quiet elegiac ending of *Wuthering Heights* and the joyful conclusion of *The Tenant of Wildfell Hall*. In both novels there are frequent references to heaven and hell to act as pointers to the theme that through suffering hell on this earth we remove hell's power over the world.

—Tom Winnifrith, "The Brontë's Religion," *The Brontës and Their Background: Romance and Reality* (1973), excerpted in *The Critical Perspective*, Vol. 7, ed. Harold Bloom (New York: Chelsea House Publishers, 1988), 4055–56

JAN B. GORDON

Anne Brontë's *The Tenant of Wildfell Hall* quickly calls attention to itself as the longest single-narrative, enclosing epistolary novel of the nineteenth century. Beginning "dear Halford," it concludes four hundred and fifty pages later with a "Till then, farewell, Gilbert Markham." It is not the characters of the individual subjects of the novel nor the contents of Markham's narrative that shape the meaning of *The Tenant of Wildfell Hall*, but rather the relative dispensation of alternative narratives competing for our attention and hence for a textual priority. Each mode of discourse must confront the recognition that in any scheme of recovery, "voice" is a privileged aspect of language, that the intrusion of the "otherness" of the listener is a necessary constitution of meaning. The engagement of a narratee is achieved by sublating a variety of second- or third-hand discourse: community gossip; the narrator's own source, a "faded old journal"; the incomplete manuscript of Helen Huntington's diary, given to the narrator because she cannot *speak* her story; a cluster of failed correspondence between Gilbert and Helen; and finally, a sort of running commentary on another and historically prior text, Helen's exegesis of the Bible, which serves to foreground all the other narratives. Each of the enclosed varieties of discourse appears as a supplement, an attempt to amend or correct either the inadequacy or the social threat posed by another "version" of the same events. Rather than seeking to establish their primacy or priority by creating a discontinuity among narratives that would furnish a ground for deconstruction, however, Anne Brontë's narrator presents the reader with another situation: a world of proliferating "texts" which cannot be contained, except by a desperate and arbitrary act of enclosure. The formal rivalry between narratives has its genetic parallel in the way *The Tenant of Wildfell Hall* encloses its originary, *Wuthering Heights*, as it strives to supplant it. This structural belatedness is paralleled by a historical belatedness—a nineteenth-century epistolary novel. ⟨. . .⟩

Figuratively speaking, Gilbert Markham must get hold of all her writings—diary as well as letters—because only then can the unfinished, mediated status that always threatens to turn her life into gossip be put to an end. Gilbert must himself write the textual supplement to her life's diary—which cannot accommodate the otherness of the listener—and pass it on in order to prevent it from lapsing back into speech or gossip. Without that transactional frame, Anne Brontë's novel threatens to revert to the world of the narrative fragment, Gothic monsters, incestuous relationships, and, of course, whispered gossip—all of which call out for the completion of a closure that will restore differentiation. And in fact, as soon as Gilbert Markham's frame encloses all the other more subversive varieties of discourse, he marries Helen and the community's gossip vanishes. This takes place contemporaneously with the settlement of the dead father's farm upon Gilbert's brother Fergus, thus maintaining a legacy and keeping it from falling into other hands. The restoration of the narrative frame takes place at the same time as the investiture of the paternal lands, falling into disrepair during the plague of gossip. Just as the Victorian novel used a finalizing marriage, the fairy-tale ending, as an antidote to the threat of less socially acceptable forms of intercourse that threatened it, so *The Tenant of Wildfell Hall* equates a sort of narrative contract—the give-and-be-given of discourse—with the marital bond: both keep other monstrous plots at bay. ⟨. . .⟩

The framed discourse that encloses more free-floating, incomplete, or discontinuous discourse in Gothic structures is not a formal component of the radical thematics of the mode, but rather serves to restrain and repress. The salvation of texts by arbitrary supplements, the recovery of subversive discourse, does for "fallen" writing what the Rev. Brontë's sermons did for the unregenerate soul: they define an ending that restores the fiction of a distinction between the elect and the babble of tongues. Closure restores metaphor—and hence likeness and difference—at the cost of containing a crisis in discourse. ⟨. . .⟩

The impulse to "enclose" sweeps all before it, including the wind and the weather that swirl about Wildfell Hall and its environs. At the beginning of Anne Brontë's novel, nature itself is part of the imperfection of the fragmented, fallen world. Wildfell Hall is shielded from the war of wind and weather only by a group of scotch firs, "themselves half-blighted with storms." It is clearly an environment of incomplete closure where "the close green wall of privet, that had bordered the principal walk, were two-thirds withered away." By the time we reach the novel's end, however, a marvelous image of the conservative powers of enclosure appears. Helen Huntington wishes for her future husband, Gilbert, to be accepted by her aging aunt, now, like Helen, a widow. He must agree to the aunt's residence at the Staningley household, which has passed into Helen's inheritance. The aunt's avocation is the gentle nurturing of flowers out of season, a pastime made possible by the existence of an indoor *conservatory* to which Gilbert must pay homage. It is a fitting supplement to the bluebells in the gentle breeze which blows on the last page of *Wuthering Heights*.

This arrangement enables three generations to live under one roof, much as Gilbert Markham's framing letter to Halford, a letter outside the novel's first chapter, enables discontinuous narrative to become suddenly continuous. The domestication of potentially anarchic nature, the nurture of roses in winter, is achieved by the same gesture that brings the civilizing influence of inheritance, marriage, the enclosure of unfinished texts, and the containment of the narrative rivalry that was part of the publication history of Anne Brontë's novel. Only then, safely passed on, is the fiction of the family and the family of fictions secure against those forces which would confuse narrative or generational lines.

    —Jan B. Gordon, "Gossip, Diary, Letter, Text: Anne Brontë's Narrative *Tenant* and the Problematic of the Gothic Sequel," *ELH*, no. 4 (Winter 1984), reprinted in *Victorian Fiction*, ed. Harold Bloom (New York: Chelsea House Publishers, 1989), 241–42, 254, 259–60

EDWARD CHITHAM

Anne's artistic and moral challenge to the content of her sisters' novels comes in *Wildfell Hall*. Until this is recognized, readers may see the book as a pale version of *Wuthering Heights*, when it is in some aspects a critique of it. ⟨. . .⟩

    As *Wildfell Hall* developed from common ground with Emily, Anne used her story to show how very different was her 'moral' view from Emily's 'poetic' one. This argument, involving matters of realism, morality and indeed differing world views, began to pervade the new book. It does, finally, become Anne's considered 'answer' to *Wuthering Heights*. ⟨. . .⟩

    A constant factor in Anne's mind, too, was her vocation, that of teacher. In this respect she took after her father, whose character is often thought to be so different from hers. In the 1790s at Glascar he had been an almost inspired teacher, using exciting methods to illustrate his lessons, pursuing pupils to their farmhouses when they underachieved, and sought after by different classes of people. In *Agnes Grey* Anne had shown her excitement, through her heroine, at the very idea of guiding youngsters, and in exile at Thorp Green she had made headway in counselling the Robinsons. At last those weary years were bearing fruit; the girls voluntarily turned to Anne this winter when their mother began to try to persuade them against their natures to attract men whom they did not like. ⟨. . .⟩

    Ever since she had been a young girl Anne had been used to hearing of the affairs of married men and women with other married men and women. Adultery was the stock in trade of the Brontës' childhood and adolescent writing. This obsession did not come from the life patterns of the Brontë elders; it must be entirely from literary roots. ⟨. . .⟩

But Anne considered she knew more about human nature than the others. She had lived more in the world, and when it came to writing about immorality in high society she doubtless thought she could tackle the question with more realism. During her five years at Thorp Green she had seen many of the gentry, though usually at a distance, and occasionally some of the aristocracy. On holiday at Scarborough she had lived in lodgings with them. Social calls were made and there were meetings at the spa and along the shopping streets. Bessy and Mary gossiped. The younger Lydia, Anne's own pupil, eloped with an actor she must have been meeting in Anne's presence at Scarborough, and the runaway had been tolerated. In drawing Rosalie for *Agnes Grey*, Anne found herself understanding the actions of a self-centred flirt. Now she came to write of a worse seductress, and she amazingly gave the woman her own name: *Anna*bella. Lady Lowborough's character represents the punishable, irresponsible facets of Anne, against which her hymns at Thorp Green are a plea.

In *Wuthering Heights* the narrative dealt with a host of attractive villains whose names begin with H: Heathcliff, Hindley, Hareton. Anne replied with a list of unattractive villains whose names also begin with H: Hattersley, Hargrave, Huntingdon. This element surely must be a parody of Emily's novel. Meanwhile one of the most sinister, Hargrave, produces arguments suggesting that Helen should go to live with him that seem to satirize Rochester's pleas to Jane Eyre. In Anne's eyes, the very attractiveness of Rochester and Heathcliff adds a pernicious element to the novels in which they appear. Her own anti-heroes would be made to seem unattractive, and thus leave the reader unmoved by vice.

—Edward Chitham, "Artistic Independence," *A Life of Anne Brontë* (Oxford: Blackwell, 1991), 134, 142, 146, 148–49.

Susan Meyer

Late in Anne Brontë's first novel, the cultivated and diligent governess-heroine, Agnes Grey, is taken to task by her employer concerning the behavior of her hoydenish student, Matilda. "If you will only think of these things and try to exert yourself a *little* more . . . then, I am convinced, you would *soon* acquire that delicate tact which alone is wanting to give you a proper influence over the mind of your pupil," Mrs. Murray tells Agnes. It seems for a moment as if the long-suffering and much-criticized Agnes is finally going to respond to one of the many unjust attacks to which she has been subjected in the course of her employment. But Agnes is never able, throughout the events the novel narrates, to "talk back" to her employers. "I was about to give the lady some idea of the fallacy of her expectations," Agnes writes, "but she sailed away as soon as she had concluded her speech. Having said what she wished, it was no part of her plan to await my answer: it was my business to hear, and not to speak" (207).

In this novel about a heroine who is, at crucial moments, nearly speechless, Anne Brontë explores the nature of a society that makes it quite literally the "business" of some of its members "not to speak": that requires silence and acquiescence of some due to the conditions of their employment or of their social position. But *Agnes Grey* is written in the form of a first-person autobiography by this silenced heroine: in the form of the novel itself Agnes "talks back," and in the course of the novel Anne Brontë both subtly criticizes and resists the unjust silencing and disempowerment of the poorer classes by an autocratic and immoral British ruling class. At the same time, however, the novel hints that some of the same problems that characterize the relationship between classes characterize the relationships between men and women, and these problems remain more irresolvable at the novel's close. ⟨. . .⟩

Agnes Grey is, as critics have noted, characterized by a quiet, emotionally restrained tone. But the coolness and restraint are both deliberate on Anne Brontë's part and important to the novel's aims, because in *Agnes Grey* Anne Brontë offers the chronicle of a life of emotional and verbal repression. And if the plot of *Agnes Grey* is simple, the social criticism it offers, through this chronicle of repression, is complex. ⟨. . .⟩

In answer to the problem of verbal repression, Anne Brontë posits the act of novel-writing itself. In *Agnes Grey*, Brontë narrates a tale from the perspective of a woman who works in the house but nonetheless presumes to think for herself, who refuses, at least in written form, to be tongue-tied by the social order, and who offers a scathing account of what her self-styled social superiors say and do in the privacy of their own homes. Agnes shows the people from wealthy families with whom she lives to be vain, frivolous, and unprincipled, prone to drinking and gluttony, quarrelsome, and self-centered. She recounts domestic altercations between husband and wife that have taken place in her presence, as if she were an automaton, shows a mother determined to marry her daughter to the wealthiest possible man, and displays the mutual hatred that substitutes for love in upper-class marriages. And while the novel describes what *really* goes on in upper-class homes, it takes issue, subtly, with some of the central ideas of that class, the ideas by which they justify the class hierarchy to themselves. ⟨. . .⟩

The return of the subtle cues of a problematic hierarchy in the marriage with which *Agnes Grey* draws to a close suggests Anne Brontë's consciousness that, while she may have brought the issue of an unjust class hierarchy to a solution satisfactory to herself, she has not yet done so with the problem of gender inequality. It remains an issue that she will continue to pursue in her next novel, *The Tenant of Wildfell Hall.* And so when Agnes Grey ends her narrative with the sentence "And now I think I have said sufficient," it remains ambiguous what degree of completion or satisfaction her cessation of speech indicates. Has Agnes now "said sufficient" because Anne Brontë has made her critique of the British upper class in the words indited on the "great vulgar sheets" of the novel? Or has Agnes "said sufficient" because the solution to the problem of hierarchy, insidiously entering the relationship between loving men and women, remains, for now, inconceivable, for now beyond the scope of Anne Brontë's resistant words?

> —Susan Meyer, "Words on 'Great Vulgar Sheets': Writing and Social Resistance in Anne Brontë's *Agnes Grey* (1847)," *The New Nineteenth Century: Feminist Readings of Underread Victorian Fiction*, eds. Barbara Leah Harman and Susan Meyer (New York: Garland Publishing, 1996), 3–5, 8, 15

BIBLIOGRAPHY

Poems by Currer, Ellis, and Acton Bell (with Charlotte and Emily Brontë). 1846.

Agnes Gray. 1847.

The Tenant of Wildfell Hall. 1848.

Wuthering Heights and Agnes Gray with a Biographical Notice of the Authors, a Selection from Their Literary Remains, and a Preface by Currer Bell (Charlotte Brontë). 1850.

The Life and Works of Charlotte Brontë and her Sisters (7 vols.). 1872–73.

The Works of Charlotte, Emily, and Anne Brontë (12 vols.). 1893.

The Life and Works of the Sisters Brontë (7 vols.). 1899–1903.

Poems by Charlotte, Emily, and Anne Brontë. 1902.

The Brontës: Life and Letters (2 vols.). 1908.

The Shakespeare Head Brontë (with Charlotte and Emily Brontë) (19 vols). 1931–38.

The Brontës: Their Lives, Friendships, and Correspondence (4 vols.). 1932.

The Novels of Charlotte, Emily, and Anne Brontë. 1976.

Selected Poems (with Charlotte and Emily Brontë). 1985.

The Brontës: Selected Poems. 1985.

CHARLOTTE BRONTE
1816~1855

CHARLOTTE BRONTË was born on April 21, 1816, in Thornton, Yorkshire. The eldest of the three literary Brontë sisters, she was actually the third child of her parents, Patrick Brontë and Maria Branwell Brontë. Her father came from a poor family in County Down, Ireland, but managed to take a degree from Cambridge University in 1806, which enabled him to enter the Church of England. In 1820, he obtained a curacy at Haworth, Yorkshire, and moved his family there. His wife died the next year, and although the Reverend Brontë would make several attempts to remarry, he would have to rely on his unmarried sister-in-law to run the household.

With her sister Emily, Charlotte attended the Cowan Bridge Clergy Daughters' School, whose harsh environment she would later immortalize as Lowood in her novel *Jane Eyre*. It was at Cowan Bridge that Charlotte's two older sisters, Maria and Elizabeth, died of tuberculosis in 1825. After this catastrophe, the Reverend Brontë educated his remaining four children at home. The children were left to their own devices for much of the time; with Emily and Anne and brother Branwell, Charlotte wrote imaginary stories and poems about exotic worlds. Emily and Anne, in fact, contributed to their Gondal saga for twenty years. But Charlotte would abandon her world, Angria, in 1839 at age 23.

In 1831, Charlotte attended Miss Wooler's School at Roe Head. The experience was far happier than her short time at Cowan Bridge. While at Roe Head, Charlotte befriended Ellen Nussey, who would later provide Mrs. Gaskell with information about the Brontë family for her *Life of Charlotte Brontë*. Charlotte returned in 1835 to work as a teacher at Roe Head. This experience would prove useful, since all three sisters became governesses when they finished their schooling. Charlotte disliked her first two posts and dreamed of starting a school of her own with Emily and Anne. In 1842 she and Emily attended the Pensionnat Heger in Brussels to help them realize this goal. While there, Charlotte suffered greatly from unrequited love for the school's priggish proprietor M. Constantin Heger. The sisters' plan for a school was attempted in 1844, but failed.

In 1846 Charlotte privately printed *Poems by Currer, Ellis, and Acton Bell* (pseudonymns for the three sisters). It was indifferently received, but in the next year all three sisters published novels. Charlotte had a great success with *Jane Eyre*, published in 1847 by Smith, Elder & Co.

Charlotte and Anne travelled to London in 1848 to prove that Anne, and not Charlotte, was the author of *The Tenant of Wildfell Hall*. After returning Charlotte suffered the loss of her three remaining siblings; Branwell and Emily died in 1848, Anne in 1849. Charlotte's circumstances were now extremely limited and very depressing, since she alone was left at Haworth with her ill and aging father. Nevertheless, *Shirley*, set in a small country parish, was published in 1849 and *Villette*, which takes place in a pensionnat in Belgium, came out in 1853.

During these years, Brontë occasionally traveled to London, where her publisher, George Smith, introduced her to William Makepeace Thackeray, to whom she had dedicated the second edition of *Jane Eyre*. This dedication caused a scandal, arising from Brontë's ignorance of Thackeray's personal life (literary London had been quick to connect the "madwoman" of *Jane Eyre* to Thackeray's own insane wife). In 1850, Brontë met Elizabeth Gaskell. The two women became admiring friends. After accepting a proposal of marriage from her father's curate, Arthur Nicholls, Brontë experienced less than a year of married life.

She died on March 31, 1855, supposedly from complications of pregnancy (although it has never been verified that she was actually pregnant at the time of her death). Her novel *The Professor* was published posthumously in 1857, ten years after it had first been rejected. That same year, Mrs. Gaskell's biography, *Life of Charlotte Brontë*, appeared. *Emma*, a fragment of Brontë's last novel, appeared posthumously in the *Cornhill Magazine* with an introduction by Thackeray.

C R I T I C A L   E X T R A C T S

ELIZABETH RIGBY

Jane Eyre is throughout the personification of an unregenerate and undisciplined spirit, the more dangerous to exhibit from that prestige of principle and self-control which is liable to dazzle the eye too much for it to observe the inefficient and unsound foundation on which it rests. It is true Jane does right, and exerts great moral strength, but it is the strength of a mere heathen mind which is a law unto itself. No Christian grace is perceptible upon her. She has inherited in fullest measure the worst sin of our fallen nature—the sin of pride. Jane Eyre is proud, and therefore she is ungrateful too. It pleased God to make her an orphan, friendless, and penniless—yet she thanks nobody, and least of all Him, for the food and raiment, the friends, companions, and instructors of her helpless youth—for the care and education vouchsafed to her till she was capable in mind as fitted in years to provide for herself. On the contrary, she looks upon all that has been done for her not only as her undoubted right, but as falling far short of it. The doctrine of humility is not more foreign to her mind than it is repudiated by her heart. It is by her own talents, virtues, and courage, that she is made to attain the summit of human happiness, and, as far as Jane Eyre's own statement is concerned, no one would think that she owed anything either to God above or to man below. She flees from Mr. Rochester, and has not a being to turn to. Why was this? The excellence of the present institution at Casterton, which succeeded that of Cowan Bridge near Kirkby Lonsdale—these being distinctly, as we hear, the original and the reformed Lowoods of the book—is pretty generally known. Jane had lived there for eight years with 110 girls and 15 teachers. Why had she formed no friendship among them? Other orphans have left the same and similar institutions, furnished with friends for life, and puzzled with homes to choose from. How comes it that Jane had acquired neither? Among that number of associates there were surely some exceptions to what she so presumptuously stigmatises as 'the society of inferior minds.' Of course it suited the author's end to represent the heroine as utterly destitute of the common means of assistance, in order to exhibit both her trials and her powers of self-support—the whole book rests on this assumption—but it is one which, under the circumstances, is very unnatural and very unjust.

Altogether the autobiography of Jane Eyre is preeminently an anti-Christian composition. There is throughout it a murmuring against the comforts of the rich and against the privations of the poor, which, as far as each individual is concerned, is a murmuring against God's appointment—there is a proud and perpetual assertion of the rights of man, for which we find no authority either in God's word or in God's providence—there is that pervading tone of ungodly discontent which is at once the most prominent and the most subtle evil which the law and the pulpit, which all civilized society in fact, has at the present day to contend with. We do not hesitate to say that the tone of mind and thought which has overthrown authority and violated every code human and divine abroad, and fostered Chartism and rebellion at home, is the same which has also written Jane Eyre.

Still we say again this is a very remarkable book. We are painfully alive to the moral, religious, and literary deficiencies of the picture, and such passages of beauty and power as we have quoted cannot redeem it, but it is impossible not to be spellbound with the freedom of the touch. It would be mere hackneyed courtesy to call it 'fine writing.' It bears no impress of being written at all, but is poured out rather in the heat and hurry of an instinct, which flows ungovernably on to its object, indifferent by what means it reaches it, and unconscious too. As regards the author's chief object, however, it is a failure— that, namely, of making a plain, odd woman, destitute of all the conventional features of feminine attraction, interesting in our sight. We deny that he has succeeded in this. Jane Eyre, in spite of some grand things about her, is a being totally uncongenial to our feelings from beginning to end. We acknowledge her firmness—we respect her determination—we feel for her struggles; but, for all that, and setting aside higher considerations, the impression she leaves on our mind is that of a decidedly vulgar-minded woman—one whom we should not care for as an acquaintance, whom we should not seek as a friend, whom we should not desire for a relation, and whom we should scrupulously avoid for a governess.

—Elizabeth Rigby (Lady Eastlake), [review of Jane Eyre], *Quarterly Review*, no. 167 (December 1848), 172–74

VIRGINIA WOOLF

A novelist, we reflect, is bound to build up his structure with much very per-ishable material which begins by lending it reality and ends by cumbering it with rubbish. As we open *Jane Eyre* once more we cannot stifle the suspicion that we shall find her world of imagination as antiquated, mid-Victorian, and out of date as the parsonage on the moor, a place only to be visited by the curious, only preserved by the pious. So we open *Jane Eyre*; and in two pages every doubt is swept clean from our minds.

> Folds of scarlet drapery shut in my view to the right hand; to the left were the clear panes of glass, protecting, but not separating me from the drear November day. At intervals, while turning over the leaves of my book, I studied the aspect of that winter afternoon. Afar, it offered a pale blank of mist and cloud; near, a scene of wet lawn and storm-beat shrub, with ceaseless rain sweeping away wildly before a long and lamentable blast.

There is nothing there more perishable than the moor itself, or more sub-ject to the sway of fashion than the 'long and lamentable blast'. Nor is this exhilaration short-lived. It rushes us through the entire volume, without giv-ing us time to think, without letting us lift our eyes from the page. So intense is our absorption that if someone moves in the room the movement seems to take place not there but up in Yorkshire. The writer has us by the hand, forces us along her road, makes us see what she sees, never leaves us for a moment or allows us to forget her. At the end we are steeped through and through with genius, the vehemence, the indignation of Charlotte Brontë. Remarkable faces, figures of strong outline and gnarled feature have flashed upon us in passing; but it is through her eyes that we have seen them. Once she is gone, we seek for them in vain. Think of Rochester and we have to think of Jane Eyre. Think of the moor, and again there is Jane Eyre. Think of the drawing-room, even, those 'white carpets on which seemed laid brilliant garlands of flowers', that 'pale Parian mantelpiece' with its Bohemia glass of 'ruby red' and the 'general blending of snow and fire'—what is all that except Jane Eyre? ⟨. . .⟩

Charlotte Brontë, at least, owed nothing to the reading of many books. She never learnt the smoothness of the professional writer, or acquired his ability to stuff and sway his language as he chooses. 'I could never rest in communication with strong, discreet, and refined minds, whether male or female', she writes, as any leader-writer in a provincial journal might have written; but gathering fire and speed goes on in her own authentic voice 'till I had passed the outworks of conventional reserve and crossed the threshold of confidence, and won a place by their hearts' very hearthstone'. It is there that she takes her seat; it is the red and fitful glow of the heart's fire which illumines her page. In other words, we read Charlotte Brontë not for exquisite observation of character—her characters are vigorous and elementary; not for comedy—hers is grim and crude; not for a philosophic view of life—hers is that of a country parson's daughter; but for her poetry. Probably that is so with all writers who have, as she has, an overpowering personality, so that, as we say in real life, they have only to open the door to make themselves felt. There is in them some untamed ferocity perpetually at war with the accepted order of things which makes them desire to create instantly rather than to observe patiently. This very ardour, rejecting half shades and other minor impediments, wings its way past the daily conduct of ordinary people and allies itself with their more inarticulate passions. It makes them poets, or, if they choose to write in prose, intolerant of its restrictions. Hence it is that both Emily and Charlotte are always invoking the help of nature. They both feel the need of some more powerful symbol of the vast and slumbering passions in human nature than words or actions can convey. It is with a description of a storm that Charlotte ends her finest novel *Villette*. 'The skies hang full and dark—a wrack sails from the west; the clouds cast themselves into strange forms.' So she calls in nature to describe a state of mind which could not otherwise be expressed. But neither of the sisters observed nature accurately as Dorothy Wordsworth observed it, or painted it minutely as Tennyson painted it. They seized those aspects of the earth which were most akin to what they themselves felt or imputed to their characters, and so their storms, their moors, their lovely spaces of summer weather are not ornaments applied to decorate a dull page or display the writer's powers of observation—they carry on the emotion and light up the meaning of the book.

—Virginia Woolf, *"Jane Eyre and Wuthering Heights"* (1916), *Collected Essays*, ed. Leonard Woolf, Vol. 1 (1967), excerpted in *The Critical Perspective*, Vol. 7, ed. Harold Bloom (New York: Chelsea House Publishers, 1988), 4194–95

KATE MILLETT

Villette reads, at times, like another debate between the opposed mentalities of Ruskin and Mill. Lucy is forever alternating between hankering after the sugared hopes of chivalric rescue, and the strenuous realism of Mill's analysis. Brontë demonstrates thereby that she knows what she is about. In her circumstances, Lucy would not be creditable if she were not continuously about to surrender to convention; if she were not by turns silly as well as sensible. So there are many moments when she wishes she were as pretty as Fanshawe, as rich as Polly, occasions when she would happily forgo life itself at a sign that Graham recognizes she was alive. Born to a situation where she is subject to life-and-death judgments based on artificial standards of beauty, Lucy is subject to a compulsive mirror obsession, whereby each time she looks in the glass she denies her existence—she does not appear in the mirror. One of the most interesting cases of inferiority feelings in literature, Lucy despises her exterior self, and can build an inner being only through self-hatred. Yet living in a culture which takes masochism to be a normal phenomenon in females, and even conditions them to enjoy it, Lucy faces and conquers the attractions Paul's sadism might have held.

Charlotte Brontë has her public censor as well as her private one to deal with. This accounts for the deviousness of her fictional devices, her continual flirtation with the bogs of sentimentality which period feeling mandates she sink in though she be damned if she will. Every Victorian novel is expected to end in a happy marriage; those written by women are required to. Brontë pretends to compromise; convention is appeased by the pasteboard wedding of Paulina Mary and Prince John; cheated in Lucy's escape.

Escape is all over the book; *Villette* reads like one long meditation on a prison break. Lucy will not marry Paul even after the tyrant has softened. He has been her jailer all through the novel, but the sly and crafty captive in Lucy is bent on evading him anyway. She plays tame, learns all he has to teach her of the secrets of the establishment—its mathematics and Latin and self-confidence. She plays pupil to a man who hates and fears intelligent women and boasts of having caused the only woman teacher whose learning ever challenged his own to lose her job. Lucy endures the baiting about the "natural inferiority of females" with which Paul tortures her all through the lesson, and understands that only the outer surface of his bigotry melts when she proves a good student and thereby flatters his pedagogic vanity. Yet in his simplicity he has been hoodwinked into giving her the keys. The moment they are in her hand, and she has beguiled him into lending her money, renting her a school of her own, and facilitated her daring in slipping from the claws of Madame Beck—she's gone. The keeper turned kind must be eluded anyway; Paul turned lover is drowned.

Lucy is free. Free is alone; given a choice between "love" in its most agreeable contemporary manifestation, and freedom, Lucy chose to retain the individualist humanity she had shored up, even at the expense of sexuality. The sentimental reader is also free to call Lucy "warped," but Charlotte Brontë is hard-minded enough to know that there was no man in Lucy's society with whom she could have lived and still been free. On those occasions when Brontë did marry off her heroines, the happy end is so fraudulent, the marriages so hollow, they read like satire, or cynical tracts against love itself. There was, in Lucy's position, just as in the Brontës' own, no other solution available.

As there is no remedy to sexual politics in marriage, Lucy very logically doesn't marry. But it is also impossible for a Victorian novel to recommend a woman not marry. So Paul suffers a quiet sea burial. Had Brontë's heroine "adjusted" herself to society, compromised, and gone under, we should never have heard from her. Had Brontë herself not grown up in a house of half-mad sisters with a domestic tyrant for father, no "prospects," as marital security was referred to, and with only the confines of governessing and celibacy staring at her from the future, her chief release the group fantasy of "Angria," that collective dream these strange siblings played all their lives, composing stories about a never-never land where women could rule, exercise power, govern the state, declare night and day, death and life—then we would never have heard from Charlotte either. Had that been the case, we might never have known what a resurrected soul wished to tell upon emerging from several millennia of subordination. Literary criticism of the Brontës has been a long game of masculine prejudice wherein the player either proves they can't write and are hopeless primitives, whereupon the critic sets himself up like a schoolmaster to edit their stuff and point out where they went wrong, or converts them into case histories from the wilds, occasionally prefacing his moves with a few pseudo-sympathetic remarks about the windy house on the moors, or old maidhood, following with an attack on every truth the novels contain, waged by anxious pedants who fear Charlotte might "castrate" them or Emily "unman" them with her passion. There is bitterness and anger in *Villette*—and rightly so. One finds a good deal of it in Richard Wright's *Black Boy*, too. To label it neurotic is to mistake symptom for cause in the hope of protecting oneself from what could be upsetting.

What should surprise us is not Lucy's wry annoyance, but her affection and compassion—even her wit. *Villette* is one of the wittier novels in English and one of the rare witty books in an age which specialized in sentimental comedy. What is most satisfying of all is the astonishing degree of consciousness one finds in the work, the justice of its analysis, the fairness of its observations, the generous degree of self-criticism. Although occasionally flawed with mawkish nonsense (there is a creditable amount of Victorian syrup in *Villette*), it is nevertheless one of the most interesting books of the period and, as an expression of revolutionary sensibility, a work of some importance.

—Kate Millett, "The Sexual Revolution, First Phase: Literary," *Sexual Politics* (1970), excerpted in *The Critical Perspective*, Vol. 7, ed. Harold Bloom (New York: Chelsea House Publishers, 1988), 4198–99

TERRY EAGLETON

Where Charlotte Brontë differs most from Emily is precisely in this impulse to negotiate passionate self-fulfilment on terms which preserve the social and moral conventions intact, and so preserve intact the submissive, enduring, everyday self which adheres to them. Her protagonists are an extraordinarily contradictory amalgam of smouldering rebelliousness and prim conventionalism, gushing Romantic fantasy and canny hard-headedness, quivering sensitivity and blunt rationality. It is, in fact, a contradiction closely related to their roles as governesses or private tutors. The governess is a servant, trapped within a rigid social function which demands industriousness, subservience and self-sacrifice; but she is also an 'upper' servant, and so (unlike, supposedly, other servants) furnished with an imaginative awareness and cultivated sensibility which are precisely her stock-in-trade as a teacher. She lives at that ambiguous point in the social structure at which two worlds—an interior one of emotional hungering, and an external one of harshly mechanical necessity—meet and collide. ⟨. . .⟩

Part of what we see happening in these novels, in fact, is a marriage of identifiably bourgeois values with the values of the gentry or aristocracy—a marriage which reflects a real tendency of the 'spirit of the age'. The Brontës were born at a time when a centuries-old system of cloth-making in the West Riding was coming to an end with the advent of water-power and then steam; they grew up in a context of rapid industrialisation and the growth of a wealthy manufacturing middle-class. It was this phenomenon, as Phyllis Bentley has pointed out, which created the demand for governesses who would give the children of wealthy manufacturers an education equivalent to that of the gentry; and in this sense the sisters were involved in the process of social transition. (As the daughters of an Irish peasant farmer's son who had married into socially superior Cornish stock, they also knew something of social transition in a more direct way). But if the West Riding was undergoing rapid industrialisation, it was also a traditional stronghold of the landed gentry, and among the gentry were men who had gone into manufacturing. ⟨. . .⟩

Shirley is perhaps the best novel to demonstrate this theme, since the historical incidents it deals with do in fact closely concern the relations between Tory squirearchy and Whig manufacturers in the West Riding in the early years of the nineteenth century. The central dramatic action of the novel—the Luddite attack on Robert Moore's mill—re-creates the assault in 1812 on William Cartwright's mill at Rawfolds in the Spen Valley; and Cartwright's ruthless repulsion of the Luddites signalled, in Edward Thompson's words, 'a profound emotional reconciliation between the large mill-owners and the authorities at a time when squire and mill-owner were bitterly hostile to one another over the war and the Orders in Council. That the novel's main thrust is to re-create and celebrate that class-consolidation, achieved as it was by the catalyst of working-class militancy, is obvious enough in the figure of Shirley herself. Shirley is a landowner, but half her income comes from owning a mill; and even though her attitudes to the mill are significantly Romantic (she is 'tickled with an agreeable complacency' when she thinks of it), she is adamant that trade is to be respected, and determined to defend her property 'like a tigress'. 'If once the poor gather and rise in the form of the mob', she tells Caroline Helstone, 'I shall turn against them as an aristocrat'. The novel registers a few feeble liberal protests against this position: Caroline ventures to point out the injustice of including all working people under the term 'mob', and elsewhere Shirley (with no sense of inconsistency, and conveniently enough for herself in the circumstances) can denounce all crying up of one class against another. But her 'spirited' attitude is in general endorsed, not least because it has behind it the weight of her ancient Yorkshire lineage, with its traditions of paternalist care for the poor. Indeed, because she is a conservative paternalist, Shirley's position can accommodate a fair amount of reformism: she objects to the Church's insolence to the poor and servility to the rich, and believes it to be 'in the utmost need of reformation'. In this sense Shirley differs from Robert Moore, whose neglect of philanthropy as a manufacturer is implicitly connected with his ill-luck in not having been born a Yorkshireman; but although Moore is critically measured against the robust traditions of Yorkshire paternalism, it is, significantly, Shirley herself who finally comes to the defence of his callousness. He is, she points out, a man who entered the district poor and friendless, with nothing but his own energies to back him; and it's unfair to upbraid him for not having been able to 'popularize his naturally grave, quiet manners, all at once'. (Moore's original, Cartwright, who defended his property with soldiers, spiked barricades and a tub of vitriol, and is reputed to have refused injured Luddites water or a doctor unless they turned informer, seems less easily excusable on the grounds of shyness). It is, in other words, the representative of the gentry who comes to the moral rescue of the bourgeois manufacturer; and Moore is in any case defended by the novel by a use of the 'split self' image which suggests that a sensitive dreamer lurks behind his 'hard dog' social exterior.

As a hybrid of progressive capitalist and traditional landowner, then, Shirley provides an important defence of trade; but her charismatic presence in the novel is also needed to defend Romantic conservatism against bourgeois ideology. ⟨. . .⟩

Commerce, in the novel's view, represents a genuine threat to (such) hierarchical harmony: the mercantile classes, Charlotte Brontë remarks, deny chivalrous feeling, disinterestedness and pride of honour in their narrowly unpatriotic scramble for gain. They deny, in fact, the aristocratic, Romantic-conservative virtues: and part of the point of the novel is to validate those neglected virtues without adopting too obviously the bigoted 'Church-and-King' posture of Helstone, Caroline's military-parson guardian. This is simple enough, given the novel's structure, since between the formalist Helstone on the one hand and the free-thinking Yorke on the other stands Shirley, paradigm of the desired union between Romanticism and reform, gentry and capitalist, order and progress. By the end of the novel, indeed, the union is literal as well as symbolic: Moore, having recovered his fortunes by the repeal of the Orders in Council, and having been suitably humanised as an employer by Caroline's influence, will add to the income of Shirley (who has married his brother), double the value of her mill-property and build cottages which Shirley will then let to his own workmen. The bond between squire and mill-owner is indissolubly sealed.

—Terry Eagleton, "Class, Power and Charlotte Brontë," *Critical Quarterly* (Autumn 1972), excerpted in *The Critical Perspective*, Vol. 7, ed. Harold Bloom (New York: Chelsea House Publishers, 1988), 4201–204

ELLEN MOERS

Charlotte Brontë ⟨was⟩ by nature a romantic of passionate strain, who remained all her life in awe of the call of her own imagination, both to genius and to madness. When Brontë wrote as a realist, therefore, it was with deliberation and from conviction. Thus it was as a Christian, as a modern (i.e., a

Victorian), as a native of industrial Yorkshire, as an adult (a status painfully won by the children of her family), and finally as a woman that she committed herself to the sober portrayal of the realities of everyday modern life at the outset of her career as a novelist. The results were interestingly original. "I had adopted a set of principles," she later wrote of her first novel. "I said to myself that my hero should work his way through life as I had seen real living men work theirs—that he should never get a shilling he had not earned—. . . that whatever small competency he might gain, should be won by the sweat of his brow. . . ." ⟨. . .⟩

Charlotte Brontë's first novel, *The Professor*, was published only after her death, and barely entered history at all except as a literary curiosity to those concerned with the development of the Brontë masterpiece *Villette*, which deals wholly, as *The Professor* deals in part, with Charlotte Brontë's experience as teacher in a Brussels school. In *Villette*, her last novel, Brontë provides one of the best literary accounts ever written of what it is like to face a classroom of the disagreeable, stupid, and intractable young. But her first novel, especially the opening six chapters, has an interest of its own, for *The Professor* is truly the sober, unromantic story of a man intended as a hero, and as at least the social equal of his readers, who works for a living. I do not know any previous work of English fiction carried out upon such principles.

William Crimsworth is well-born and well-educated but penniless, and driven by various necessities to forget family patronage and consider "engaging in trade." He works as second clerk in a textile manufacturing establishment in ——shire, charged with translating and copying the firm's foreign correspondence. (Clerk then meant secretary, man's work before the late-Victorian invention of the typewriter, and the ensuing opening of office employment to women.) No exciting incident, no upsweep of fortune, no romance, no amusement other than reading and walking, and very few social encounters break the routine of his office life. He lives on his meager salary in lodgings, a rented bedroom where the sluttish servant regularly lets the fire go out. The interest of the opening chapters is the peculiar atmosphere Brontë evokes—a kind of sooty, acrid, coldness—and the peculiar character of her hero. For sensibility, refinement, youth, and individuality, the qualities with which her hero is endowed at birth, are swallowed up by the character of the job-holder. ⟨. . .⟩

Subservience and self-denial are here the essentials of the white-collar working character. Whatever the defects of *The Professor*—whatever its conscious drabness of atmosphere, which I for one like to savor—the novel does not belong to the self-improving, success-worshiping genre of popular fiction.

The only burst of enthusiasm for work in itself that Brontë permits herself is, interestingly enough, in her delineation of the happy marriage that ends the novel. For an essential ingredient in its happiness is the working wife: it is she (a lace-mender turned schoolteacher) who craves employment for its own sake, she who finds fulfillment in work for pay. Crimsworth accedes to his wife's need, though at the end his income, amassed through school-managing and careful investing, makes her earnings a spiritual rather than an economic necessity.

> I put no obstacle in her way; raised no objection; I knew she was not one who could live quiescent and inactive, or even comparatively inactive. Duties she must have to fulfil, and important duties; work to do—and exciting, absorbing, profitable work; strong faculties stirred in her frame, and they demanded full nourishment, free exercise; mine was not the hand ever to starve or cramp them. . . .

Here and throughout the elaboration in the last chapters of *The Professor* of the ideal of work for married women—something of a landmark in that area, I imagine, for 1846—Brontë lets down her guard and reveals herself a woman novelist, whistling in the Victorian dark.

—Ellen Moers, "Money, the Job, and Little Women," *Commentary* (January 1973), excerpted in *The Critical Perspective*, Vol. 7, ed. Harold Bloom (New York: Chelsea House Publishers, 1988), 4205–206

Thomas A. Langford

The many references in the novel to "presentiments, sympathies and signs" scarcely need pointing out. From Jane's prophetic dreams just before her wedding day, to the lightning-blasted chestnut tree foreshadowing Rochester's tragedy, to the telepathic call which comes to Jane at Marsh End—the reader is seldom free from the influence of these prophetic suggestions and revelations. They provide a continuing source, frequently unnoticed, of the novel's sense of continuity and unity.

Perhaps the most striking example of the author's use of "presentiments" is the three pictures in chapter thirteen. Lawrence Moser has interpreted the pictures as surrealistic, insisting upon "the surrealistic tenet that art of necessity mirrors the artist's personality and mentality, in this case both Jane's and Charlotte's, and tends violently toward a complete revelation of self." That the pictures do indeed mirror certain aspects of the personality of both Jane and Charlotte is easily evident, but they seem to me to go beyond this level in a way only indirectly hinted by Professor Moser, when, in interpreting the second picture, he sees the "two critical junctures in Jane's career," the traumatic breaking off of relationships with Rochester and St. John Rivers, suggested. The pictures are, of course, painted long before Jane meets either of these men. To interpret the pictures so as to include these men and other events following the creation of the paintings is to acknowledge "presentiment," or the prophetic quality in the act of artistic creation. ⟨. . .⟩

While Rochester looks at the pictures, Jane points out that their conception surpassed their execution, that each was "but a pale portrait of the thing I had conceived." There are other hints that the pictures were reflections of some kind of prophetic vision. She says that she "saw them with the spiritual eye," and Rochester says, after viewing them, "you have secured the shadow of your thought; but no more." He further suggests that parts of the pictures are strange, such that she "must have seen in a dream." Whether or not the content of the pictures may be said to be prophetic, one must conclude that they reflect the strong intuitive sense of things to come. As Jennifer Gibble has suggested, "the effect is to show how Jane's sensitive response to her experience can foresee, through the transmuting and organizing activity of the dream, the calamity implicit in what has already been lived through."

With these clues, I submit that the pictures represent the three major sections of Jane's life—Lowood, Thornfield, and Marsh End—each representing a major stage in the development of her character. If the three pictures are prophetic visions, or at least artistic reflections of the "presentiments" Jane believed in, it is not illogical to assume that they may symbolize the dominant action of the major sections of the novel. If the reader objects to the element of prophecy, I suggest that the novel must be taken on its own assumptions and that prophetic visions are no more difficult to accept than the telepathic call Jane receives from Rochester later in the novel. All are a part of the imaginative and highly sensitive world of Jane Eyre.

Interpreting the pictures in the light of these assumptions, we observe that the first picture presents an accurate symbolic portrayal of Jane's childhood and adolescence. ⟨. . .⟩

The second picture is clearly a vision of the goddess of love and is connected in various ways with Thornfield. It is in this section of the novel that Jane feels most strongly her womanly instincts and is awakened to the exhilarating and happy prospects of a transcendent love. Of the three pictures, only this one is specifically discussed by Rochester; this is the part of the total vision which concerns him most directly. The visionary quality of this picture is enhanced by his recognition and identification of Latmos, a hill he is sure the picture portrays, but which Jane cannot have seen except in dream. ⟨. . .⟩

The final picture is drawn in sharp contrast to the second. Where the other reveals the warmth and passion of love, this last is the pictorialization of ascetic austerity. This picture is a dream vision of Jane's coming experience with the cold crusader, St. John Rivers. ⟨. . .⟩

The pictures reflect the melange of experience which had been Jane's traumatic past, but in her sensitivity to that experience and the world of the spirit, she is able to envision the future storm for which the past has prepared her. To use her own words from another context: "It is the work of nature. She was roused, and did—no miracle—but her best" (p. 399).

Embraced in the scope of the pictures, therefore, are the three major sections of Jane Eyre's life and the three most crucial situations of the novel. Coming early in the novel, the pictures thus provide a subtle foreshadowing of the developments to come and a delicate vehicle for unity and cohesion among otherwise rather disparate sections. This interpretation of the pictures demonstrates that, contrary to the view of many critics, the novel is an intricate unit, a work of careful artistry.

—Thomas A. Langford, "Prophetic Imagination and the Unity of *Jane Eyre*," *Studies in the Novel* (Summer 1974), excerpted in *The Critical Perspective*, Vol. 7, ed. Harold Bloom (New York: Chelsea House Publishers, 1988), 4206–209

NANCY PELL

A large number of critics insist that the dream qualities of Charlotte Brontë's writing comprise its highest, if not its only merits. Heilman, among them, asserts that in the struggle between imagination's trackless waste and the safe fold of common sense, "imagination's trackless waste turns out to be exactly the route to Jane's well-being." Kathleen Tillotson says of *Jane Eyre* that "such social commentary as it may offer is oblique, limited, incidental. It is both in purpose and effect primarily a novel of the inner life, not of man in his social relations; it maps a private world." Yet her view is qualified, if not contradicted, when she calls attention to contemporary attacks on *Jane Eyre* that 'testify indirectly to its timeliness in [1847], hearing it as a voice from the dangerous north and the dangerous class of oppressed or 'outlawed' women." ⟨. . .⟩

In *Jane Eyre* Charlotte Brontë's romantic individualism and rebellion of feeling are controlled and structured by an underlying social and economic critique of bourgeois patriarchal authority. Although this does not describe the entire scope of the novel, which includes countercurrents and qualifications as well, the formal and dramatic elements of a social critique are manifest in Jane's resistance to the illegitimate power of John Reed, Mr. Brocklehurst, and St. John Rivers; allusions to actual historical incidents involving regicide and rebellion; and, finally, the dynamics of Rochester's two marriages—both his marriage to Jane and his earlier marriage to Bertha Mason. ⟨. . .⟩

There is indeed a grim justice in the fact that Rochester's only instance of open, public involvement with Bertha comes at the moment of his physical crippling. Their secret has all along crippled his life socially and psychologically. He has been determined to deny this throughout the past fifteen years; his marriage and all that has followed from it are his experiences-of-the-world on which he claimed superiority to Jane. Jane challenges this claim during their first conversation in the library, and it seems to me that Bertha is the psychological symbol, not of Charlotte Brontë's repressed hostility against the male universe, but of Edward Rochester's repressed awareness of his true social situation. ⟨. . .⟩

Rochester's bitterness against society is thus personally cynical rather than socially perceptive like Jane's. He describes himself at the time of their meeting as in "a harsh, bitter frame of mind . . . corroded with disappointment, sourly disposed against all man- and especially against all *woman*kind (for I began to regard the notion of an intellectual, faithful, loving woman as a mere dream)" (398). He indulges in the luxury of scorn for Blanche Ingram. He has no sympathy for one who, like himself in his youth, is compromised in her choice of a mate by an elder brother's precedence in the family economy and who is, in addition, excluded because of her sex from ever inheriting entailed family land (200). ⟨. . .⟩

The legacy that Jane receives from her uncle in Medeira makes possible her reunion with Rochester and also significantly redefines her relationship to patriarchal structures. "An independent woman now," Jane proceeds to redefine the term. Previously she has rejected the independence exemplified in Helen and St. John, who despise the natural and human realms of life. She has refused as well the mockery of independence found in Eliza Reed's advice to her sister Georgiana.

> "Take one day; share it into sections; to each section apportion its task: leave no stray unemployed quarters of an hour, ten minutes, five minutes,—include all; do each piece of business in its turn with method, with rigid regularity. The day will close almost before you are aware it has begun; and you are indebted to no one for helping you to get rid of one vacant moment: you have had to seek no one's company, conversation, sympathy, forbearance; you have lived, in short, as an independent being ought to do." (295–96)

Similarly, Jane turns down the role of heiress, which St. John urges upon her, and prefers a competency to a fortune. ⟨. . .⟩

Jane's affirmation of interdependence rather than of autonomy helps to explain the genuineness of her acceptance of Rochester, but it also points to the problem of their reabsorption into the system of inheritance and primogeniture that has made their earlier lives so difficult. Jane's division of her legacy among her cousins to secure each a competency is an important gesture, as I have indicated, but the larger society remains unaltered. Both Rochester and Jane have acquired their wealth in untimely or arbitrary ways through the deaths of their predecessors in the line of inheritance. Together they have a son, who, in his turn, doubtless will inherit their combined estates.

—Nancy Pell, "Resistance, Rebellion, and Marriage: The Economics of *Jane Eyre*," *Nineteenth-Century Fiction* (March 1977), excerpted in *The Critical Perspective*, Vol. 7, ed. Harold Bloom (New York: Chelsea House Publishers, 1988), 4209–10, 4213–15

SANDRA M. GILBERT AND SUSAN GUBAR

Since *Shirley* is about impotence, Brontë had to solve the problem of plotting a story about characters defined by their very inability to initiate action. ⟨. . .⟩

To underline this point, the book begins with the curates called away from their meal to help mill-operator Robert Moore, who is waiting for the arrival of machinery that finally appears smashed to pieces by the angry workers. Throughout the novel, Moore waits, hoping to alter his waning fortunes but unable to take any real initiative. Finally he is reduced to the morally reprehensible and pitifully ineffective decision not to marry Caroline Helstone because she is poor, and instead to propose to Shirley Keeldar because she is rich. The novel is centrally concerned with these two young women and the inauspicious roles assigned them. But while none of the characters can initiate effective action because of the contingencies of a costly war abroad, Brontë's heroines are so circumscribed by their gender that they cannot act at all. Though many readers have criticized *Shirley* for a plot which consistently calls attention to its own inorganic development, we shall see that Brontë deliberately seeks to illustrate the inextricable link between sexual discrimination and mercantile capitalism, even as she implies that the coercion of a patriarchal society affects and infects each of its individual members. With this the case, it is not easy to provide or describe escape routes. ⟨. . .⟩

Although Brontë exposes the ways in which the exploitation of women that the Bible seems to justify perpetuates mercantile capitalism and its compulsive manipulation of human and physical nature, her characters cannot escape the confinement of Biblical myth: haunted by Eden, Caroline wants to return to Hollow's Cottage "as much almost as the first woman, in her exile, must have longed to revisit Eden" (chap. 13); but she and Shirley, knowing the power of Paul's use of the story of the garden, also realize that men imagine women as either angels of submission or monsters of aggression:

> The cleverest, the acutest men are often under an illusion about women: they do not read them in a true light: they misapprehend them, both for good and evil: their good woman is a queer thing, half doll, half angel; their bad woman almost always a fiend.
>
> (chap. 20)

Increasingly aware that instead of inhabiting Eden they actually live on the edge of Nunnwood with its ruins of a nunnery, Shirley and Caroline feel that men do not read women in a true light and that the heroines of male-authored literature are false creations. But Shirley knows as well how subversive her critique of male authority is, explaining to Caroline that if she were to give her "real opinion of some [supposedly] first-rate female characters in first-rate works," she would be "dead under a cairn of avenging stones in half-an-hour (chap. 20). ⟨. . .⟩

Because she so consciously experiences herself as monstrous, deviant, excluded, powerless, and angry, Shirley sees through the coercive myths of her culture that imply and even condone inequality and exploitation. Because she understands the dehumanizing effect of patriarchal capitalism, moreover, she is the only wealthy person in the novel who "cannot forget, either day or night, that these embittered feelings of the poor against the rich have been generated in suffering" (chap. 14), for her experience of her gender as it is circumscribed by available sexual roles gives her insight into the misery of the poor. This does not mean, however, that she has a solution to the class conflict she watches with such ambivalence. Sympathizing with Moore as he defends her property, she knows that his cruelty and the workers' misery have erupted in violence she can only deplore, and although her own rather matriarchal relationship with the laborers allows for more kindness between classes, it too is fraught with potential violence, since she retains economic control over their lives and they, in their masculine pride, are angered by what they see as her unnatural authority. ⟨. . .⟩

It looks as if Brontë began *Shirley* with the intention of subverting not only the sexual images of literature but the courtship roles and myths from which they derive. But she could find no models for this kind of fiction; as she explains in her use of the Genesis myth, the stories of her culture actively endorse traditional sexual roles, even as they discourage female authority. In spite of all the rationales Brontë provides, therefore, the absence and inactivity of her heroes seem contrived, just as the problems faced by her heroines seem unrelated to the particular historical framework in which they are set, in spite of the fact that at least one of her major statements in *Shirley* concerns the tragic consequences of the inability of women to shape the public history that necessarily affects their own lives. The tension between Brontë's personal allegiances and the dictates of literary conventions is especially evident when she seeks to write a story of female strength and survival. She has herself explained to the reader in the course of the novel why the only "happy ending" for women in her society is marriage. She gives us that ending, but, like Jane Austen, she never allows us to forget that marriage is a suspect institution based on female subordination, and that women who are not novel heroines probably do not fare even as well as Caroline and Shirley.

—Sandra M. Gilbert and Susan Gubar, "The Genesis of Hunger According to Shirley," *The Madwoman in the Attic: The Woman Writer and the Nineteenth-Century Literary Imagination* (1979), reprinted in *The Brontës*, ed. Harold Bloom (New York: Chelsea House Publishers, 1987), 111–12, 120–22, 127–28

JANICE CARLISLE

Recounting one of the more famous anecdotes of the fabled life at Haworth parsonage, Patrick Brontë once described the result of his desire to know what his very young children were thinking: "happening to have a mask in the house, I told them all to stand and speak boldly from under the cover of that mask." The father suspected that the everyday behavior of his children was itself a mask, an assumed pose of innocence that veiled "more than [he] had yet discovered." By means of his ruse he hoped to counter that deception; the mask would conceal the face and identity of the speaker in order to reveal the child's heart. The episode is one of those telling revelations of both character and the forces that mold character. Even at the age of eight, Charlotte Brontë was being encouraged to adopt subversive modes of self-expression. The form of this little drama would become the form of her art. Like Thackeray, who fled the responsibilities of speaking *in propria persona* by creating narrators such as Barry Lyndon or Arthur Pendennis, Brontë was most comfortable when presenting narratives mediated through a consciousness other than her own; from the earliest extant juvenilia to the fragment of the novel begun just before her death, she spoke with most freedom when she spoke through the voices of characters like Captain Tree or Charles Wellesley Townshend, Jane Eyre or Mrs. Chalfont. This mode was never more central to Brontë's art than in the case of *Villette*. Lucy Snowe is the mask under cover of which Brontë conceals her identity in order to reveal the unappealing reality of her emotional life and its central figures, M. Heger and George Smith. The mask, however, performs this function in the service of art. The novel is a mirror in which reality is transformed to grant the emotional and aesthetic satisfactions that life invariably withholds.

 Villette, the result of this process, is indeed a private document, but its privacy is a function of Lucy Snowe's life and character, not its author's. Brontë was able to distance herself from her own experience and even from facets of her own personality so that we do not need the facts of her life to explain or justify the novel. Yet *Villette* is genuinely puzzling, and it presents mysteries that we might be tempted to unlock with the key of biography. ⟨. . .⟩

Yet if we begin to look more closely at Lucy Snowe, at the shape and form of Brontë's mask, what has seemed perplexing or contradictory about her story reveals a clarity and persuasive emotional logic that shine through even the most apparently trivial or irrelevant detail.

The qualities that Lucy displays as the narrator of her own life and the qualities of *Villette* as the mirror of her experience are most easily defined if we set the novel in the context of its contemporary tradition, the art of autobiography at the Victorian midcentury. 〈. . .〉

Finding 〈. . .〉 fugitive modes of self-expression is a central convention of nineteenth-century autobiography. The writer whose work is a mirror of his experience naturally emphasizes those events or characters within it which serve as miniature reflections of self. The pretence of distance between the writer and his reflection is, however, absolutely essential to the success of this kind of self-analysis. 〈. . .〉

The art of autobiography, like Tennyson's dream, rests on such projections of self. Patrick Brontë's mask, seemingly the bright idea of a concerned parent, is a device that has a natural role in autobiography. By exploring self as if it were another identity, the autobiographer can confront its hidden facets with honesty and often profoundly acute scrutiny. Lucy's use of this device is usually only because it invariably achieves for her an otherwise unattainable emotional gratification. 〈. . .〉

Lucy has said of her younger self that she has lived "two lives"; that sense of division is appropriate to her narrative activity as well. The moments of clarity she achieves in volume 3 fade in the "Finis" with which *Villette* ends. Here again memory too painful for expression must be evasively cloaked in vague generalizations and patently ironic statements of resolution. 〈. . .〉

During the childhood sections of *Villette*, Lucy is a ghost-like presence on the periphery of the action. Later she finds herself "happier, easier, more at home" in the past as she has felt during her stay at La Terrasse. But the comfort offered by memory is a promise of inevitable dispossession. The fact of Paul's death makes the past as uninhabitable as Lucy's earlier need to earn a living has made La Terrasse. Yet in the interval before she must acknowledge the fact of her ultimate and continuing deprivation, Lucy makes at least partial peace with her past. In her hands the already highly developed conventions of autobiography reach a new level of complexity and subtlety. Both character and creator construct a narrative mirror in which self appears vindicated against the slights experience has dealt them and consoled for the indifference with which others have treated them.

—Janice Carlisle, "The Face in the Mirror: *Villette* and the Conventions of Autobiography," *ELH*, no. 2 (Summer 1979), reprinted in *The Brontës*, ed. Harold Bloom (New York: Chelsea House Publishers, 1987), 131–32, 148, 152–53

ROSEMARIE BODENHEIMER

On the first page of *Jane Eyre*, Jane is ordered to keep silent; at the end of the novel her voice becomes the central source of perception for her blind and captive audience, Mr. Rochester, "impressing by sound on his ear what light could no longer stamp on his eye." How Jane acquires and uses the power of speech, and with whom, are subjects that bear both upon the story of her development as a character and upon the first-person narrative stance that Charlotte Brontë invented for her first successful novel. At many points in the telling, Jane's story calls attention to the questions, "How shall I learn to tell the story of my life?" and "What kind of a story is it?" And her narrative is persistently set in relation to other, more conventional kinds of stories—not only the fairy tales, Gothics, and "governess tales" which have received critical attention, but also the internal, interpolated narratives like Rochester's story about his affair with Céline Varens, St. John Rivers's version of Jane's inheritance story, or the innkeeper's tale about the burning of Thornfield. Jane's insistence on the originality of her character and voice must therefore be seen as taking shape in a world full of fictions, which often prove to be in curiously unstable relations with her own. ⟨. . .⟩

Jane Eyre's history may be read as the story of an empowered narrator, which describes her gradual, though partial release from conventional bondages, both social and fictional. Such a reading, emphasizing the literary self-consciousness of *Jane Eyre*, shows that the "problem" of speaking out in a single and singular voice is not only Brontë's narrative voice, but an explicit and complexly argued theme in the substance of the fiction. ⟨. . .⟩

Brontë's interest in stressing Jane's responsibility to her audience is particularly clear when she makes a special point of telling us that Jane withholds the "supernatural" experience of hearing Rochester's voice calling her. Even though she has earlier proclaimed the belief that the event was nature doing "her best," Jane feels that Rochester's tendency to "gloom, needed not the deeper shade of the supernatural." The passage seals Jane's commitment to "credible narrative," and to the shaping and pruning of experience that it demands. The implication for her development is clear: Jane has grown up into a purveyor of tales realistic and moral, suspenseful and heartwarming. Since the time of her lonely pacing in Thornfield's third story, her tale has acquired form and social content, while she has acquired an endless supply of audience and the concomitant power and responsibility to shape a vision of the world for him.

A private and dependent audience of one in a secluded manor may not seem so triumphant a development from that internal continuous narrative—though it is not a bad image for the single and private relationship of novelist and reader. But in Jane's career the search for audience is essentially a search for love and human connection. And maintaining the connection means withholding some truths. Thus, the act of withholding so curiously stressed at the end of the novel is a guarantee of the social connection of Jane and Rochester, even as it suppresses the mystic connection implied by the supernatural calls through the night. It is Jane's assertion of control, both over Rochester and over forces in the universe, and in the psyche, that belie the desire to shape and control experience.

While the "internal" plot presents Jane's repression as a moral choice, the larger narrative remains in command of both the shapely story and what it leaves out. Jane is represented as having been moved to find Rochester by that "supernatural" event for which she claims full reality; the fact that she rejects it as material to be told to Rochester shows again the tension between Brontë's character and her narrative, which retrieves and includes the irrational sources that Jane learns to repress in order to achieve her social, loving, and controlling ends. If Jane grows up to be a successful narrator, she is not—at least not yet—the narrator of *Jane Eyre*, whose vision depends on the tense truth of the discontinuity between fierce feeling and credible story.

—Rosemarie Bodenheimer, "Jane Eyre in Search of Her Story," *Papers on Language and Literature* 16, no. 3 (Summer 1980), reprinted in *The Brontës*, ed. Harold Bloom (New York: Chelsea House Publishers, 1987), 155–56, 161

JOHN MAYNARD

Jane's subsequent description of their ten years of life together continues the emphasis throughout the Ferndean scenes on their physical closeness. Jane feels supremely blest just because she is fully Rochester's life as he is hers: "No woman was ever nearer to her mate than I am: even more absolutely bone of his bone, and flesh of his flesh." They have been knit especially closely by the early years of Rochester's dependence on her sight. Now they share heartbeats and conversation all day long. Few readers, even the most happily married in our divorcing age, will believe such a degree of exclusive mutual company, even between an engaging ex-governess and a man with a West Indian and European past, could be entirely satisfactory. This is a storybook ending, a paradise of satisfied love. The interesting point is that it is love conceived of as exceptionally physical, a meeting of bodies as well as true minds and hearts. Lest there be any question about the potency of this, Jane casually alludes to their first-born, leaving open how many children issued from their fruitful union.

Jane Eyre ends, somewhat unfortunately, with a very brief account of St. John's missionary activity and his hope for the next world. If Brontë won't allow Jane, probably rightly in character, any irony over St John's disposal of all earthly joys, she nonetheless concludes the novel as a whole with a clear assertion of loving sexual union. Jane herself has manifestly been brought to a decisive choice between the alternatives of ascetic self-suppression and sexual fulfillment. Yet far more than *The Professor*, the work as a whole also speaks most clearly about the myriad obstacles, within and without the individual, to mature sexual awakening. Brontë uses lesser characters and symbolic structures to indicate the difficulties she sees in sexual openness. She shows how fears, conscious suppressions, and undeliberate repressions work within Jane's mind to drive her into anxiety and, finally, a panicked flight. She even builds into the plot of the book as a series of obstacles that suggest her own anxieties: Rochester really is in some sense an illegal seducer; sex has helped drive Bertha mad; Rochester does pay a heavy price for his sins, however much this is qualified and ultimately requited. Because such fears of sexuality become actually incorporated into the world of the tale, they require balancing assertions of sexual growth within the plot, especially the timely elimination of Bertha and the marvelous call to Jane. The same nice balancing of forces of suppression and assertion is at work in the mythic world of the novel's action as in the finer analysis of Jane's psychological response or in the examination of sexual alternatives.

In all cases Brontë comes down finally on the side of sexual initiation—with caution. But the assertion on the side of the life force is far less valuable than the quality of the analysis. Brontë shows us on every level of the novel the complex interweaving strands in sexual life that make it at once so central to experience and so easily miswoven or unraveled. Jane's childhood, her early relations with those loving or unloving to her, her position in the world and her degree of independence, her relative inexperience, her moral and religious values, her sense of belonging to a family, her relation to supportive females or female images, her perception of the uses of sexual energies to different lovers, her need to sacrifice herself or others, all affect her capacity to undergo sexual awakening successfully. Brontë, unlike many of her critics, makes no simple case for how a complex individual functions. She lets Jane tell her tale, reveal her delicate and complicated responses, and challenge us to comprehend sexual experience in its complex totality. The result, for all its occasional naivetés, is one of the finest novels in English and a particularly splendid examination of the process of sexual awakening. Good as the studies of Caroline Vernon's seduction or Elizabeth Hastings's flight from sexuality were, this is miles further along. With tact and infinite delicacy Brontë unfolds and examines the sexual life. For this area of experience, so close to the unconscious world of symbolic language, she needs and finds language rarely drawn upon by as subtle a predecessor in psychological analysis as Jane Austen: strong symbols, dreams, mythic overlays, Gothic plot devices, descriptions of buildings or nature and the seasons. Yet the marvel is that in all this welter of

large symbols and emotional signs there is the fundamental focus on the delicate workings of and adjustments to Jane's continuous inner life. She is no
vague human counter moving through a turbulent world of symbols, though
Lawrence's heroes and heroines sometimes are. Jane remains the center of
human complexity around which Brontë's vision of the need for sexual fulfillment and its obstacles focus and concentrate. When we have read the work
with the attention it deserves, we feel we have come perhaps as close as we
shall in language to the infinitely subtle but not totally inexplicable process of
sexual growth.
    —John Maynard, *Charlotte Brontë and Sexuality* (Cambridge: Cambridge University Press,
    1984), 143–44

MARGARET HOMANS

The Gothic's literalization of imaginative or other subjective states often coin-
cides with representations of a rather different kind of literalization, the experience or idea of childbirth. That women bear children and men do not is the
simple origin of this complex and troubling tradition that associates women
with the literal and with nature, an association that at once appeals to and
repels women writers. Both ⟨*Wuthering Heights* and *Jane Eyre*⟩ foreground a curious connection between their most Gothic elements and motherhood. The
transitory experience of being a mother is the central and recurring metaphor
for the abundant sense of danger in *Jane Eyre* (just as the plot of *Wuthering
Heights* turns on the main character's death in childbirth and her subsequent
transformation into a ghost). The specific connection between the literalization of subjective states and childbirth's actual passage from internal to external takes place in dreams about children. Like other internal states in the
Gothic mode, dreams are literalized in the object world, and the ambiguous
process of their literalization mirrors and reinforces an ambivalence that is
almost always integral to the imagery of childbearing in the two novels. ⟨. . .⟩

    Jane Eyre establishes a complex series of connectives between danger or
trouble and figures of childbirth or of mother-child relationships, comprising
the prophetic dreams of children and also the narrative use of such figuration.
⟨. . .⟩

    These dreams of children represent Jane's unconscious investigation of the
state of becoming other than herself or of deferring altogether to projections,
and the process of this investigation is repeated in the literalization or coming
true of the dreams that characterizes the Gothic pattern. All the dreams come
true in some way, but from one dream to the next they come true in increasingly literal ways. ⟨. . .⟩

Dreams also literalize each other: just as the second of the pair of dreams extends the action and implications of the first, the third dream, in which Jane explicitly dreams of herself as the child, realizes the unpleasant implication of the first two dreams, that Jane is herself the child as well as the mother. Looking further back, the third dream also appears to spell out and explain the morally ambiguous ghost that confused Jane as a child in the red-room. Set in the same scene, the more recent vision soothes where Mr. Reed terrified; but the vision of the shining human form "inclining a glorious brow earthward" and speaking words of comfort literalizes what the child had only imagined to be the ultimate terror. Her fear then was that her grief would "waken a preter-natural voice to comfort me, or elicit from the gloom some haloed face, bend-ing over me with strange pity," and that is exactly what happens in the dream. The passage from "theory" to "realization" was what was "terrible" in the red-room, and the same turns out to be true here, in the passage from the dream to the next few days' actual experience. Jane finds the dream's figures enacted in the object world, and like other literalizations, these threaten her life.

In the waking scenes of flight and wandering that directly follow, the prophetic dream comes true in the literalization of the dreamt mother: "I have no relative but the universal mother, Nature: I will seek her breast and ask repose" (chap. 28). Mother Nature is a mother only figuratively, yet because Jane names the landscape in this way and insists on and extends the figure, the dreamt mother must be connected to this very tangible one. Naming nature "mother," Jane accepts the tradition that identifies the feminine with the object world, an identification that at this point seems very appealing. The visionary mother encouraged Jane to flee temptation, and when Jane wanders into nature after leaving Rochester, the landscape appears maternal because it appears to help on her flight from temptation. This positive view of nature may represent what Nancy Chodorow would identify as the daughter's con-tinued close connection to her mother long past her entry into androcentric culture, a connection that, however, a daughter who is a figure for the novel-ist, whose main allegiance is to the father's symbol making, finds very difficult to sustain and finally rejects. ⟨. . .⟩

The true child of Mother Nature, one that finds "permanent shelter" in her breast, is the lizard or the bee, never the living woman. Jane's wish that she had died in the night and the temptation as she walks to stop and "submit resistlessly to the apathy that clogged heart and limb" represent nature's resid-ual pressure and conflict with "life, . . . with all its requirements, and pains, and responsibilities," which prevents Jane from yielding. Nature is now a danger-ous tempter, in contrast to that mother within Jane's mind who told Jane to "flee temptation." She returns to her starting point at Whitcross, to begin again; soon she is again on the verge of giving in to nature's temptation when she is recalled to consciousness by the chime of a church bell and then by the sight of a village and cultivated fields that, by representing human life, help her resist the literality of the wild moor.

—Margaret Homans, "Dreaming of Children: Literalization in *Jane Eyre*," *Bearing the Word: Language and Female Experience in Nineteenth-Century Women's Writing* (1986), reprinted in *Charlotte Brontë's Jane Eyre*, ed. Harold Bloom (New York: Chelsea House Publishers, 1987), 117–19, 123–25, 127

Bibliography

Poems by Currer, Ellis, and Acton Bell (with Emily and Anne Brontë). 1846.

Jane Eyre: An Autobiography (3 vols.). 1847.

Shirley: A Tale (3 vols.). 1849.

Villette (3 vols.). 1853.

The Professor: A Tale (2 vols.). 1857.

The Life and Works of Charlotte Brontë and Her Sisters (7 vols.). 1872–73.

The Works of Charlotte, Emily, and Anne Brontë (12 vols.). 1893.

The Adventures of Ernest Alembert: A Fairy Tale. 1896

The Life and Works of the Sisters Brontë (7 vols.). 1899–1903.

Poems by Charlotte, Emily, and Anne Brontë. 1902.

The Brontës: Life and Letters. Ed. Clement K. Shorter (2 vols.). 1908.

Richard Coer de Lion and Blondel: A Poem. 1912.

Saul and Other Poems. 1913.

The Violet: A Poem Written at the Age of Fourteen. 1916.

Lament Befitting "These Times of Night." 1916.

The Red Cross Knight and Other Poems. 1917.

The Swiss Emigrant's Return and Other Poems. 1917.

The Orphans and Other Poems (with Emily and Branwell Brontë). 1917.

The Four Wishes: A Fairy Tale. 1918.

Latest Gleaning: Being a Series of Unpublished Poems from Her Early Manuscripts. 1918.

Napoleon and the Spectre: A Ghost Story. 1919.

Darius Codomannus: A Poem Written at the Age of Eighteen Years. 1920.

Complete Poems. 1923.

An Early Essay. 1924.

The Twelve Adventurers and Other Stories. 1925.

The Spell: An Extravaganza. 1931.

The Shakespeare Head Brontë (with Emily and Anne Brontë) (19 vols.). 1931–38.

The Brontës: Their Lives, Friendships, and Correspondence (4 vols.). 1932.

Legends of Angria: Compiled from the Early Writings of Charlotte Brontë. 1933.

The Professor; Tales from Angria; Emma, a Fragment; Together with a Selection of Poems (with Emily and Anne Brontë). 1954.

The Search after Happiness. 1969.

Five Novelettes. 1971.

The Novels of Charlotte, Emily, and Anne Brontë. 1976.

Two Tales. 1978.

Poems. 1984.

A Leaf from an Unopened Volume; or, The Manuscript of an Unfortunate Author: An Angia Story. 1985.

Poems: A New Text and Commentary. 1985.

Selected Poems (with Anne and Emily Brontë). 1985.

The Brontës: Selected Poems. 1985.

The Juvenilia of Jane Austen and Charlotte Brontë. 1986.

An Edition of the Early Writings of Charlotte Brontë. 1987.

EMILY BRONTE

1818-1848

EMILY BRONTË was born in Thornton, Yorkshire, on July 30, 1818, two years after her sister Charlotte and two years before her sister Anne. In 1820, her father, Patrick Brontë, moved the family to Haworth, the parsonage on the Yorkshire Moors that fueled the sisters' imaginations and that will always be associated with Emily's work. A year after the move to Haworth, Emily's mother, Maria Branwell Brontë, died, and the children and the house were left in care of an aunt. Emily was sent away to school on three different occasions. The first school she attended was the poorly run Cowan Bridge Clergy Daughters' School, where she was miserable and where her two oldest sisters became ill with tuberculosis and died. Her father then removed his remaining daughters from the school, and Emily was educated at home with Charlotte, Anne, and her brother, Branwell.

Although the four siblings were extremely close, having virtually no other company, Emily was particularly close to Anne, and the two spent countless hours writing poems and stories about a fictional realm called Gondal (Charlotte and Branwell wrote a parallel saga about a kingdom named Angria). Anne and Emily would continue writing these stories for the next twenty years, and Emily, more than Anne, would show the influences of the Gondal saga in her mature work.

Emily's second attempt at education away from home was at Miss Wooler's school at Roe Head. Eventually Emily worked as a governess for a family at Law Hill, near Halifax, but was temperamentally unsuited for the work and soon returned home. In 1842 she accompanied Charlotte to Brussels to attend the Pensionnat Heger. She had traveled to Brussels with the hope that it would train her and her sisters to open their own school in Yorkshire. While at the Pensionnat Heger, Emily displayed a gift for languages but made few friends. After their return to Haworth, the Brontë sisters attempted to start their school in 1844, but the venture failed.

Meanwhile, Emily continued to write poetry about Gondal. In 1845, Charlotte discovered the poems and convinced Emily to allow her to submit them for publication. In 1846, her poems were published in a volume with her sisters': *Poems by Currer, Ellis, and Acton Bell*. After the volume was published, Emily focused on her novel, *Wuthering Heights*, whose characters resemble those who people the Gondal poems. *Wuthering Heights* was published in 1847 with Anne's *Agnes Grey* by London publisher Thomas Newby. The book was not nearly as well received as Charlotte's *Jane Eyre*, which was published the same year. Despite its initial reception, however, its stature has continued to grow; it is now considered a masterpiece of British fiction. In September of 1848, the Brontë sisters' only brother, Branwell, drank himself to death. Tuberculosis, which was to be the scourge of the entire family, claimed Emily next. She died on December 19, 1848, at the age of 30.

CRITICAL EXTRACTS

CHARLOTTE BRONTË

With regard to the rusticity of *Wuthering Heights*, I admit the charge, for I feel the quality. It is rustic all through. It is moorish, and wild, and knotty as a root of heath. Nor was it natural that it should be otherwise; the author being herself a native and nursling of the moors. Doubtless, had her lot been cast in a town, her writings, if she had written at all, would have possessed another character. Even had chance or taste led her to choose a similar subject, she would have treated it otherwise. Had Ellis Bell been a lady or a gentleman accustomed to what is called "the world," her view of a remote and unreclaimed region, as well as of the dwellers therein, would have differed greatly from that actually taken by the home-bred country girl. Doubtless it would have been wider—more comprehensive: whether it would have been more original or more truthful is not so certain. As far as the scenery and locality are concerned, it could scarcely have been so sympathetic: Ellis Bell did not describe as one whose eye and taste alone found pleasure in the prospect; her native hills were far more to her than a spectacle; they were what she lived in, and by, as much as the wild birds, their tenants, or as the heather, their produce. Her descriptions, then, of natural scenery, are what they should be, and all they should be.

Where delineation of human character is concerned, the case is different. I am bound to avow that she had scarcely more practical knowledge of the peasantry amongst whom she lived, than a nun has of the country people who sometimes pass her convent gates. My sister's disposition was not naturally gregarious; circumstances favoured and fostered her tendency to seclusion; except to go to church or take a walk on the hills, she rarely crossed the threshold of home. Though her feeling for the people round was benevolent, intercourse with them she never sought; nor, with very few exceptions, ever experienced. And yet she knew them: knew their ways, their language, their family histories; she could hear of them with interest and talk of them with detail, minute, graphic, and accurate; but *with* them, she rarely exchanged a word. Hence it ensued that what her mind had gathered of the real concerning them, was too exclusively confined to those tragic and terrible traits of which, in listening to the secret annals of every rude vicinage, the memory is sometimes compelled to receive the impress. Her imagination, which was a spirit more sombre than sunny, more powerful than sportive, found in such traits material whence it wrought creations like Heathcliff, like Earnshaw, like Catherine. Having formed these beings, she did not know what she had done. If the auditor of her work, when read in manuscript, shuddered under the grinding influence of natures so relentless and implacable, of spirits so lost and fallen; if it was complained that the mere hearing of certain vivid and fearful scenes banished sleep by night, and disturbed mental peace by day, Ellis Bell would wonder what was meant, and suspect the complainant of affectation. Had she but lived, her mind would of itself have grown like a strong tree, loftier, straighter, wider-spreading, and its matured fruits would have attained a mellower ripeness and sunnier bloom; but on that mind time and experience alone could work: to the influence of other intellects, it was not amenable.

Having avowed that over much of *Wuthering Heights* there broods "a horror of great darkness;" that is, in its storm-heated and electrical atmosphere, we seem at times to breathe lightning: let me point to those spots where clouded daylight and the eclipsed sun still attest their existence. For a specimen of true benevolence and homely fidelity, look at the character of Nelly Dean; for an example of constancy and tenderness, remark that of Edgar Linton. (Some people will think these qualities do not shine so well incarnate in a man as they would do in a woman, but Ellis Bell could never be brought to comprehend this notion: nothing moved her more than any insinuation that the faithfulness and clemency, the long-suffering and loving-kindness which are esteemed virtues in the daughters of Eve, become foibles in the sons of Adam. She held that mercy and forgiveness are the divinest attributes of the Great Being who made both man and woman, and that what clothes the Godhead in glory, can disgrace no form of feeble humanity). There is a dry saturnine humour in the delineation of old Joseph, and some glimpses of grace and gaiety animate the younger Catherine. Nor is even the first heroine of the name destitute of a certain strange beauty in her fierceness, or of honesty in the midst of perverted passion and passionate perversity. ⟨. . .⟩

Wuthering Heights was hewn in a wild workshop, with simple tools, out of homely materials. The statuary found a granite block on a solitary moor; gazing thereon, he saw how from the crag might be elicited a head, savage, swart, sinister; a form moulded with at least one element of grandeur—power. He wrought with a rude chisel, and from no model but the vision of his meditations. With time and labour, the crag took human shape; and there it stands colossal, dark, and frowning, half statue, half rock: in the former sense, terrible and goblin-like; in the latter, almost beautiful, for its colouring is of mellow grey, and moorland moss clothes it; and heath, with its blooming bells and balmy fragrance, grows faithfully close to the giant's foot.

—Charlotte Brontë, "Preface," *Wuthering Heights and Agnes Grey* (1850), excerpted in *Emily Brontë's Wuthering Heights*, ed. Harold Bloom (New York: Chelsea House Publishers, 1996), 29–32

MRS. HUMPHRY WARD

Wuthering Heights is a book of the later Romantic movement, betraying the influences of German Romantic imagination, as Charlotte's work betrays the influences of Victor Hugo and George Sand. The Romantic tendency to invent and delight in monsters, the *exaltation du moi*, which has been said to be the secret of the whole Romantic revolt against classical models and restraints; the love of violence in speech and action, the preference for the hideous in character and the abnormal in situation—of all these there are abundant examples in *Wuthering Heights*. The dream of Mr. Lockwood in Catherine's box bed, when in the terror of nightmare he pulled the wrist of the little wailing ghost outside on to the broken glass of the window, 'and rubbed it to and fro till the blood ran down and soaked the bed-clothes'—one of the most gruesome fancies of literature!—Heathcliff's long and fiendish revenge on Hindley Earnshaw; the ghastly quarrel between Linton and Heathcliff in Catherine's presence after Heathcliff's return; Catherine's three days' fast, and her delirium when she 'tore the pillow with her teeth;' Heathcliff dashing his head against the trees of her garden, leaving his blood upon the bark, and 'howling, not like a man, but like a savage beast being goaded to death with knives and spears;' the fight between Heathcliff and Earnshaw after Heathcliff's marriage to Isabella; the kidnapping of the younger Catherine, and the horror rather suggested than described of Heathcliff's brutality towards his sickly son:—all these things would not have been written precisely as they were written, but for the 'Germanism' of the thirties and forties, but for the translations of *Blackwood and Fraser*, and but for those German tales, whether of Hoffmann or others, which there is evidence that Emily Brontë read both at Brussels and after her return.

As to the 'exaltation of the Self,' its claims, sensibilities and passions, in defiance of all social law and duty, there is no more vivid expression of it throughout Romantic literature than is contained in the conversation between the elder Catherine and Nelly Dean before Catherine marries Edgar Linton.

And the violent, clashing egotisms of Heathcliff and Catherine in the last scene of passion before Catherine's death, are as it were an epitome of a whole *genre* in literature, and a whole phase of European feeling.

Nevertheless, horror and extravagance are not really the characteristic mark and quality of *Wuthering Heights*. If they were, it would have no more claim upon us than a hundred other forgotten books—Lady Caroline Lamb's *Glenarvon* amongst them—which represent the dregs and refuse of a great literary movement. As in the case of Charlotte Brontë, the peculiar force of Emily's work lies in the fact that it represents the grafting of a European tradition upon a mind already richly stored with English and local reality, possessing at command a style at once strong and simple, capable both of homeliness and magnificence. The form of Romantic imagination which influenced Emily was not the same as that which influenced Charlotte; whether from a secret stubbornness and desire of difference, or no, there is not a mention of the French language, or of French books, in Emily's work, while Charlotte's abounds in a kind of display of French affinities, and French scholarship. The dithyrambs of *Shirley* and *Villette*, the 'Vision of Eve' of *Shirley*, and the description of Rachel in *Villette*, would have been impossible to Emily; they come to a great extent from the reading of Victor Hugo and George Sand. But in both sisters there is a similar *fonds* of stern and simple realism; a similar faculty of observation at once shrewd, and passionate; and it is by these that they produce their ultimate literary effect. The difference between them is almost wholly in Emily's favour. The uneven, amateurish manner of so many pages in *Jane Eyre* and *Shirley*; the lack of literary reticence which is responsible for Charlotte's frequent intrusion of her own personality, and for her occasional temptations to scream and preach, which are not wholly resisted even in her masterpiece *Villette*; the ugly tawdry sentences which disfigure some of her noblest passages, and make quotation from her so difficult:—you will find none of these things in *Wuthering Heights*. Emily is never flurried, never self-conscious; she is master of herself at the most rushing moments of feeling or narrative; her style is simple, sensuous, adequate and varied from first to last; she has fewer purple patches than Charlotte, but at its best, her insight no less than her power of phrase, is of a diviner and more exquisite quality.

—Mrs. Humphry Ward, "Introduction," *Wuthering Heights* (New York: Harper & Brothers, 1900), xxv–xxvii

DOROTHY VAN GHENT

The strangeness that sets *Wuthering Heights* apart from other English novels does not lie alone in the attitude that it expresses and the level of experience that it defines, for something of the same quality of feeling exists, for instance, in Conrad's work. Its strangeness is the perfect simplicity with which it presents its elemental figures almost naked of the web of civilized habits, ways of thinking, forms of intercourse, that provides the familiar background of other fiction. Even Conrad's adventurers, no matter how far they may go into the "heart of darkness," carry with them enough threads of this web to orient them socially and morally. We can illustrate what we mean by this simplicity, this almost nakedness, if we compare Emily Brontë's handling of her materials with Richardson's handling of materials that, in some respects, are similar in kind. For example, the daemonic character of Heathcliff, associated as it is with the wildness of heat and moors, has a recognizable kinship with that of Lovelace, daemonic also, though associated with town life and sophisticated manners. Both are, essentially, an anthropomorphized primitive energy, concentrated in activity, terrible in effect. But Emily Brontë insists on Heathcliff's gypsy lack of origins, his lack of orientation and determination in the social world, his equivocal status on the edge of the human. When Mr. Earnshaw first brings the child home, the child is an "it," not a "he," and "dark almost as if it came from the devil"; and one of Nelly Dean's last reflections is, "Is he a ghoul or a vampire?" But Richardson's Lovelace has all sorts of social relationships and determinations, an ample family economic orientation, college acquaintances, a position in a clique of young rakes; and Richardson is careful, through Lovelace's own pen, to offer various rationalizations of his behavior, each in some degree cogent. So with the whole multifold *Clarissa*-myth: on all sides it is supported for the understanding by historically familiar morality and manners. But *Wuthering Heights* is almost bare of such supports in social rationalization. Heathcliff might *really* be a demon. The passion of Catherine and Heathcliff is too simple and undeviating in its intensity, too uncomplex, for us to find in it any echo of practical social reality. To say that the motivation of this passion is "simple" is not to say that it is easy to define: much easier to define are the motivations that are somewhat complex and devious, for this is the familiar nature of human motivations. We might associate perfectly "simple" motivations with animal nature or extrahuman nature, but by the same token the quality of feeling involved would resist analysis.

But this nakedness from the web of familiar morality and manners is not quite complete. There is the framework formed by the convention of narration (the "point of view"): we see the drama through the eyes of Lockwood and Nelly Dean, who belong firmly to the world of practical reality. Sifted through the idiom of their commonplace vision, the drama taking place among the major characters finds contact with the temporal and the secular. Because Lockwood and Nelly Dean have witnessed the incredible violence of the life at the Heights, or rather, because Nelly Dean has witnessed the full span and capacity of that violence and because Lockwood credits her witness, the drama is oriented in the context of the psychologically familiar. There is also another technical bulwark that supports this uneasy tale in the social and moral imagination, and that is its extension over the lives of two generations and into a time of ameliorated and respectable manners. At the end, we see young Cathy teaching Hareton his letters and correcting his boorishness (which, after all, is only the natural boorishness consequent on neglect, and has none of the cannibal unregeneracy of Heathcliff in it); the prospect is one of decent, socially responsible domesticity. For this part of the tale, Lockwood alone is sufficient witness; and the fact that now Nelly Dean's experienced old eyes and memory can be dispensed with assures us of the present reasonable-ness and objectivity of events, and even infects retrospection on what has hap-pened earlier—making it possible for the dream-rejecting reason to settle complacently for the "naturalness" of the entire story. If ghosts have been men-tioned, if the country people swear that Heathcliff "walks," we can, with Lockwood at the end, affirm our skepticism as to "how anyone could ever imagine unquiet slumbers for the sleepers in that quiet earth."

Let us try to diagram these technical aspects of the work, for the compo-sitional soundness of *Wuthering Heights* is owing to them. We may divide the action of the book into two parts, following each other chronologically, the one associated with the earlier generation (Hindley and Catherine and Heathcliff, Edgar and Isabella Linton), the other with the later generation (young Cathy and Linton and Hareton). The first of these actions is centered in what we shall call a "mythological romance"—for the astonishingly raven-ous and possessive, perfectly amoral love of Catherine and Heathcliff belongs to that realm of the imagination where myths are created. The second action, centered in the protracted effects of Heathcliff's revenge, involves two sets of young lives and two small "romances": the childish romance of Cathy and Linton, which Heathcliff manages to pervert utterly; and the successful asser-tion of a healthy, culturally viable kind of love between Cathy and Hareton, asserted as Heathcliff's cruel energies flag and decay. Binding the two "actions" is the perduring figure of Heathcliff himself, demon-lover in the first, paternal ogre in the second. Binding them also is the framing narrational convention or "point of view": the voices of Nelly Dean and Lockwood are always in our ears; one or the other of them is always present at a scene, or is the confidant of someone who was present; through Lockwood we encounter Heathcliff at the beginning of the book, and through his eyes we look on Heathcliff's grave at the end. Still another pattern that binds the two actions is the repetition of what we shall call the "two children" figure—two children raised virtually as brother and sister, in a vibrant relationship of charity and passion and real or possible metamorphosis. The figure is repeated, with variation, three times, in the relationships of the main characters. ⟨. . .⟩

What, concretely, is the effect of this strict patterning and binding? What does it "mean"? The design of the book is drawn in the spirit of intense compositional rigor, of *limitation;* the characters act in the spirit of passionate immoderacy, of *excess.* Let us consider this contrast a little more closely. Essentially, *Wuthering Heights* exists for the mind as a tension between two kinds of reality: the raw, inhuman reality of anonymous natural energies, and the restrictive reality of civilized habits, manners, and codes. The first kind of reality is given to the imagination in the violent figures of Catherine and Heathcliff, portions of the flux of nature, children of rock and heath and tempest, striving to identify themselves as human, but disrupting all around them with their monstrous appetite for an inhuman kind of intercourse, and finally disintegrated from within by the very energies out of which they are made.

—Dorothy Van Ghent, "On Wuthering Heights," *The English Novel: Form and Function* (1953), reprinted in *Emily Brontë's Wuthering Heights*, ed. Harold Bloom (New York: Chelsea House Publishers, 1987), 10–13

INGA-STINA EWBANK

If the moral consciousness which is part of her total vision makes Emily Brontë more *of* her period than we might at first think, the structural and stylistic means whereby she develops that vision set her apart. If we speak of the novelist in Emily Brontë being a poet, we are also speaking of the way in which, in her novel, all the parts are subordinated to the whole. In what follows I want to examine more closely this aspect of *Wuthering Heights*. The typical Victorian novel is large and leisurely, incorporating a great deal of material for its own intrinsic interest: descriptions of nature, historical events, social life, and so on. In Anne Brontë's first novel, the simplicity of the story and theme gives the novel a *conte*-like unity of form, but when she tries to cover a larger canvas in *The Tenant of Wildfell Hall*, her structure becomes dangerously unbalanced. Charlotte Brontë tries in *Shirley* to give the kind of social panorama which *Jane Eyre*, in its concentration on its heroine, does not have, but her curates and her Luddite elements do not become very integral parts of a whole. Even *Villette* has passages of slack writing, where one feels that she is just trying to bring the story forward. What is outstanding about *Wuthering Heights* is the sense of form displayed by Emily Brontë—a sense which, before her, had been shown only by Jane Austen. Like Jane Austen, she achieves a structure which, in every part, is the visible embodiment of the theme, by the exclusion from the novel of anything not necessary, anything that would dissipate concentration. No more than in Jane Austen do we, in *Wuthering Heights*, have any references to the historical period of the novel, to the goings on at the time in the world at large. But here the similarity stops, for what Jane Austen includes—'parties, picnics, and country dances' (Virginia Woolf)—is just what Emily Brontë excludes.

The concentration on the world limited geographically by Wuthering Heights to the north and Thrushcross Grange to the south-west, with the chapel, churchyard and Gimmerton brook between them, is complete. We never follow anybody outside it. Hindley just reappears on his father's death, with a wife whom he has found somehow, somewhere. For three and a half years Heathcliff is just gone, and nobody is told where he has been or what he has done. There is not one word about where Isabella and Heathcliff go on their ghastly honeymoon; we pick up their story again with a characteristic sentence: 'The sun set behind the Grange, as we turned on to the moors', and all we hear of it from Isabella is that her heart 'returned to Thrushcross Grange in twenty-four hours after I left it'. Isabella herself vanishes, except for the barest account of facts, as soon as she leaves the Grange carrying the unborn Linton. The events in the novel stem from the moment that old Mr. Earnshaw brings Heathcliff into that world, carried under his coat from the streets of Liverpool; the central conflict from the moment that the first Catherine and Heathcliff peep in through the parlour window at the Grange. The novel is resolved with the second Catherine and Hareton going to live at Thrushcross Grange, leaving the Heights to 'the use of such ghosts as choose to inhabit it'. There is no sense of a geographical or social world outside this—it never occurs, for example, to Edgar Linton that his daughter might find a husband other than Linton Heathcliff.

For all its exclusiveness, this world is also inclusive. It has everything that matters: birth, death, love, hatred, nature, the seasons. And so it gets a larger than naturalistic significance, becomes a microcosm of the human condition.

—Inga-Stina Ewbank, "Emily Brontë: The Woman Writer as Poet," *Their Proper Sphere: A Study of the Brontë Sisters as Early-Victorian Female Novelists* (1968), excerpted in *The Critical Perspective*, Vol. 7, ed. Harold Bloom (New York: Chelsea House Publishers, 1988), 3929–30

DENIS DONOGHUE

It is proper to begin with the recognition of *Wuthering Heights* as a novel, even if we find it necessary to admit other elements which are uncomfortable in that description. If we take the book, in the first instance, as a novel, we acknowledge the fact that it is firmly grounded in a particular society, the Yorkshire moors, at a particular time, the years from 1757 to 1803. C. P. Sanger has demonstrated in detail the care Emily Brontë took to anchor the book in place and time. We are made to feel that between Wuthering Heights and Thrushcross Grange there is solid land, a distance of four English miles, and it is only a short way to Gimmerton, and beyond Gimmerton there are other villages and towns. In this land people live and die, farm their acres, furnish their homes, hire lawyers to make wills, act as magistrates, walk to Pennistone Crags, and scandalize the neighbors. Six men carried Heathcliff's coffin; we know nothing more of them, but we are not allowed to forget that, behind the violent events at Wuthering Heights and Thrushcross Grange, there are ordinary people going about their business. It is the novel's business, too. Manners, morals, families, relations, houses, property: these are the novel's traditional instruments. In *Wuthering Heights* much of this concern reaches us through Mrs. Dean. It has often been maintained that she is an unreliable guide; if she is, it follows, according to the argument, that Emily Brontë means us to think of the domestic moralities as inadequate, irrelevant, beside the point. At least one reader has thought of Mrs. Dean as the villain of the whole piece. But this is perverse. Mrs. Leavis has no such doubts: "Nelly Dean is most carefully, consistently and convincingly created for us as the normal woman, whose truly feminine nature satisfies itself in nurturing all the children in the book in turn." This is reasonable. Mrs. Dean is not the omniscient narrator, the detached observer; she has her likes and dislikes, in the quarrel between Earnshaws and Lintons she is a Linton, she has been cruel to the child Heathcliff. But she is undoubtedly a reliable witness: we know her faults only because she confesses them. Finally, there is no reason to think that Emily Brontë wants us to hold aloof from Isabella's testimony, in Chapter XIII, when she says, "How did you contrive to preserve the common sympathies of human nature when you resided here?"—meaning Wuthering Heights. It seems clear that Mrs. Dean maintains the common sympathies; this is her chief function in the narrative. While others aspire to the metaphysics, she consults the physics, she is the spirit of the English novel.

But Emily Brontë does not confine her imagination to these matters. Living at Haworth, she invented Gondal by an act of will, insisting upon this wild place free from clergy and morality. Correspondingly, there are forces in the novel which strain to be released from empirical allegiance. In terms of genre, *Wuthering Heights* is mixed: novel and romance. The novel strains toward the romance, to transcend its own nature. Mrs. Leavis thinks it a flaw that the relationship between Catherine and Heathcliff is not substantiated, we ought to have been shown their "shared life and interests." But this misses the point; the cause is not a question of shared life and interests but of merged natures, merged identities. Heathcliff's character is irrelevant to Catherine; she knows his cruelty, but it is irrelevant. She identifies herself with his nature as with a reality far more profound. The identification is so complete that it determines her life even when she perceives every vice in his character. She warns Isabella against him, in Chapter X, but the vices disclosed make no differences to herself; to him she responds in terms which have nothing to do with character, personality, vice or virtue. "Your bliss lies in inflicting misery," Catherine tells Heathcliff in Chapter XII: true or false, the charge is irrelevant, since it can only be relevant to morality, and morality is irrelevant. To respond to this part of the book it is necessary to acknowledge modes of being which act at a level beneath the patterns of ethics and morality: of the identification of Catherine and Heathcliff it is necessary to say that the gap separating it from considerations of morality and society is absolute. We begin to recognize this gap when, using the world "nature," we sense possibilities in its presence so primitive, so much a matter of instinct and consanguinity, that they render moral considerations irrelevant. Catherine and Heathcliff are not united by love, or even by passion; they are united by nature, and nature is unanswerable. ⟨. . .⟩

Catherine and Heathcliff are allowed to persevere in their natures; they are not forced to conform to the worldly proprieties of Thrushcross Grange. Conformity is reserved for the next generation. But this is too blunt as an account of the later chapters of the book. The juxtaposition of Wuthering Heights and Thrushcross Grange is inescapable, but it is not simple. The values of the Grange are social, political, personal, compatible with the emerging England, the cities, railways, the lapse of the old agricultural verities. Wuthering Heights is, in this relation, primitive, aboriginal, Bohemian; it rejects any pattern of action and relationships already prescribed. Finally, Emily Brontë accepts the dominance of Thrushcross Grange, since the new England requires that victory, but she accepts it with notable reluctance. Wuthering Heights has been presented as, in many respects, a monstrous place, but its violence is the mark of its own spirit, and Emily Brontë is slow to deny it. The entire book may be read as Emily Brontë's progress toward Thrushcross Grange, but only if the reading acknowledges the inordinate force of attraction, for her, in the Heights.

—Denis Donoghue, "Emily Brontë: On the Latitude of Interpretation," *The Interpretation of Narrative: Theory and Practice* (1970), excerpted in *The Critical Perspective*, Vol. 7, ed. Harold Bloom (New York: Chelsea House Publishers, 1988), 3944–46

DAVID SONSTOEM

Wuthering Heights tends to be read for its purple passions—read as though those passions and the rationale behind them were being endorsed by Emily Brontë. But such a reading does not do the novel full justice. It does not treat an important element in the actual page-by-page experience of reading, namely, the uneasiness or confusion of the reader: his vacillating allegiances, his sense of being afloat on a troubled conceptual and ethical sea. Much of the reader's confusion is due to the pervasive and obvious shortsightedness of all the characters, including Heathcliff and Catherine. The somewhat Lawrencian outlook that the two leading figures harbor at the base of their natures but only partly understand simply does not take the whole world of *Wuthering Heights* into comprehensive account. In fact their shortsightedness is very similar in kind to that of everyone else. I wish to argue that *Wuthering Heights* presents the spectacle of several limited and inadequate points of view—genteel, Christian, pragmatic, animistic—at indecisive war with one another. Far from whole-heartedly endorsing an order, Emily Brontë depicts conceptual wuthering. She addresses herself less to vision than to blindness: to man's refusal to over-look his prejudices, and his inability to discern what lies beyond his limita-tions. ⟨. . .⟩

Instead of gradually aligning the reader's outlook with some controlling point of view of her own, Emily Brontë systematically brings it into line with the various limited perspectives of her characters. We are granted no visions, only variations upon the experience of shortsightedness. Although it is not unusual for a reader, in the course of a novel, to be led to change his mind about a character or event, he is accustomed to make his revisions upward—to find his perceptions coming closer to the full truth as it is presented by the author. *Wuthering Heights* is remarkable in that the tokens of authorial guid-ance serve throughout to keep the reader down, to make him grope and stum-ble. ⟨. . .⟩

My best guess is that Emily Brontë does not pretend to an overarching vision, and that that is her point. The stumbling shortsightedness that she pre-sents in her characters and induces in her reader is in fact her own experience of the world and the burden of her message. She does not expect the reader to embrace any world view, not even the attractively Romantic, elemental, ani-mistic one implicit in the relationship between Heathcliff and Catherine. She expects the reader rather to experience with them the sense of it as looming intangibly and uncertainly just beyond their ken, even as it is naggingly gain-said, crossed by ineradicably foreground considerations. In a word, she pre-sents wuthering as basic to almost all human experience. ⟨. . .⟩

Emily Brontë is finally depicting a Victorian rather than a Romantic state of mind, one akin to Arnold's

> Hither and thither spins
> The wind-borne mirroring soul,
> A thousand glimpses wins,
> And never sees a whole
> (*Empedocles on Etna*, ll. 6–9)

One akin also to George Eliot's sense of the futility of human ordering implicit in her celebrated image of a pier-glass, "multitudinously scratched in all direc-tions," which yet presents a unique pattern of concentric circles of scratches to each candle held up to it (*Middlemarch*, chap. 27). Like many of her fellow Victorians, Emily Brontë would seem to have been impressed by multiplicity of outlook and the relativity inherent in any point of view. That she would choose to employ the Romantic vision as her primary example of a concept felt to be receding beyond human viability places her almost too neatly as a transitional figure between the literary periods.

One thing at least is clear: Whatever her intentions, Emily Brontë did not merely throw her being vicariously into the lives of Heathcliff and Catherine. That she did read herself into their fictive adventures goes without saying. But an equally strong impulse was her drawing back in acid judgment upon her Romantic characters, as well as the more conventional characters who cross their existence. By implicating the reader as well, she dramatized the truth and range of her strictures. Her Romantic impulse was severely checked, if not actually destroyed, by the critical, judicial impulse. It has been said of her that she "never casts a sidelong glance; she is innocent of irony." Clearly the remark is incorrect, insofar as irony is used in the sense given currency by T. S. Eliot, namely, a strong awareness of alternative possibilities and points of view. A sidelong glance questions every view in *Wuthering Heights*. She has also been called a visionary. It is true that she often gives her reader a sense of vital forces operating just beyond the horizons of humanity. But, far from pretending to see beyond the sight of other men, she stresses the faults and limited scope of all human sight. Her final vision—epistemological, fragmented, negative—is a very earthly one, very close to home.

—David Sonstoem, "*Wuthering Heights* and the Limits of Vision," *PMLA* 86, no. 1 (January 1971), reprinted in *Emily Brontë's Wuthering Heights*, ed. Harold Bloom (New York: Chelsea House Publishers, 1987), 27, 42–45

FRANK KERMODE

Novels, even this one, were read in houses more like the Grange than the Heights, as the emphasis on the ferocious piety of the Earnshaw library suggests. The order of the novel is a civilized order; it presupposes a reader in the midst of an educated family and habituated to novel reading; a reader, moreover, who believes in the possibility of effective ethical choices. And because this is the case, the author can allow herself to meet his proper expectations without imposing on the text or on him absolute generic control. She need not, that is, know all that she is saying. She can, in all manner of ways, invite the reader to collaborate, leave to him the supply of meaning where the text is indeterminate or discontinuous, where explanations are required to fill narrative lacunae.

Instances of this are provided by some of the dreams in the book. ⟨. . .⟩

Dreams, visions, ghosts—the whole pneumatology of the book is only indeterminately related to the "natural" narrative. And this serves to muddle routine "single" readings, to confound explanation and expectation, and to make necessary a full recognition of the intrinsic plurality of the text.

Would it be reasonable to say this: that the mingling of generic opposites—daylight and dream narratives—creates a need, which we must supply, for something that will mediate between them? If so, we can go on to argue that the text in our response to it is a provision of such mediators, between life and death, the barbaric and the civilized, family and sexual relations. The principal instrument of mediation may well be Heathcliff: neither inside nor out, neither wholly master nor wholly servant, the husband who is no husband, the brother who is no brother, the father who abuses his changeling child, the cousin without kin. And that the chain of narrators serve to mediate between the barbarism of the story and the civility of the reader—making the text itself an intermediate term between archaic and modern—must surely have been pointed out.

What we must not forget, however, is that it is in the completion of the text by the reader that these adjustments are made; and each reader will make them differently. Plurality is here not a prescription but a fact. There is so much that is blurred and tentative, incapable of decisive explanation; however we set about our reading, with a sociological or a pneumatological, a cultural or a narrative code uppermost in our minds, we must fall into division and discrepancy; the doors of communication are sometimes locked, sometimes open, and Heathcliff may be astride the threshold, opening, closing, breaking. And it is surely evident that the possibilities of interpretation increase as time goes on. The constraints of a period culture dissolve, generic presumptions which concealed gaps disappear, and we now see that the book, as James thought novels should, truly "glories in a gap," a hermeneutic gap in which the reader's imagination must operate, so that he speaks continuously in the text. For these reasons the rebus—*Catherine Earnshaw, Catherine Heathcliff, Catherine Linton*—has exemplary significance. It is a riddle that the text answers only silently; for example it will neither urge nor forbid you to remember that it resembles the riddle of the Sphinx—what manner of person exists in these three forms?—to which the single acceptable and probable answer involves incest and ruin.

I have not found it possible to speak of *Wuthering Heights* in this light without, from time to time, hinting—in a word here, or a trick of procedure there—at the new French criticism. I am glad to acknowledge this affinity, but it also seems important to dissent from the opinion that such "classic" texts as this—and the French will call them so, but with pejorative intent—are essentially naive, and become in a measure plural only by accident. The number of choices is simply too large; it is impossible that even two competent readers should agree on an authorized naive version. It is because texts are so naive that they can become classics. It is true, as I have said, that time opens them up; if readers were immortal the classic would be much closer to changelessness; their deaths do, in an important sense, liberate the texts. But to attribute the entire *potential* of plurality to that cause (or to the wisdom and cunning of later readers) is to fall into a mistake. The "Catherines" of Lockwood's inscriptions may not have been attended to, but there they were in the text, just as ambiguous and plural as they are now. What happens is that methods of repairing such indeterminacy change; and, as Wolfgang Iser's neat formula has it, "the repair of indeterminacy" is what gives rise "to the generation of meaning."

—Frank Kermode, "A Modern Way with the Classic," *The Classic: Literary Images of Permanence and Change* (1975), reprinted in *Emily Brontë's Wuthering Heights*, ed. Harold Bloom (New York: Chelsea House Publishers, 1987), 54, 56–57

ROSALIND MILES

What was the aim, the drive behind Emily Brontë's poetry, the struggle of her artistry to be at all costs accurate? She put the honesty of her energy to work at one of the most unusual and difficult task of poetry, the account of her mystical experiences. If her style is, as we have seen, sinewy, personal and impressive, how much more so is the content of this theme—uniquely personal, uniquely impressive. ⟨. . .⟩

Inevitably the more intense her visions grew, the duller in comparison lay the world outside, robbed of its colour by the vividness of the dream world. H. 184, "Ah! why, because the dazzling sun," shows us Emily Brontë going more and more into her inner existence, the night life of spirit and thought. The "glorious eyes" that watch in this poem are pretty clearly those of the stars. But their power is not only to soothe her into peace—once her spirit is lulled into serenity they provide too the stimulus for the free association of thought and feeling which lifts her into the desired but unknown state of unknowing:

> Thought followed thought—star followed star
> Through boundless regions on,
> While one sweet influence, near and far,
> Thrilled through and proved us one.

This state, virtually indescribable because virtually unimaginable by others, achieved its finest poetic rendering in the famous central section of H. 190, "Julian M. to A. G. Rochelle." This poem catches up and illuminates afresh all the vital elements of Emily Brontë's mystical experiences as we have noticed them in earlier references; possibly it was not until this stage that she had sufficiently refined and clarified her own perception of what was taking place within her. We see again, evening, wind, and stars; we have the visitant identified as "He," and for the first time set forth as a "messenger of Hope." He brings "visions," in the plural, which "rise and change," indicating plainly that for Emily Brontë mystical possession was not a static state, but one which progressed in itself and also hinted at further progression towards an even more desirable goal—"kill me with desire." There is a brief reference to her having passed through an earlier emotional stage, of strong but confused emotion, which was unlike what she now feels; this supports other suggestions of some sort of emotional apprenticeship served before the full harmonious spiritual union was realized.

The mystical experience itself is described as occurring in two stages. First comes the cessation of physical life, and especially the irritability of expectancy. Paradox again is the natural, indeed perhaps the only, mode of expression here—"mute music . . unuttered harmony." Then, in one brilliant movement, the inner self ("essence") leaps to commune with a being which can only be described in terms of negatives—the Invisible, the Unseen. Yet despite the use of these (to us) rather chilling abstracts, this being or condition is warm and welcoming to the poet; note Emily Brontë's use of the two supreme metaphors of safety and reassurance in line eighty-three, "home" and "harbour." In agonizing contrast to this certainty, this poem gives the fullest account of what Emily Brontë elsewhere refers to simply as her "bitter waking." It is clear that the freedom which she elsewhere highlights as an essential of her life is more totally hers in this state of mystical possession than in any other mode of her life. Nothing can make her lose her faith in this; again we see the flicker of doubting orthodoxy, when she concedes that her vision may be "robed in fires of Hell, or bright with heavenly shine"; but she remains insistent upon its (ultimately) divine origin.

In the face of an achievement like that of Emily Brontë, the imagination staggers, the self-esteem creeps away rebuked. The startling originality of her experiences combines with her mastery of poetic techniques to dwarf the accomplishment of many poets who are yet often higher in the general esteem. It is a final paradox that one of the most honest of our writers, who emphasized so strongly, using such passionate and authoritative rhythms because she wanted above all to make herself plain, has been taken so oddly at times; especially when the treatment of her as an instinctive, unconscious creature results in a major critic writing off *Wuthering Heights* as a "sport," as Leavis did. Yet this is the writer who consistently, and with amazing resources of technical skill, dealt on our behalf with all the great intolerables of life—pain, loss, and cruelty—who put her originality to work in the service of clarifying for us all the great unoriginal occurrences of human nature and daily existence.

Emily Brontë, as a poet and as a person, was quite devoid of that winning flirtatiousness, that capacity to charm and flatter, that gratitude for guidance and attention which is still felt in some circles, even today, to be a prerequisite of a literary female. While her true greatness has long been acknowledged, perhaps we can now pay her the further tribute of an ungrudging, *unsurprised* admiration of her achievement. We should be able to accept with grace the idea that a young female could, without faltering, create works whose only fellows in literature are the Greek tragedies, the Norse sagas, *King Lear*. We must see the beauty of her artistry and skill, or see her all wrong.

—Rosalind Miles, "A Baby God: The Creative Dynamism of Emily Brontë's Poetry," *The Art of Emily Brontë* (1976), reprinted in *The Brontës*, ed. Harold Bloom (New York: Chelsea House Publishers, 1987), 83, 88–89

J. HILLIS MILLER

The literature on *Wuthering Heights* is abundant and its incoherence striking. Even more than some other great works of literature this novel seems to have an inexhaustible power to call forth commentary and more commentary. All literary criticism tends to be the presentation of what claims to be the definitive rational explanation of the text in question. The criticism of *Wuthering Heights* is characterized by the unusual degree of incoherence among the various explanations and by the way each takes some one element in the novel and extrapolates it toward a total explanation. ⟨. . .⟩

The essays on *Wuthering Heights* ⟨. . .⟩ seem to me insufficient, not because what they say is demonstrably mistaken, but rather because there is an error in the assumption that there *is* a single secret truth about *Wuthering Heights*. This secret truth would be something formulable as a univocal principle of explanation which would account for everything in the novel. The secret truth about *Wuthering Heights*, rather, is that there is no secret truth which criticism might formulate in this way. No hidden identifiable ordering principle which will account for everything stands at the head of the chain or at the back of the back. Any formulation of such a principle is visibly reductive. It leaves something important still unaccounted for. This is a remnant of opacity which keeps the interpreter dissatisfied, the novel still open, the process of interpretation still able to continue. ⟨. . .⟩

The critic's conceptual or figurative scheme of interpretation, including my own here, is up against the same blank wall as the totalizing emblems within the novel, or up against the same impasse that blocks Heathcliff's enterprise of reaching Cathy by taking possession of everything that carries her image and then destroying it. If "something" is incompatible with any sign, if it cannot be seen, signified, or theorized about, it is, in our tradition, no "thing." It is nothing. The trace of such an absence therefore retraces nothing.

It can refer only to another trace, in that relation of incongruity which leads the reader of *Wuthering Heights* from one such emblematic design to another. Each passage stands for another passage, in the way Branderham's sermon, ⟨. . .⟩ is a commentary on Jesus's words, themselves a commentary on an Old Testament passage, and so on. Such a movement is a constant passage from one place to another without ever finding the original literal text of which the others are all figures. This missing center is the head referent which would still the wandering movement from emblem to emblem, from story to story, from generation to generation, from Catherine to Catherine, from Hareton to Hareton, from narrator to narrator. ⟨. . .⟩

Each emblematic passage in the novel is both a seeming avenue to the desired unity and also a barrier forbidding access to it. Each means the death of experience, of consciousness, of seeing, and of theory by naming the "state" or "place" that lies always outside the words of the novel and therefore can never be experienced as such, and at the same time, in itself and in its intrinsic tendency to repeat itself, each emblematic passage holds off that death. ⟨. . .⟩

Wuthering Heights ⟨. . .⟩ is an example of a special form of repetition in realistic fiction. This form is controlled by the invitation to believe that some invisible or transcendent cause, some origin, end, or underlying ground, would explain all the enigmatic incongruities of what is visible. Conrad's *Heart of Darkness* is another example of such a repetitive form, as is *Lord Jim*, discussed in chapter 2 [of *Fiction and Repetition*]. It is by no means the case that all realistic fiction takes this form. . . . The special form of "undecidability" in *Wuthering Heights* or in other narratives in which repetition takes this form lies in the impossibility, in principle, of determining whether there is some extralinguistic explanatory cause or whether the sense that there is one is generated by the linguistic structure itself. Nor is this a trivial issue. It is the most important question the novel raises, the one thing about which we ought to be able to make a decision, and yet a thing about which the novel forbids the reader to make a decision. In this *Wuthering Heights* justifies being called an "uncanny" text. To alter Freud's formulas a little, the uncanny in *Wuthering Heights* is the constant bringing into the open of something which seems familiar and which one feels ought to have been kept secret, not least because it is impossible to tell whether there is any secret at all hidden in the depths, or whether the sense of familiarity and of the unveiling of a secret may not be an effect of the repetition in difference of one part of the text by another, on the surface.

—J. Hillis Miller, "*Wuthering Heights*: Repetition and the 'Uncanny'," *Fiction and Repetition: Seven English Novels* (1982), reprinted in *The Brontës*, ed. Harold Bloom (New York: Chelsea House Publishers, 1987), 175–76, 188–90

STEVIE DAVIES

Wuthering Heights, with its story of Catherine's wilful separation from her "twin," Heathcliff, her exile at Thrushcross Grange, the riddle of her delirium and the "baby-work" of her pregnancy and delivery of the new Catherine, is an original myth of loss, exile, rebirth, and return. It has the self-contained and opaque quality of all myth. It imagines the human soul as being female, seeking a lost male counterpart. The "secret" of *Wuthering Heights* is not a displaced incest motif, nor is it asexual, as critics claim. Catherine, having betrayed the union with her own truest likeness, is involved in a sexual search, but sexual union is not the subject of the story, rather it is the metaphor for a search which is metaphysical and "human" in the largest sense. 〈. . .〉

The novel is not so much about individuals as about humanity. It is less about humanity than humanity in a setting. It is far less about humanity in the person of the male of our species ("man," "forefathers," "God the father," "masterpiece") as about humanity in the person of the female. The author of *Genesis*, looking back to our origins, had felt called upon to attribute to Adam a sort of womb where his ribcage was, by biological sleight and to the confounding of common sense, deriving woman from man. For a person as radical as Emily Brontë, and innocent of the offence her perceptions might cause the vulnerable minds of the orthodox, writing of the theme of genesis, this would simply not seem sensible, credible, or even efficient according to the laws of practical economy. She expresses instead a female vision of genesis, expulsion, and rebirth in terms of the metaphor of fertility and childbirth. Wordsworth and the Romantic poets, whom she deeply admired, had taken the imagination back to childhood, to muse over the idea of the child as "father of the man," a metaphor for our beginnings. Emily Brontë, in a way that is radical and difficult because no language has existed in patriarchal England to express it (foremothers, mistress piece, God the mother?), relived the idea according to the more natural metaphor of the child as mother of the woman. Catherine's mothering of Cathy at the centre of the book relates past to present; projects present into future, so that past and future meet at source. The ethic of this feminine way of encountering reality is that of universal forgiveness; the metaphysic is one of final but mysterious redemption; the means of expression is that of a coded, secret utterance which, though we feel we understand fully while we read, has the knack akin to that of dream-language of slipping just out of comprehension when we awaken. 〈. . .〉

In the second half of the novel, Heathcliff tries to thwart and mutilate the products of this fertility. Yet toward the end, it becomes clear that he cannot destroy anything; that he is in a strange way the agent of a harmony for which he cannot wish. Far from thieving the property of the Heights and the Grange from their rightful owners, his efforts marry the two inheritances by bringing the two heirs into proximity. The "little dark thing, harboured by a good man to his bane" as Nelly muses, is not ultimately a "bane" at all, but an instrument of regeneration and of harmonious balance between eternal oppositions. *Wuthering Heights* hinges on a fruitful but—in rational terms—baffling paradox: order and disorder, creation and destruction, being born and dying, looking in and seeing out, enclose and define each other, as if in a series of multiple parentheses. Within this pattern Heathcliff, for all his efficient manipulations, is caught static. He is, at the centre, a "piece of timber," rooted in the seasonal cycle, at whose foot the breeding birds are free to fulfil their instinctual nature. ⟨. . .⟩

The happiness of the future, Emily Brontë asserts, is built on the destruction of the past, and is seen by the reader to depend on it. In one of the most poignantly beautiful images of *Wuthering Heights*, (stated matter-of-factly two chapters later,) Nelly says of the second Catherine, whose birth had killed her mother: "For the rest, after the first six months, she grew like a larch; and could walk and talk too, in her own way, before the heath blossomed a second time over Mrs. Linton's dust." ⟨. . .⟩

The child has in her the best of the Lintons and the best of the Earnshaws, in fruitful mixture. If she is "like" her mother she is also "like" Heathcliff, since we must believe Catherine's conviction that "I *am* Heathcliff." As he stood in the terrible night of Cathy's birth amongst the larches, and shed his blood upon the bark of a tree, so Cathy "grew like a larch." In some mysterious way, Heathcliff is intrinsically linked to the second Cathy, and has given up some of his life to her.

—Stevie Davies, "Baby-Work: The Myth of Rebirth in *Wuthering Heights*," *Emily Brontë: The Artist as a Free Woman* (1983), reprinted in *Emily Brontë's Wuthering Heights*, ed. Harold Bloom (New York: Chelsea House Publishers, 1987), 121, 127–28, 133–36

SHEILA SMITH

The ballads are fundamentally important to *Wuthering Heights*, especially to the novel's version of the supernatural which records the chief characters' triumphant attainment of a spiritual life, bringing them into accord with each other and with Nature. This life transcends the restrictions of contemporary class prejudices, evades the law (Heathcliff is both metaphorically and, by his cunning, literally outside the scope of the law and with which Nelly threatens him) and disregards orthodox morality, so often used as an instrument of oppression. Wimberly emphasizes the pagan nature of the ballads: 'The remains of heathendom in folksong are especially marked . . . the ideas and practices imbedded in British balladry may be referred almost wholly to a pagan culture.' In the novel the pagan world, centred on sexual passion, expressed in the supernatural tale of Heathcliff and Cathy's enduring love, is constantly set against orthodox Christianity, of the routine kind dutifully voiced by Nelly or referred to by Lockwood or Edgar Linton; or the more lurid morality of Calvinistic sects such as Joseph's. Ironically, Joseph, who is constantly inveighing against the pleasures of this life and insisting on the demands of the next, does not convince the reader that he is possessed of the life of the spirit. Joseph's religion is a brand of individualistic materialism, insisting on the return which his outlay of good conduct will ensure him. Despite his continual and vehement references to the Devil, Joseph is not in contact with the supernatural. He remains simply a cantankerous old man, using the terms of his religion to vent his spite against youth, vigour, and love.

In *Wuthering Heights* Emily Brontë revitalizes the literary form of the novel by use of structural devices, motifs, and subjects which properly belong to the oral tradition with which all the Brontë children were familiar, particularly through the agency of Tabitha Aykroyd, the Yorkshire woman who for thirty years was servant in the Brontë household. Elizabeth Gaskell, in her biography of Charlotte, says of Tabby that 'she had known the "bottom", or valley, in those primitive days when the fairies frequented the margin of the "beck" on moonlight nights, and had known folk who had seen them'. ⟨. . .⟩

By adapting one of the newer genres of the literature of high culture elements of one of the older forms of the literature of folk culture, Emily Brontë extends and develops both Wordsworth's perception of imagination playing upon the familiar to give insight into the human condition, and Coleridge's apprehension of the supernatural as familiar. In *Wuthering Heights* imagination, in the supernatural manifestations, *is* insight, as against the cloudy perceptions of reason and orthodox morality. Her version of reality challenges the materialistic, class-ridden structure of the society of 1847, as Arnold Kettle and Terry Eagleton have suggested. But as Q. D. Leavis maintains that the allusions to fairy-tales in the novel are a sign of immaturity, so Eagleton argues that the supernatural is a weakness in the book, that Emily Brontë makes a 'metaphysical' challenge to society, but can do this 'only by refracting it through the distorting terms of existing social relations, while simultaneously, at a "deeper" level, isolating that challenge in a realm eternally divorced from the actual'. But, as I have tried to show, the novel's power lies in Emily Brontë's perception of the supernatural as an essential dimension of the actual, and this theme, central in ballad and folk-tale, is expressed by techniques which can be related to those of ballad and folk-tale. She uses the supernatural in her narrative to give direct, dramatic, and objective expression to the strength of sexual passion, as so many of the ballads do. It was this directness which so shocked Emily Brontë's first readers. 'Coarseness' and lack of orthodox morality were charges frequently levelled against the book. Even the perceptive G. H.

Lewes, who could not 'deny its truth', found it also 'rude' and 'brutal'. The more obtuse E. P. Whipple, although he acknowledged 'Acton Bell's' (*sic*) 'uncommon talents', objected to 'his subject and his dogged manner of handling it'. Miriam Allott comments that it was Whipple who regarded *Wuthering Heights* 'as the last desperate attempt to corrupt the virtues of the sturdy descendants of the Puritans'. It was left to Swinburne, who had himself been ostracized for setting his poetry against the bourgeois morality of High Victorian society, to make the most perceptive comment on the novel: 'All the works of the elder sister [Charlotte Brontë] are rich in poetic spirit, poetic feeling, and poetic detail; but the younger sister's work is essentially and definitely a poem in the fullest and most positive sense of the term.' For 'poem' read 'ballad'.

> —Sheila Smith, "'At Once Strong and Eerie': The Supernatural in *Wuthering Heights* and Its Debt to the Traditional Balad," *Review of English Studies*, no. 172 (1992), 515–17

B I B L I O G R A P H Y

Poems by Currer, Ellis, and Acton Bell (with Charlotte and Anne Brontë). 1846.

Wuthering Heights (2 vols.). 1847.

Wuthering Heights and Agnes Gray (by Anne Brontë) *with a Biographical Notice of the Authors, a Selection from Their Literary Remains, and a Preface by Currer Bell* (Charlotte Brontë). 1850.

The Life and Works of Charlotte Brontë and her Sisters (7 vols.). 1872–73.

The Works of Charlotte, Emily, and Anne Brontë (12 vols.). 1893.

The Life and Works of the Sisters Brontë (7 vols.). 1899–1903.

Poems by Charlotte, Emily, and Anne Brontë. 1902.

Poems. 1906.

The Brontës: Life and Letters (2 vols.). 1908.

Complete Works (2 vols.). 1910–11.

Complete Poems. 1923.

The Shakespeare Head Brontë (with Charlotte and Anne Brontë) (19 vols.). 1931–38.

The Brontës: Their Lives, Friendships, and Correspondence (4 vols.). 1932.

Two Poems: Love's Rebuke, Remembrance. 1934.

Gondal Poems: Now First Published from the MS in the British Museum. 1938.

Complete Poems. 1941.

Five Essays Written in French (Tr. Lorrine W. Nagel). 1948.

Complete Poems. 1951.

A Selection of Poems. 1952.

Gondal's Queen: A Novel in Verse. 1955.
Poems. 1973
The Novels of Charlotte, Emily, and Anne Brontë. 1976.
Selected Poems (with Anne and Charlotte Brontë). 1985.
The Brontës: Selected Poems. 1985.
Poems. 1992.
The Complete Poems. 1992.

FANNY BURNEY
1752-1840

FANNY BURNEY was born in King's Lynn on June 13, 1752. In 1760, her father, the musicologist Dr. Charles Burney, moved the family to London, where his services as music master were in demand in fashionable society. The Burney family had aristocratic and literary friends, including Sir Joshua Reynolds, Samuel Johnson, Edmund Burke, and David Garrick. The six Burney children were clever and accomplished. Their mother, Esther Sleepe Burney, died in 1761. In 1764, Dr. Burney sent Fanny's two sisters to school in Paris, but kept Fanny at home out of fear that she might become too attracted to Catholicism. Throughout her life, Fanny Burney was devoted to both her father and his friend, Samuel or "Daddy" Crisp, who was twenty years older than Dr. Burney and who became his daughter's beloved mentor and friend.

The young Fanny enjoyed writing, or "scribbling," as she called it, but sometime after her father's second marriage, to Elizabeth Allan, a widow, she burned her early writings and renounced authorship. Yet Burney could not repress her propensities for writing; she composed much of *Evelina* in secret before confessing to her father that she was writing a novel. *Evelina* was published anonymously in 1778 and made Fanny famous when her identity as the book's author became known. Samuel Johnson was a great admirer of the novel, as was Mrs. Thrale, who befriended its young author. *Evelina* was followed by *Cecilia* in 1882.

Burney abandoned writing between 1786 and 1791, when she was Second Keeper of the Robes to Queen Charlotte, the wife of King George III. The position was prestigious and paid a good salary, but Burney found the work physically taxing and emotionally isolating. She returned to her father's house in 1791 and resumed her writing career with *Edwy and Elgiva*, *Hubert De Vere*, *The Siege of Pevensey*, and *Elberta*—all tragedies for the stage. In 1793 she married Alexandre d'Arblay, formerly a high-ranking general in the French military, but now a refugee living in England. They had a son in 1794, and Fanny published *Camilla*, her third novel, in 1796. Due to M. D'Arblay's difficulties with his pension and his passport, the family lived in France for ten years, from 1802 to1812.

In 1814, Burney published her last novel, *The Wanderer*. The book commanded a great deal of money from her publisher, but was attacked by reviewers. Burney's style became more self-conscious and convoluted as she grew older, a result, perhaps of her desire to imitate Samuel Johnson. Burney and her husband returned to France, only to be driven out by Napoleon in 1815. In 1818, Burney's husband died in England and she set to work on assembling and editing *Memoirs of Dr. Burney*, remembrances of her father, who had died a few years before her husband. These were also written in her later style, and as a result, also attacked in the press. In 1837, Burney's son, Alexandre D'Arblay, died suddenly of influenza at the start of a promising career in the church. Burney, or Madame D'Arblay, as she was then known, died in 1840 at age 88. She had been a dedicated diarist and correspondent for her entire life, and her diaries and letters appeared posthumously as *The Diary and Letters of Madame d'Arblay* (7 vols., 1843–46) and *The Early Diary of Frances Burney* (2 vols., 1889). These have been combined in a modern, 10-volume edition of her letters and journals, edited by Joyce Hemlow (1972–81).

CRITICAL EXTRACTS

WILLIAM HAZLITT

Madame D'Arblay is ⟨. . .⟩ quite of the old school, a mere common observer of manners ⟨. . . .⟩ She is a quick, lively, and accurate observer of persons and things; but she always looks at them with a consciousness of her sex, and in that point of view in which it is the particular business and interest of women to observe them. There is little in her works of passion or character, or even manners, in the most extended sense of the word, as implying the sum-total of our habits and pursuits; her *forte* is describing the absurdities and affectations of external behaviour, or *the manners of people in company*. Her characters, which are ingenious caricatures, are, no doubt, distinctly marked, and well kept up; but they are slightly shaded, and exceedingly uniform. Her heroes and heroines, almost all of them, depend on the stock of a single phrase or sentiment, and have certain mottoes or devices by which they may always be known. They form such characters as people might be supposed to assume for a night at a masquerade. She presents, not the whole-length figure, nor even the face, but some prominent feature. ⟨. . .⟩

Women, in general, have a quicker perception of any oddity or singularity of character than men and are more alive to every absurdity which arises from a violation of the rules of society, or a deviation from established custom.

This partly arises from the restraints on their own behaviour, which turn their attention constantly on the subject, and partly from other causes. The surface of their minds, like that of their bodies, seems of a finer texture than ours; more soft, and susceptible of immediate impulses. They have less muscular strength; less power of continued voluntary attention—of reason, passion, and imagination: but they are more easily impressed with whatever appeals to their senses or habitual prejudices. The intuitive perception of their minds is less disturbed by any abstruse reasonings on causes or consequences. They learn the idiom of character and manners, as they acquire that of language, by rote, without troubling themselves about the principles. Their observation is not the less accurate on that account, as far as it goes; for it has been well said, that 'there is nothing so true as habit.'

There is little other power in Miss Burney's novels, than that of immediate observation: her characters, whether of refinement or vulgarity, are equally superficial and confined. The whole is a question of form, whether that form is adhered to or infringed upon. It is this circumstance which takes away dignity and interest from her story and sentiments, and makes the one so teazing and tedious, and the other so insipid. The difficulties in which she involves her heroines are too much 'Female Difficulties'; they are difficulties created out of nothing. ⟨. . .⟩

To mention the most painful instance—*The Wanderer*, in her last novel, raises obstacles, lighter than 'the gossamer that idles in the wanton summer air,' into insurmountable barriers; and trifles with those that arise out of common sense, reason, and necessity. Her conduct is not to be accounted for directly out of the circumstances in which she is placed, but out of some factitious and misplaced refinement on them. It is a perpetual game at cross-purposes. There being a plain and strong motive why she should pursue any course of action, is a sufficient reason for her to avoid it; and the perversity of her conduct is in proportion to its levity—as the lightness of the feather baffles the force of the impulse that is given to it, and the slightest breath of air turns it back on the hand from which it is thrown. We can hardly consider this as the perfection of the female character!

—William Hazlitt, *Lectures on the English Comic Writers* (1818), excerpted in *The New Moulton's Library of Literary Criticism*, Vol. 7, ed. Harold Bloom (New York: Chelsea House Publishers, 1989), 4039–40

THOMAS BABINGTON MACAULAY

The truth is, that Madame D'Arblay's style underwent a gradual and most pernicious change, a change which, in degree at least, we believe to be unexampled in literary history, and of which it may be useful to trace the progress.

When she wrote her letters to Mr. Crisp, her early journals, and her first novel, her style was not indeed brilliant or energetic; but it was easy, clear, and free from all offensive faults. When she wrote *Cecilia* she aimed higher. She had then lived much in a circle of which Johnson was the centre; and she was herself one of his most submissive worshippers. It seems never to have crossed her mind that the style even of his best writings was by no means faultless, and that even had it been faultless, it might not be wise in her to imitate it. Phraseology which is proper in a disquisition on the Unities, or in a preface to a Dictionary, may be quite out of place in a tale of fashionable life. Old gentlemen do not criticize the reigning modes, nor do young gentlemen make love, with the balanced epithets and sonorous cadences which, on occasions of great dignity, a skilful writer may use with happy effect.

In an evil hour the author of *Evelina* took the *Rambler* for her model. This would not have been wise even if she could have imitated her pattern as well as Hawkesworth did. But such imitation was beyond her power. She had her own style. It was a tolerably good one; and might, without any violent change, have been improved into a very good one. She determined to throw it away, and to adopt a style in which she could attain excellence only by achieving an almost miraculous victory over nature and over habit. She could cease to be Fanny Burney; it was not so easy to become Samuel Johnson.

In *Cecilia* the change of manner began to appear. But in *Cecilia* the imitation of Johnson, though not always in the best taste, is sometimes eminently happy; and the passages which are so verbose as to be positively offensive, are few. There were people who whispered that Johnson had assisted his young friend, and that the novel owed all its finest passages to his hand. This was merely the fabrication of envy. Miss Burney's real excellences were as much beyond the reach of Johnson, as his real excellences were beyond her reach. He could no more have written the Masquerade scene, or the Vauxhall scene, than she could have written the "Life of Cowley" or the "Review of Soame Jenyns." But we have not the smallest doubt that he revised *Cecilia*, and that he retouched the style of many passages. We know that he was in the habit of giving assistance of this kind most freely. Goldsmith, Hawkesworth, Boswell, Lord Hailes, Mrs. Williams, were among those who obtained his help. Nay, he even corrected the poetry of Mr. Crabbe, whom, we believe, he had never seen. When Miss Burney thought of writing a comedy, he promised to give her his best counsel, though he owned that he was not particularly well qualified to advise on matters relating to the stage. We therefore think it in the highest degree improbable that his little Fanny, when living in habits of the most affectionate intercourse with him, would have brought out an important work without consulting him; and, when we look into *Cecilia*, we see such traces of his hand in the grave and elevated passages as it is impossible to mistake.

When next Madame D'Arblay appeared before the world as a writer, she was in a very different situation. She would not content herself with the simple English in which *Evelina* had been written. She had no longer the friend who, we are confident, had polished and strengthened the style of *Cecilia*. She had to write in Johnson's manner without Johnson's aid. The consequence was, that in *Camilla* every passage which she meant to be fine is detestable; and that the book has been saved from condemnation only by the admirable spirit and force of those scenes in which she was content to be familiar. ⟨. . .⟩

It is from no unfriendly feeling to Madame D'Arblay's memory that we have expressed ourselves so strongly on the subject of her style. On the contrary, we conceive that we have really rendered a service to her reputation. That her later works were complete failures, is a fact too notorious to be dissembled: and some persons, we believe, have consequently taken up a notion that she was from the first an overrated writer, and that she had not the powers which were necessary to maintain her on the eminence on which good luck and fashion had placed her. We believe, on the contrary, that her early popularity was no more than the just reward of distinguished merit, and would never have undergone an eclipse, if she had only been content to go on writing in her mother tongue. If she failed when she quitted her own province, and attempted to occupy one in which she had neither part nor lot, this reproach is common to her with a crowd of distinguished men. Newton failed when he turned from the courses of the stars, and the ebb and flow of the ocean, to apocalyptic seals and vials. Bentley failed when he turned from Homer and Aristophanes, to edite the *Paradise Lost*. Inigo failed when he attempted to rival the Gothic churches of the fourteenth century. Wilkie failed when he took it into his head that the Blind Fiddler and the Rent Day were unworthy of his powers, and challenged competition with Lawrence as a portrait painter. Such failures should be noted for the instruction of posterity; but they detract little from the permanent reputation of those who have really done great things.

—Thomas Babington Macaulay, "Madame D'Arblay" (1843), *Critical, Historical, and Miscellaneous Essays* (1860), excerpted in *The New Moulton's Library of Literary Criticism*, Vol. 7, ed. Harold Bloom (New York: Chelsea House Publishers, 1989), 4050–52

RONALD PAULSON

Fanny Burney's *Evelina* (1778), [one] critic [Montague and Martz] has observed, uses "*Humphry Clinker* as a base for operations in the direction of Jane Austen." Austen was a careful reader of Burney, and Burney owes an obvious debt to Smollett. Although the plot of *Evelina* receives a great deal more emphasis than that of *Humphry Clinker*, both novels are structurally a series of letters describing a series of places visited, an itinerary held together by a conventional sentimental plot. Unacknowledged fathers, the lowly who turn out to be highborn, and brothers who find their lost sisters are all ingredients of the sentimental plot in both novels. The themes in both—though different— are conveyed by the cities and country houses visited. Evelina goes from the country to London with the acceptable Mirvan family; then back to the country and again to London, this time in the company of the impossible, vulgar Branghtons and Mme. Duval; then back to the country and to Bristol Hot Well with people of quality, the Beaumonts; and finally to Bath with Lord Orville. The effect here is not too different from that of a scene in London or Bath seen through the eyes of Bramble, then Jery, and then Winifred Jenkins and Tabitha. In a more formalized, static way, these letters serve the function of Evelina's different guides, revealing and opposing "different points of view and incompatible ways of meeting the same experience" (Baker). In this sense *Humphry Clinker* points away from the true-false world of formal verse satire toward the infinitely qualified world of the novel of manners. ⟨. . .⟩

The chief difference between the two novels, however, lies in the fact that in *Evelina* the places and scenes not only are part of a satiric survey of society, but also are stages in the social climb of a young girl. One difficulty in Smollett's novels up to *Humphry Clinker* was his inability to merge his sentimental plot conventions and his real center of interest (the satiric scene); *Evelina* carries Smollett's work a step further, fitting his psychological form to the logical form of the courtship. For this aspect of her novel, Burney drew upon *Sir Charles Grandison*, omitting the melodramatic end of the spectrum. But the plot Burney follows in *Evelina* is not solely made up of the stages of a courtship; it simultaneously consists of the stages in the social ascent of a young girl. Evelina, the chief letter writer of the novel, has much in common with Harriet Byron, but she has more with Sir Charles Grandison's young ward, Emily Jervois, a naive observer without Harriet's certainty in her own judgment; Emily's horrible mother becomes Evelina's Mme. Duval, with the implications more fully developed.

Evelina is sharp and critical, and her standards are high; but as Bramble is isolated by his illness, she (like Humphry Clinker) is isolated by her birth. She is outside society, of obscure parentage, and comes from a sheltered life in the country which sets off the vice of London in vivid relief. However, the function of her equivocal position is no longer simply to make her a touchstone or a satirist (though she is a little of both) but to put her outside society—a "nobody" as Lovel calls her—so that she literally does not know who she is; her progression then is not, like Harriet's, toward fulfillment, but toward self-definition and identity. ⟨. . .⟩

Evelina has too much of the Smollettian character in her to lose all traces of the satiric device. Her embarrassment—the effect of the Branghtons' faux pas on her delicate sensibility—can be taken as another mutation of Bramble's violent reaction to sociomoral corruptions. At any rate, the reactions of cultivated heroines in scenes with boors are gentle cousins to the satiric outburst. ⟨. . .⟩

The embarrassment of Evelina is more personal than Bramble's; her future with an aristocratic husband is at stake, and so, in the celebrated scene at the opera, her enlightened self-importance is caught in the same satiric situation as the Branghtons' stupid self-importance. Both roles are still distinct enough to make her derivation from the English satiric tradition plain, and yet they dramatically merge as they lead her toward abduction at the hands of the proper gentleman Willoughby.

Smollett always stops short of this treatment of the personal problem because, although he reduces his satirical spokesman's attitude to just one way of looking at the world, he still shares with his satirical forebears the assumption that the individual's quest is not as important as the many different endeavors of the people surrounding him. This may offer an explanation for the form of the anatomy he employs, where person after person and scene after scene receive varying but not disproportionate emphasis; the whole human organism is the important consideration, and the satirist feels that a hand or a foot should never make one lose sight of the larger meaning of the whole. In this sense *Evelina* is a careful balance of the old and new: the anatomy of society is still present, and the protagonist is still functioning as a satiric device, but the fictional form given these matters is about to absorb and subordinate them all to the single theme of the protagonist's growing self-awareness.

—Ronald Paulson, "*Evelina*: Cinderella and Society," *Satire and the Novel in Eighteenth-Century England* (1967), reprinted in *Fanny Burney's Evelina*, ed. Harold Bloom (New York: Chelsea House Publishers, 1988), 5–7, 11–12

SUSAN STAVES

There is a remarkable degree of critical consensus on the merits of *Evelina*, Fanny Burney's popular novel. This consensus is for the most part sound, but it has one aspect which strikes me as peculiar. Descriptions of the novel make it appear to be a combination of the usual romance with cheerful, albeit occasionally malicious, satire. The primary criticism of the book is that it is hopelessly trivial. Yet Evelina's predominant emotion seems to me to be an acute anxiety which is painful, real, and powerful. ⟨. . .⟩

We may notice immediately that Evelina's anxiety is partly provoked by physical violence and threats of violence. She is subjected to assaults which—though they could happen in Richardson—could not conceivably be made on heroines in Jane Austen or even in Dickens. ⟨. . .⟩

Evelina's progress through the public places of London is about as tranquil as the progress of a fair-haired girl through modern Naples. Every time she is accidentally separated from her protectors she is addressed with indelicate freedom, pursued, and usually grabbed. ⟨. . .⟩

Evelina's anxiety, however, is more often provoked by psychic threats than by the possibilities of physical assault. She worries constantly that her delicacy will be wounded or that it will appear to be compromised. "Delicacy" seems to be a central concept in the novel and is worth trying to define. As a positive virtue it arises from awareness of the sensibilities and needs of others. ⟨. . .⟩

Female delicacy can be wounded and, if wounded often enough or seriously enough, actually killed. Delicacy is in part like virginity: once lost it cannot be regained. Yet it is still more fragile and precarious than virginity, since it can be eroded by the social ambiance in which one finds oneself. ⟨. . .⟩

What, finally, are the female difficulties which are a subject of *Evelina?* First, there are the physical limitations which make women too weak to resist men who grab them and even too slow to run away. Then, there are the psychological restraints which force real and pretended ignorance about subjects from sexuality to money. Lord Orville wants to tell Evelina about the marriage settlements, but like all her sisters in the family of heroines, she assures him she is "almost ignorant of the word." Violations of the code of female delicacy, however minor, lead to anxiety that a woman will become a sort of outlaw who has lost her claim to the protection of society, protection which young women desperately need. Of course, many of Evelina's embarrassments seem all too familiar to anyone, male or female, who has memories of a sensitive adolescence. Indeed, many female difficulties were rapidly becoming human difficulties as the passivity and modesty here required of Evelina were shortly to be required of the romantic heroes of Scott and Cooper. Nevertheless, the special vulnerability of a young woman in traditional society gives her anxieties a sharper edge.

Evelina tells and shows how difficult it is to be a young lady. With the sincerest desire for correctness, the heroine is forced into situations where she must offend punctilio. Her own grandmother orders her to accept ball tickets from a vulgar young man she barely knows. Her supposedly wise guardian abandons her to the authority of such a woman—and then warns that Madame Duval's judgment is poor and her associates of a kind likely to compromise Evelina. Beginning to know the world, Evelina reflects bitterly, "But I knew not, till now, how requisite are birth and fortune to the attainment of respect and civility." In short, much of the novel dwells upon the special helplessness of women to determine their own fates.

—Susan Staves, "*Evelina;* or, Female Difficulties," *Modern Philology* 73, no. 4 (May 1976), reprinted in *Fanny Burney's Evelina,* ed. Harold Bloom (New York: Chelsea House Publishers, 1988), 13, 15, 18, 20–21, 28–29

PATRICIA MEYER SPACKS

As Fanny Burney discovered more and more emphatically the uses of fear as a principle of guidance in her life, she found also the way to tell her own story and came to understand the nature of the story she was constructing. "The act of journalizing," a theorist of autobiography writes, "intensifies the conflict in any autobiographer between life and pattern, movement and stasis, identification and definition, world and self." The observation applies hardly at all to Miss Burney as journalizer. Writing down her experience, she seems, on the contrary, to resolve potential conflicts between life and pattern and world and self. Discovering the structures of her life, she finds out how to feel about the world. As a result she contradicts also, essentially if not technically, the common generalization that, however highly wrought its individual entries, a "diary or journal as a complete work will never reflect the conscious shaping of a whole life for one informing purpose." One can speculate about how conscious the diarist's structuring could have been, but the sense of an informing purpose shaping her existence in the living and in the recording becomes increasingly strong. That purpose—to defend the freedom of the self by asserting fear of wrongdoing and commitment to virtue—involved familial, social, and literary relations, dictated action and restraints, and resolved as well as created conflict. ⟨. . .⟩

If the collection of Fanny Burney's journals and letters creates the effect of autobiography, a coherent narrative implying an imaginative grasp of experience, her four novels also have aspects of psychic autobiography. One can readily perceive in them versions of the journals' central theme: the discipline and the liberation of a woman's fears of disapproval and of being found wanting—fear, in fact, of the other people who comprise society. But novels, with their capacity to express wish and fantasy as well as reality, allow Fanny Burney to enlarge her communication of her own nature. Her fiction illustrates complex feminine identities of indirection. ⟨. . .⟩

No one now reads Fanny Burney's novels, except for *Evelina*, where comedy and youthful exuberance qualify the pervasive anxiety and one can even smile at the anxiety, for its causes are, by and large, so trivial. Yet the later novels, creaky of plot and increasingly impenetrable in rhetoric, seriously explore the possibilities for women to assert individual identities. More clearly than Fanny Burney's letters and diaries, the novels betray her anger at the female condition, although she also acknowledges the possibility of happiness within that condition. Imagining female defiance, she imagines also its futility in those heroines dominated, like herself, by fears of doing wrong. The atmosphere of anxiety she vividly evokes suggest what conflicts attend a woman's search for identity. The Burney female characters face endless struggle between what they want to have (independence, specific husbands, friends, pleasure, work) and what they want to be (angelically perfect): between the impulses to action and to avoidance. However important or negligible the specific images of this conflict, it stands behind the action and the characterization of all the novels. ⟨. . .⟩

Fiction, finally, may constitute autobiography. Through Fanny Burney's novels, through their flaws and their positive achievements, she conveys her private self more emphatically, more explicitly, than she does in the diaries. Not needing to exercise reductive moral control over every character, she can use her fantasies to communicate her feelings and her conflicts, the interior drama that her decorous life largely concealed. She quotes Mme. de Genlis: "The life of every Woman is a Romance!" The remark, implying an interpretation of actual experience in terms of literary categories, suggests a useful way to read the diaries and letters—perceiving the extent to which, even in her personal record, it is Fanny Burney's fictions that reveal herself. Writing novels, she allows herself to convey the impermissible sides of her nature and to enlarge the permissible. Writing journals, she confines herself largely to the surfaces of her life; yet she uncovers the depths by the unchanging form of her self-interpretation, by her wistful, persistent fantasy of flawless virtue, and by her insistence on shaping her account of all that happens to her in terms of the struggle for virtue. She tells the story of an uneventful life as a romance rich in drama.

Fanny Burney's novels and her journals alike reveal the dynamics of fear in a woman's experience. They also reveal some ways in which the imagination deals with emotion, demonstrating how useful are the disguises of fiction in clarifying the truths of personality and how much the forms and perceptions of fiction become necessary material for the autobiographer.

—Patricia Meyer Spacks, "Dynamics of Fear: Fanny Burney," *Imagining a Self* (1976), reprinted in *Fanny Burney's Evelina,* ed. Harold Bloom (New York: Chelsea House Publishers, 1988), 35–36, 48, 53–54, 56–57

JANET TODD

The search for the correct female friend forms part of the ⟨. . .⟩ complicated plots of Fanny Burney, the main painter of sentimental female friendship in England and France in the late eighteenth century. Although less perfect than *Evelina,* her first, triumphant novel, her later works more engagingly depict female relationships, and both *Cecilia* and *The Wanderer* deeply probe the dangers and rewards of female ties. If in the main Burney paints with dark colors, the sombreness conveys regret for a lightness she rejects from both fear and principle. Haywood and Lennox find friendship an asylum in a predatory world; Mme de Grafigny wishes it were so but cannot discover it. Burney seems close to Richardson in seeing it not only rare but dangerously tempting.

In *Cecilia*, the heroine's path is strewn with uncomfortable women. She inherits some from childhood and has no strength to repudiate the legacy; others she takes to meet her psychic needs. Lonely and rich, she wants mother-figures to guide her (feeling betrayed when they prove flexible), and daughters to call forth her benevolence. Like Wollstonecraft's Mary, similarly rich and isolated, she seems unable to find and like an equal. ⟨. . .⟩

Many of the motifs of female friendship recur in Fanny Burney's final, little appreciated novel, *The Wanderer; or, Female Difficulties*, which presents her most ambiguous and complex portrait of female relationships. Like Cecilia, the heroine of this work is degraded to the depths of society, severed from friends and relatives, and deprived of all signs of domestic worth. Like Cecilia again, she treads a bitter path through defective women who fail her at every turn and, worse, humiliate her with a nastiness not seen in fiction since the whores baited the saintly Clarissa. But at the end her suffering is rewarded and she receives the sentimental prize denied Cecilia—a sister-friend. ⟨. . .⟩

In *The Wanderer*, friendship reaches new heights in sisterly love. Yet in its success it reveals its flaws. If the novel supports the display of friendship, it seems to vitiate its substance. Elinor, though given room to show her force, is rejected, and Aurora herself is more a rapturous shade of Juliet than an equal. Women in both *Cecilia* and *The Wanderer* may console each other and compensate for loss, but they can rarely spur to action. Both heroines ultimately act alone, if they act at all, and come to grief in solitude. The most promising tie of Juliet with Elinor is rejected in ridicule, although their union might have released the androgynous power Wollstonecraft described. Certainly Juliet could have used such a union as psychic model when she sought her own feminine strength. As it is, Elinor is cast out and the feminine left to grow effeminate.

Sentimental friendship in the novel is extreme and radical in expression but limited in action. In the works of Richardson, Lennox, Haywood, Grafigny, Burney and a host of other writers, it seems an ideal, avidly sought for its promise of female growth and autonomy. It provides a relationship into which two women can enter with passion and propriety, and it supplies a code of behavior that eases them toward each other. Yet, when it approaches fulfillment as it does in *The Wanderer*, its limitation appears. Seemingly the last bastion of the female self against the reductive claims of patriarchy, it yet fearfully retrenches when it might subvert, rendering the woman more accepting, not more desperate. In the structure of the novel, too, sentimental friendship defuses. The heroine avoids working out her difficult tie with the man who will define her, but instead flees him or simply accepts him on the final page.

Left with an impotent friendship, the two women may become not androgynous but schizophrenic, while the model of the female alliance remains the duplication of sisters.

> —Janet Todd, "The Literary Context," *Women's Friendship in Literature* (1980), excerpted in *The Critical Perspective*, Vol. 7, ed. Harold Bloom (New York: Chelsea House Publishers, 1988), 3866–68

JUDITH LOWDER NEWTON

Burney's *Evelina* ⟨. . .⟩ presents us with a world dominated by the imposition of men upon women, a world in which male control takes the form of assault, and a world in which male assault is the most central expression of power.

That the author of *Evelina*, herself a young woman of good family, should give this emphasis to male control, that she should portray male control as violation, and that she should virtually equate a young lady's entry into the world with her subjection to abuse expresses something pointed about the situation of genteel unmarried women in 1778. It evokes the fact that the status of young middle-class women was in doubt; it suggests that men felt a special authority to impose their will upon them; and it implies that respectable unmarried women were essentially powerless to avoid if not to resist this imposition. ⟨. . .⟩

Evelina finds Burney firmly committed to the ideology that marriage is a woman's natural and only destiny and to the understanding that she achieves that destiny by displaying herself and waiting to be chosen. Given Burney's own trauma on the marriage market, this is a commitment which suggests how impoverished any other options must have appeared. Evelina's entrance into the world, like Fanny Burney's, is patently an entry onto the marriage market, and the assemblies, operas, plays, and pleasure gardens, while initiating her into knowledge of society, also function as occasions upon which she is displayed. Indeed, there is some fun early in the novel when Evelina describes the sensation of turning herself out London-style: "You can't think how oddly my head feels; full of powder and black pins, and a great cushion on the top of it." Being an object is odd, but it is also amusing, and it is even thrilling when the princely Lord Orville asks one to dance. But being on display, which is necessary to secure a husband, to fulfill one's destiny, and to be supported, is pleasant only when one is regarded as a fascinating treasure. Unfortunately, the logic of women's economic situation dictates that she may also be regarded as something of lower value—as overstocked merchandise, for example, by men of the lower orders or, at best, by gentlemen as prey.

The workings of this logic are widely, though intuitively, evoked in *Evelina*, for it is women's economic dependency which lurks behind men's easy assumption that Evelina may be pursued, imposed upon, and controlled. Burney, moreover, although she never protests or makes a point of the fact that it *is* a woman's destiny to display herself on the market, is one of the few writers in the century to describe the experience in such a way as to emphasize its discomfort and oppression—and she is one of the very few to take this discomfort seriously. The language of Evelina's response to male assault—she is "provoked," "distressed," "terrified," "angered"—impresses upon us what ought to be obvious—that Evelina finds it oppressive to be raped—and that critics have not noticed this aspect of the novel is merely a comment on what we have come to accept as women's due.

But, while intuitively evoking the discomfort of being forcibly reduced to merchandise or prey, Burney maintains another ideological version of a genteel woman's situation and of her relation to society, a version which is much in conflict with the first. This second version suggests not only that genteel women are not merchandise at all but that there are no shared economic conditions which would tend to impose that identity upon them. And it is this vision of a genteel woman's lot that ameliorates the inescapable experience of being assailed and that ultimately helps establish an eighteenth-century patriarchy, with all its restrictions on young women, as something bearable by and indeed beneficial to young women of the middle classes. ⟨. . .⟩

But *Evelina*, of course, is more than a simple endorsement of patriarchy—as run by gentlemen—and of the ideologies with which it justifies and mitigates its power. It is also the history of a young woman's progress, a form of Erbildungsroman. It is possible to see in Evelina's progress, for example, some reflections of a traditional male quest plot or initiation story. Like many a young man, Evelina enters the world, is initiated into the nature of her society, and, one might argue, grows in prudence and good judgment. For the first two volumes of the novel, in fact, she satirizes male conceit, resists male control, and becomes increasingly skillful at exerting what in this novel is a highly significant form of power—the power of self-defense, a form of power as autonomy. To a limited degree, in fact, *Evelina* entertains a fantasy of female power which is in some tension with the novel's endorsement and idealization of landed male control. The nature of that autonomy is subtle and it is also deliberately qualified, for Burney feared above all things "ridicule or censure as a female." But, as George Eliot has put it, "yoked creatures" may have their "private opinions," and it is Evelina's private opinions which are the source of what we must call her power in this novel.

—Judith Lowder Newton, *"Evelina:* A Chronicle of Assault," *Women, Power and Subversion: Social Strategies in British Fiction, 1778–1860* (1981), excerpted in *Fanny Burney's Evelina,* ed. Harold Bloom (New York: Chelsea House Publishers, 1988), 59–60, 63–64, 74–75

MARY POOVEY

Fanny Burney's first novel, written when she was in her early twenties, and Mary Shelley's last novel, published when Shelley was nearly forty, have few superficial similarities. The sometimes ribald comedy of *Evelina* (1778) provides an obvious contrast to the sentimental, decidedly melodramatic plot of *Falkner* (1837), and the extreme passivity of Burney's heroine highlights even the limited assertiveness of Elizabeth Raby. But in at least one respect the novels do bear a remarkable similarity to each other. In both works, the writers develop their plots so as to introduce the likelihood of what is potentially the most traumatic moment in a young girl's maturation: the clash between her duty towards her father and her affection for a lover. Typically in modern society, girls have tended to remain dependent upon parents—and, specifically, their fathers—longer than boys, and, for both social and psychological reasons, girls have also tended to fix their affections upon their fathers, as lords in the patriarchal mansion and as necessary replacements for their earlier libidinal attachments to their mothers. Yet at least since the middle of the eighteenth century, as personal preference rather than parents' will has increasingly dictated the choice of a marriage partner, girls have enjoyed at least one moment of theoretical autonomy. The brief period of courtship, the moment at which a woman acquiesces to the imploring suitor or exercises her legitimate "negative," has seemed to signal her independence from her father's will and from her emotional fixation upon him. This moment of putative autonomy, then, more than any other, potentially brings the young woman into conflict both with the social imperative that she have only tractable desires and with the psychological necessity that she love her father so as to wrench her libidinal fixation from her mother. In other words, the moment at which a young girl transfers her affection from her father to a lover threatens to create a collision between roles and psychological postures which have been previously mutually exclusive; and the subsequent conflicts—between duty and inclination, between the behavior proper to a daughter and that demanded of an autonomous individual—seem inevitably to mark the threshold of adult identity, to separate the girl from the woman she struggles to become. ⟨. . .⟩

In *Evelina*, Fanny Burney prepares her reader for this paradigmatic confrontation in three important ways. In the first place, the plot contains not one father but two, and, in the second place, Burney ties her heroine's almost reluctant quest for social maturity to *both* the discovery and reunion with her father *and* Evelina's marriage to Lord Orville. And finally, in the course of the novel Burney provides two prominent examples of confrontations between fathers and lovers, and in each case, the conflict not only causes emotional anguish, but also precipitates the crises that punctuate the central plot. Yet, despite the apparent amassing of circumstantial support, Evelina is spared the emotional turmoil of a conflict between duty and desire. By a last-minute, decidedly awkward contrivance of the plot, Burney effectively decenters the very crisis which she had prepared us to expect. Through what amounts to narrative sleight of hand, Evelina becomes the acknowledged daughter of Sir John Belmont and the wife of Lord Orville in such rapid succession that Evelina has literally no opportunity to suffer an emotional conflict. And, to further defuse this potential crisis, the lover who ushers Evelina into a new set of roles and responsibilities is more like a father to her than is the real father she has so recently found. ⟨. . .⟩

What should be a moment of social autonomy for a girl is therefore not really one at all. Indeed, far from allowing the expression of autonomous desire, this moment brings to the surface the complex facets of the girl's psychological immaturity. The promise of social autonomy is in fact false: as wife, the young woman will be as dependent as she was as daughter. Nevertheless, the demands of the situation are real; the moment of choice dictates that the woman take the initiative—or at least the responsibility—for rejecting her father and installing another man in his place. The consequence of these demands—in the face of the girl's inability to meet them—is the exposure of two critical truths of the female situation: the girl sees that her relationship with her father has been largely idealized; and she intuits, however dimly, that the man she has idealized is, in fact, the tyrant of patriarchal society. For Fanny Burney and Mary Shelley, these truths both delimit the opportunities for female self-expression and constitute the foundation for woman's power.

—Mary Poovey, "Fathers and Daughters: The Trauma of Growing Up Female," *Men by Women* (1981), excerpted in *Fanny Burney's Evelina*, ed. Harold Bloom (New York: Chelsea House Publishers, 1988), 85–87, 95–96

JENNIFER A. WAGNER

Evelina is a novel that examines the interplay between the public and the private—public and private spaces, public and private opinion, and particularly the title character's tense and problematic experience of physical and emotional privacy. The brutality of Richardson's *Clarissa*, an obvious precursor, is precisely society's denial of *any* right of possession or privacy whatsoever to that unfortunate young lady. The interest of *Evelina* is in its heroine's subtle strategies to preserve her identity by evading societal demands upon her privacy. The fact that her identity is so problematic—that she does not know, quite literally, who she is and even has a made-up name—provides both the context for the privacy problem and the solution to it: Evelina's very anonymity becomes a powerful screen from society's demands on her integrity and will. ⟨. . .⟩

Fanny Burney's original inscription, dedication, and preface were all published, of course, like the novel, anonymously. Professional anonymity was a way of protecting one's reputation—and one's privacy. And one needn't look far to discover in Burney's own journals an almost obsessive fear of being identified as the author of *Evelina* ⟨. . .⟩

Burney seems to have lived in constant fear that her journal and her novel-in-progress would be discovered. And the journal was discovered finally, by her father, who, adding to her mortification, said nothing of it until she had stood silently at his study doorway for at least a half-hour. "All I can say for myself," Burney adds in her diary, "is that I have always feared discovery, always sought concealment, and always known that no success should counterbalance the publishing of my name."

Far from "owning" or acknowledging *her* authorial identity, Burney does everything possible to obscure that identity: "Without name, without recommendation, and unknown alike to success and disgrace, to whom can I so properly apply for patronage, as to those who publicly profess themselves inspectors of all literary performances?" Like Evelina herself, Burney seeks admission into a society to which she *must* expose herself, but she is capable of doing so only while "happily wrapped up in a mantle of impenetrable obscurity."

It is consistent with the novel as a whole that Fanny Burney ultimately defers entirely to male judgment; the very act of authorship is displaced upon Dr. Burney: "Oh, Author of my being!—far more dear / To me than light." The first three stanzas of the inscription suggest that perhaps the only truly acceptable literary effort would be one that simply traced "thy num'rous virtues"; she becomes then not Author, but mere "Recorder of thy worth." It is not only fear of Dr. Burney's disapproval that is registered in *Evelina*'s introductory material; it is also the fear of disapproval from her father's literary counterparts—the critics. Burney acknowledges the right of both her father and the critics not only to censure but also to censor, or silence, her work. "Concealment is the only boon" she claims in the original inscription; obscurity, for Burney as for her Evelina, is always the best defense.

—Jennifer A. Wagner, "Privacy and Anonymity in *Evelina*," *Fanny Burney's Evelina*, ed. Harold Bloom (New York: Chelsea House Publishers, 1988), 99, 107–9

JULIA L. EPSTEIN

Fanny Burney had a compulsion to write—she repeatedly refers to a writing "mania" in her journals and letters. At the same time, she understood that for her time and circumstances, to write was to defy convention, and this understanding emerges in covert and coded ways in her fiction. In particular, the epistolary *Evelina or the History of a Young Lady's Entrance into the World* (1778) can be interpreted as a treatise on the appropriate uses of language for young women in the late eighteenth century, and on the methods by which that apparent appropriateness may be manipulated to subvert social oppression. This first novel maps the terrain of eighteenth-century social decorum, in relations between the sexes and between youth and age, as a minefield waiting to explode. Like Burney's third novel, *Camilla; or, A Picture of Youth* (1796), *Evelina* contains tongue-tied and sabotaged conversations, misread gestures, and unfinished communications. Evelina's letters represent an expressly "feminine" art: the art of coaxing, flattering, and mystifying; the art of requesting and granting permission or forgiveness; and the verbal ingenuity of the woman whose survival depends upon her appearing to remain ingenuous and innocent, and whose only tool of power lies in her use of language to manipulate both her situation and the way it is presented to others. In *Evelina*, Burney excavates beneath the eighteenth-century social virtues of "feminine" decorum and artlessness professed by her heroine to a gritty and subterranean exposure of the language that controls both propriety and rebellion against it. ⟨. . .⟩

The major clue to how Evelina understands and responds to her situation lies in the epistolary documents with which the novel present us. Letter-writing in *Evelina* is a synecdochic gesture: it stands, in miniature, for the tenuous and danger-fraught communication process between authority and its charge, between the empowered and the powerless. A well-behaved young woman, Evelina knows, must be innocent and artless, and the "art" of letter-writing—that "feminine" accomplishment for cultured ladies—should reflect this. But innocence and artlessness get Evelina continually into trouble, so self-preservation demands that she replace those traits with experience as fast as she can. Her guardian, the Reverend Arthur Villars, affects not to understand this exigency (though Evelina's grandmother Madame Duval knows and promotes it); so as Fanny Burney herself had not wanted to appear studious in public, Evelina also must disguise her burgeoning intelligence about the ways of the fashionable world. Letters are the vehicles for this deceit and for the rhetorical repossession it engenders. Letters became an especially licensed mode of writing for eighteenth-century women writers and their heroines precisely because letter-writing was a sanctioned female activity. Because it was licensed, the letter also presented a potential arena for subversion. As a feminine narrative form, letters pretend to spontaneity and absolute sincerity. But they can never be utterly sincere, as no crafted piece of writing can be without artifice. Evelina makes sophisticated use of this potential, as did Burney herself. ⟨. . .⟩

The crucial issue in Evelina's use of letters and signatures is reader- and writer-context. The recognized conventions of eighteenth-century epistolary fiction and the general tone of comedic benevolence cultivated by Fanny Burney in Evelina make it too easy to forget that Villars, the primary reader of Evelina's letters as well as her guardian, has decision-making along with moral power over her. He represents the source of all permission. If she angers or offends him, all is lost—on his approval rests her tenuous foothold in polite society. We cannot expect, then, that her letters to this guardian, to whom she writes most regularly and frequently, will be straightforward. She has no choice but to edit them carefully. Most critics of Evelina have ignored this crucial facet of Evelina's narrative strategy. She is a storyteller with an ulterior motive. The covert distortions her self-editing necessarily prompts control the narrative Evelina's letters ultimately produce.

The epistolary format of the novel, an expected enough fictional mode in 1778, allows Burney to play with tone, sincerity, and narrative truth. Evelina uses her letters as emissaries to her guardian: they plead her case without offending her judge. Each volume of Evelina presents a problem of education—both in how to behave and in how to phrase and organize an account of one's behavior—and this education ultimately serves to train Evelina in the procedures for conducting a search for a father, a husband, a name, and a proper and publicly sanctionable social status. In volume 1, she learns aristocratic manners: how to refuse to dance at an assembly without creating gossip; what to wear and where to sit at the opera; how to distinguish the fashionable from the vulgar. In volume 2, she joins the London middle class, learns the dangers of the city and its pleasure gardens for an unescorted woman, and applies her new knowledge of social rules, now sometimes to her own advantage. By volume 3, she actually controls the behavior of others towards her and determines her own social position. From the outset, however, she has a facility with words and their arrangement, though her education also makes her more adept with language's tyrannies and its argumentative potential.

—Julia L. Epstein, "Evelina's Deceptions: The Letter and the Spirit," Fanny Burney's Evelina, ed. Harold Bloom (New York: Chelsea House Publishers, 1988), 111–13, 115–16

BIBLIOGRAPHY

Evelina; or, The History of a Young Lady's Entrance into the World (2 vols.). 1778.

Cecilia; or, Memoirs of an Heiress (2 vols.). 1782.

Brief Reflections Relative to the Emigrant French Clergy: Earnestly Submitted to the Humane Considerations of the Ladies of Great Britain. 1793.

Camilla; or, A Picture of Youth (5 vols.). 1796.

The Wanderer; or, Female Difficulties (5 vols.). 1814.

The Memoirs of Dr. Burney. 1832.

Diaries and Letters of Madame D'Arblay (7 vols.). 1842–54.

The Early Diary of Frances Burney (2 vols.). 1889.

Letters and Journals (10 vols.). 1972–81.

GEORGE ELIOT

1819-1880

GEORGE ELIOT was born Mary Anne Evans in Arbury, Warwickshire, on November 22, 1819. Her father, Robert Evans, was a land agent in the service of the Newdigate family of Arbury Hall. During her childhood, Eliot was extremely attached to her older brother, Isaac; a fictionalized portrait of their relationship appeared in Eliot's early work, *The Mill on the Floss* (1860). Eliot attended local schools in Griff, Attleborough, and Nuneaton. When she was thirteen, she was sent to a girls' school in Coventry, where she remained until she was sixteen. The following year, her mother died, leaving Mary Anne to keep house for her father. Eliot's precocious intellect was already apparent. She read widely, and was influenced, in particular, by the Romantic poets and works of theology (she had coverted to Evangelicalism while at school).

In the early 1840s she met Charles and Cara Bray, whose freethinking ways she found attractive. This led to her refusal to attend church with her father in 1842. Bray also introduced her to journalism, and in 1844 she published her translation of Strauss's *Life of Jesus*. Robert Evans died in 1949, leaving Marian (she had changed her name from Mary Anne to Marian) a small inheritance. That year she took her first trip to the continent, accompanied by the Brays. She met John Chapman in 1850 and took up work for the *Westminster Review*, which Chapman edited, writing articles on a variety of subjects. For a time she lived with Chapman and his wife, but she had to leave when her love for Chapman made the arrangement impossible. Eliot had a difficult affair with Herbert Spencer in 1852, who rejected her because of her physical appearance, which, by all accounts, was not that prepossessing. That same year, however, she met George Henry Lewes, with whom she was involved for the next twenty-five years. Lewes was a married man who had agreed to let his wife live with her lover, Thornton Hunt. Because he had not objected to his wife's adultery, Lewes could not divorce. He set up house with Eliot, who referred to herself as Mrs. Lewes, but the couple was often snubbed by Victorians who were less freethinking than they were. This liason also led to Eliot's estrangement from her brother.

Eliot began to write fiction in 1856 with encouragement from Lewes. In 1857, *Scenes of Clerical Life* appeared in *Blackwood's Magazine*, which was kept ignorant, initially, of the identity of their pseudonymous contributor. However, when *Adam Bede* was published in 1859,

Eliot's identity was revealed. Eliot's next novel, *The Mill on the Floss* (1860), was her most autobiographical, and it cemented her literary reputation. *The Mill on the Floss* was followed by *Silas Marner* (1861) and *Romola*, a novel of fifteenth-century Florence. Offered a huge sum by George Smith, the proprietor of the *Cornhill Magazine*, Eliot deserted *Blackwood's Magazine* to serialize *Romola* in Smith's magazine. *Romola* was not a success, however, and Eliot returned to her first publisher with her last three novels. Meanwhile, the money she earned from *Romola* enabled her and Lewes to purchase the Piory, an expensive house which would be the scene of their salon, held on Sunday afternoons. *Felix Holt, The Radical* was published in 1868 followed by *Middlemarch*, which first appeared in eight free-standing serial parts in 1871–72. Eliot's last novel, *Daniel Deronda*, was published in the same way. Its subject matter, Judaism, was a departure for Eliot, but unlike *Romola*, which had also strayed from "provincial life," *Daniel Deronda* was a success. It was followed by her final work, *Impressions of Theophrastus Such*, in 1879. In 1878, just two years after Eliot and Lewes moved to a new house near Haslemere, Lewes died of cancer, and the following year Eliot married John Cross, a man twenty years her junior. The marriage lasted less than a year. Eliot died of a kidney disorder on December 22, 1880.

CRITICAL EXTRACTS

HENRY JAMES

Middlemarch is at once one of the strongest and one of the weakest of English novels. Its predecessors as they appeared might have been described in the same terms; *Romola*, is especially a rare masterpiece, but the least *entraînant* of masterpieces. *Romola* sins by excess of analysis; there is too much description and too little drama; too much reflection (all certainly of a highly imaginative sort) and too little creation. Movement lingers in the story, and with it attention stands still in the reader. The error in *Middlemarch* is not precisely of a similar kind, but it is equally detrimental to the total aspect of the work. We can well remember how keenly we wondered, while its earlier chapters unfolded themselves, what turn in the way of form the story would take—that of an organized, moulded, balanced composition, gratifying the reader with a sense of design and construction, or a mere chain of episodes, broken into accidental lengths and unconscious of the influence of a plan. We expected the actual result, but for the sake of English imaginative literature which, in this line is rarely in need of examples, we hoped for the other. If it had come we should have had the pleasure of reading, what certainly would have seemed to us in the immediate glow of attention, the first of English novels. But that pleasure has still to hover between prospect and retrospect. *Middlemarch* is a treasure-house of details, but it is an indifferent whole. ⟨. . .⟩

A work of the liberal scope of *Middlemarch* contains a multitude of artistic intentions, some of the finest of which became clear only in the meditative after-taste of perusal. This is the case with the balanced contrast between the two histories of Lydgate and Dorothea. Each is a tale of matrimonial infelicity, but the conditions in each are so different and the circumstances so broadly opposed that the mind passes from one to the other with that supreme sense of the vastness and variety of human life, under aspects apparently similar, which it belongs only to the greatest novels to produce. The most perfectly successful passages in the book are perhaps those painful fireside scenes between Lydgate and his miserable little wife. The author's rare psychological penetration is lavished upon this veritably mulish domestic flower. There is nothing more powerfully real than these scenes in all English fiction, and nothing certainly more *intelligent*. ⟨. . .⟩

English readers may fancy they enjoy the "atmosphere" of *Middlemarch;* but we maintain that to relish its inner essence we must—for reasons too numerous to detail—be an American. The author has commissioned herself to be real, her native tendency being that of an idealist, and the intellectual result is a very fertilizing mixture. The constant presence of thought, of generalizing instinct, of *brain*, in a word, behind her observation, gives the latter its great value and her whole manner its high superiority. It denotes a mind in which imagination is illumined by faculties rarely found in fellowship with it. In this respect—in that broad reach of vision which would make the worthy historian of solemn fact as well as wanton fiction—George Eliot seems to us among English romancers to stand alone. Fielding approaches her, but to our mind, she surpasses Fielding. Fielding was didactic—the author of *Middlemarch* is really philosophic. These great qualities imply corresponding perils. The first is the loss of simplicity. George Eliot lost hers some time since: it lies buried (in a splendid mausoleum) in *Romola*. Many of the discursive portions of *Middlemarch* are, as we may say, too clever by half. The author wishes to say too many things, and to say them too well; to recommend herself to a scientific audience. Her style, rich and flexible as it is, is apt to betray her on these transcendental flights; we find, in our copy, a dozen passages marked "obscure." *Silas Marner* has a delightful tinge of Goldsmith—we may almost call it: *Middlemarch* is too often an echo of Messrs. Darwin and Huxley. In spite of these faults—which it seems graceless to indicate with this crude rapidity—it remains a very splendid performance. It sets a limit, we think, to the development of the old-fashioned English novel. Its diffuseness, on which we have touched, makes it too copious a dose of pure fiction. If we write novels so, how shall we write History? But it is nevertheless a contribution of the first importance to the rich imaginative department of our literature.

   —Henry James, *Galaxy* (March 1873), excerpted in *The New Moulton's Library of Literary Criticism*, Vol. 9, ed. Harold Bloom (New York: Chelsea House Publishers, 1989), 5092–94

DOROTHY VAN GHENT

In Chapter 17 of *Adam Bede*, "the story pauses a little" and George Eliot sets forth her aim as a novelist, an aim which she describes as "the faithful representing of commonplace things," of things *as they are*, not "as they never have been and never will be"; and we are reminded of a similar aim as expressed by Defoe's Moll Flanders, who said, "I am giving an account of what was, not of what ought or ought not to be." It is the vocation of the "realistic" novelist to represent life in this way; . . . but, as Defoe brought us to a consideration of the shaping changes which the "real" undergoes as it is submitted to art, even to the most "realistic" art, so George Eliot brings us back to the same consideration of the transforming effect of composition upon things-as-they-are. Her strongest effort, she says, is to avoid an "arbitrary picture," and

> to give a faithful account of men and things as they have mirrored themselves in my mind. The mirror is doubtless defective; the outlines will sometimes be disturbed, the reflection faint or confused; but I feel as much bound to tell you as precisely as I can what that reflection is, as if I were in the witness-box, narrating my experience on oath.

We cannot avoid observing that the "mirror" is at times defective, but since it is for the most part clear and well lighted we are not primarily concerned with the defects; more interesting is the analogy of the mirror itself—the novelist's mind as a mirror from whose "reflections" of "men and things" he draws his account. Men and things, then, do not leap to his page directly out of the "real" but, before they get there, take a journey through the "mirror." But the mirror which the mind offers is not at all like other mirrors; even—leaving out of consideration defective glasses—very clear minds are not like very clear mirrors. Dangerous as analogies are, a spoon would be a better one, where, in the concave, as we tip it toward us, we see our head compressed and a half-moon scooped out of it on top as if it were a dime-store flowerpot for our viney hair, our body tapered to vanishing at the hips, and the whole upside down; or, in the convex, our eyelids are as large as foreheads, our forehead is as small as an eyelid, our cheeks hang down from our face like shoulders, and our shoulders hide under them like little ears. The "mirror" of the mind shapes what it sees. It does not passively "reflect" things-as-they-are, but creates thing-as-they-are. Though we can clearly discriminate the quality of intention shown by a realistic art—and it usually reduces finally to a choice of materials from the field of the quotidian, the commonplace, the mediocre—yet its aim of veraciousness is necessarily one of veraciousness to what the artist sees in the shape-giving, significance-endowing medium of his own mind, and in this sense the mythopoeic art of *Wuthering Heights* is as veracious as the realistic art of *Adam Bede*.

The singularity of the world of *Wuthering Heights* is its innocence of "good" and "evil" in any civilized ethical meaning of these terms; it is a world shaped by kinetic rather than by ethical forces, and its innocence is that of the laws of dynamics (Catherine's fatal choice, for instance, is essentially a choice of stasis and a denial of motion; it is as if an electron or a star should "choose" to stand still). *Adam Bede* offers the radical contrast of a world shaped through and through by moral judgment and moral evaluation. We are prone, perhaps, to think of a perfectly amoral vision, such as Emily Brontë's, as a vision not of things-as-they-are but as a subjective creation of things-as-they-never-were-but-might-be, and, on the other hand, to think of an ethical vision, such as George Eliot's, as closer to things-as-they-are, more "objective," because of our own familiar addiction to moral judgments (however inapropos or cliché) and our difficulty in turning ethics out of doors. But, on a thought, it should be clear that a through and through ethically shaped world is as "created" a world as the other. The question is not one of *whether* things are really this way or that way, for either vision touches responsive similitudes within us, and God knows what things really are. The question is one of different organizations and different illuminations of the infinite possible qualities of things-as-they-are.

Technique is that which selects among the multitude of possible qualities, organizes them in the finite world of the novel, and holds them in a shape that can catch the light of our own awareness, which, without shapes to fall upon, is ignorant. Technique is like the concave or convex surface of the spoon, and the different turnings and inclinations to which it is liable; technique elongates or foreshortens, and while the rudimentary relationships of common experience remain still recognizable, it reveals astonishing bulges of significance, magnifies certain parts of the anatomy of life, of whose potentialities we had perhaps not been aware, humbles others. The massively slow movement of *Adam Bede* is one such shapemaking technique. ⟨. . .⟩

The clock is a monument not to time merely as time, but to the assured and saving values stored up through ages of experience. In one of her books

George Eliot says, "There is no private life which has not been determined by a wider public life." In *Adam Bede*, this is the mute recognition by which the community lives: as imaginatively realized here, it is a recognition that personal good has communal determinations, that it is contingent upon the preservation of common values. But the statement bears also its converse, which might be phrased thus: "There is no public life which has not been determined by the narrower private life"; for the story of *Adam Bede* is a story of the irreparable damage wrought on the community by a private moment's frivolity.

—Dorothy Van Ghent, *"Adam Bede," The English Novel: Form and Function* (1953), reprinted in *George Eliot*, ed. Harold Bloom (New York: Chelsea House Publishers, 1986), 27–29, 33

JOHN HOLLOWAY

George Eliot was a profoundly, perhaps excessively serious writer, and her novels are coloured through and through by her view of the world. ⟨. . .⟩

It would, with George Eliot, be ⟨therefore⟩ a mistake to begin by noticing incidents, metaphors, snatches of conversation, or similar details. What must be given primary stress is the broad outline, the whole movement of her novels as examples of life that claim to be typical. 'How unspeakably superior', wrote Matthew Arnold, 'is the effect of the one moral impression left by a great action treated as a whole, to the effect produced by the most striking single thought or by the happiest image'. This is as true of the work of the sage-novelist as it is of classical drama or the epic poem. To ignore it is to miss the wood for the trees.

Silas Marner, perhaps because it is simple and short, shows this most plainly.

Various things lend the tale its distinctive quality. First, the characters and their doings seem to belong to the same order of things as the non-human world that surrounds them. The little village, off the beaten track in its wooded hollow, is half submerged in the world of nature. The villagers are 'pressed close by primitive wants.' The passage of time and the rotation of the seasons affect humans and animals and plants all alike. Individuals are dominated by their environment. 'Marner's face and figure shrank and bent themselves into a constant mechanical relation to the objects of his life, so that he produced the same sort of impression as a handle or a crooked tube, which has no meaning standing apart'. It follows from this that all the people in the book are humble and obscure; they may be attractive or virtuous, but they are all nobodies. Silas is a poor weaver who finds hard words in the prayer-book, Godfrey Cass is a squireen's son and a barmaid's husband, Eppie marries a gardener—even Nancy Lammeter, Godfrey's second wife, is only a trim farmer's daughter who does the baking and says ' 'oss'. Such, the tale implies, is the staple of men and women.

The pattern of events in which these people are involved is one of 'poetic justice': vice suffers, virtue is rewarded. Silas, though unfortunate at first, is a good man, and at last is made happy. Godfrey Cass, who refused to acknowledge his daughter, has no children by his second marriage. Dunstan Cass the rake, stealing Silas's money at night, falls into the pond and is drowned. But this justice is rough and partial. It is not vindictively stern, so much as impersonal and aloof and half-known; it takes a slow chance course, and meets human imperfections not with definite vengeance but with a drab pervasive sense of partial failure or limited success. For the peasantry of such places as Raveloe 'pain and mishap present a far wider range of possibilities than gladness and enjoyment'. For Silas in his time of misfortune the world is a strange and hopeless riddle. His money is taken, Eppie arrives, through the operation of forces that he venerates without comprehending. Done injustice by a sudden twist of fate, he comes to trust in the world again over a long period of years, as the imperceptible influence of Eppie gradually revives long-dead memories and emotions; over the same period his estrangement from the other villagers is slowly replaced by intimacy. His life is governed by habit, and so is theirs. We never learn whether his innocence ever became clear to the congregation that expelled him as a thief.

Though the book is so short, its unit of measurement is the generation: Silas young and old, Eppie the child and the bride, Godfrey the gay youth and the saddened, childless husband. The affairs of one generation are not finally settled except in the next, when Silas's happiness is completed by Eppie's marriage, and Godfrey's early transgressions punished by her refusal to become Miss Cass. Dunstan Cass's misdeeds are not even discovered until, twenty years after the robbery, his skeleton is found clutching the money-bags when the pond is drained; and this is brought to light through, of all things, Godfrey's activities as a virtuous, improving landlord. Well may the parish-clerk say 'there's windings i' things as they may carry you to the fur end o' the prayer-book afore you get back to 'em'. All in all, the world of the novel is one which, in its author's own words, 'never *can* be thoroughly joyous'. The unhappiness in it comes when natural generous feelings are atrophied by selfishness: Dunstan steals, Godfrey denies his daughter. And the consequences of sin are never quite obliterated; Godfrey must resign himself to childlessness, though resignation is itself a kind of content. Real happiness comes when numb unfeeling hardness, the state of mind for example of the grief-stricken and disillusioned Silas, slowly thaws to warmer emotions of kindliness and love.

This novel contains, therefore, though in little, a comprehensive vision of human life and the human situation. It does so through its deep and sustained sense of the influence of environment and of continuity between man and the rest of nature, through its selection as characters of ordinary people living drab and unremarkable lives, and through the whole course of its action, working out by imperceptible shifts or unpredictable swings of chance to a solution where virtue is tardily and modestly rewarded, and vice obscurely punished by some dull privation. The details of George Eliot's treatment operate within this broader framework.

   —John Holloway, "'Silas Marner' and the System of Nature," *The Victorian Sage: Studies in Argument* (1953), reprinted in *George Eliot,* ed. Harold Bloom (New York: Chelsea House Publishers, 1986), 39–41

U. C. KNOEPFLMACHER

The Mill on the Floss is divided into seven books, which can be separated into two movements: in the first, Mr. Tulliver, like Amos Barton, vainly tries to shore his present against the impending future; in the second, where that future becomes the present of his children, Tom and Maggie vainly try to recover their childhood at Dorlcote Mill. The first movement concludes with Mr. Tulliver's death at the end of book 5; the second culminates with the drowning of Tom and Maggie. Like *Antony and Cleopatra,* the novel thus contains two related tragedies, which I shall examine individually only for the sake of making critical distinctions. In Shakespeare's play, Cleopatra's sacrifice is meant to exalt Antony's bungling death; in her tragic novel, George Eliot likewise intends Maggie's sacrifice to lend a wider meaning to the little world ignobly lost through Mr. Tulliver's recklessness. The miller's gradual ruin and self-destruction are deftly handled by a novelist sure of her control. The rash miller is in his way as convincing a tragic figure as the impetuous Antony. But George Eliot could not handle Maggie's fate with the same assurance. For reasons which I shall examine in the last section of this chapter, George Eliot failed to convert Maggie's immolation into an action as world-stirring as that of Shakespeare's Cleopatra. ⟨. . .⟩

   In an essay entitled "Tragedy and the Common Man," Arthur Miller once argued that the terror and fear of tragedy could still be evoked in a modern everyman's exposure to the pressures of social change. Defending *Death of a Salesman,* the playwright contended: "I believe that the common man is as apt a subject for tragedy in its highest sense as kings were." ⟨. . .⟩

   But George Eliot's superior miller is a much more tragic figure than Miller's Loman; there is more poetry in the loss of an ancestral mill than in an aging salesman's loss of his former "territory." Like Willy Loman, Mr. Tulliver, incapable of adjusting himself to the ways of the future, escapes into a dreamworld and ponders what might have been. But Willy's end is pathetic, whereas there is a magnificence in Mr. Tulliver's impenitent death. The miller who demands a "retributive justice" barely recognizes that he also must pay for his mistakes.

Yet his nemesis does inspire us with the true terror of tragedy. The impersonal order which pushes him aside seems more fearsome than Willy's displacement by a boss who plays with a tape recorder. Willy smashes his car so that his wife and children can collect his insurance money; his death is a deliberate act by which he intends to repair the damage he has done. Mr. Tulliver's injuries to his family, however, cannot be repaired. His fall is more momentous. The indifference with which Mr. Deane and Mr. Glegg regard their brother-in-law's lost "water-power" is far closer, artistically, to the indifference which Goneril and Regan display toward Lear's regal attributes than it is to Howard's refusal to augment Willy Loman's Social Security payments. In the eyes of St. Ogg's, Mr. Tulliver is incompetent. In his archaic world, however, Maggie's fond and foolish father remains a "lofty personage." Accordingly, his fall is far more princely than that of the "hardworking, unappreciated prince" who is the father of the neurotic Biff. ⟨. . .⟩

In a tragedy like *King Lear*, the forces of circumstances are as prominent as in a "realistic" novel like *The Mill on the Floss*. The unexpected reversal of the French army, Edmund's deception, the protracted distraction of Albany and Edgar at the very moment that Cordelia is hanged contribute to the final tragedy. But it is Lear's initial act of willfulness, committed at the height of his powers, which has precipitated the ensuing concatenation of events. Maggie's one act of willfulness, itself blamed on the hypnotic influence of her seducer and on her Tulliver blood, is unrelated to the cataclysmic circumstances of her death. Had Lear not banished Cordelia, the carnage of his house would have been avoided; but had Maggie not fled with Stephen, she could still have drowned like the "helpless cattle" washed away by the Floss. Notwithstanding George Eliot's identification of the overflowing river with those deterministic "laws" within and without the girl's psyche, the drowning is not tragic. For all her queenly attributes, despite the carefully implanted parallels to figures like the drowning Ophelia, despite Maggie's own firsthand knowledge about "Shakespeare and everything," she remains a figure of pathos, the prey of circumstances that are capricious and accidental. There is no causal connection between her flight and the destiny assigned to her.

—U. C. Knoepflmacher, "Tragedy and the Flux: *The Mill on the Floss*," *George Eliot's Early Novels: The Limits of Realism* (1968), reprinted in *George Eliot's The Mill on the Floss*, ed. Harold Bloom (New York: Chelsea House Publishers, 1988), 23, 29–30, 41

RAYMOND WILLIAMS

It is proper to trace the continuity of moral analysis from Jane Austen to George Eliot, but we can do this intelligently only if we recognise what else is happening in this literary development: a recognition of other kinds of people, other kinds of country, other kinds of action on which a moral emphasis must be brought to bear. For just as the difference between Jonson and Crabbe is not the historical arrival of the 'poor laborious natives' but a change in literary bearings which allows them suddenly to be seen, so the difference between Jane Austen and George Eliot, and between both and Thomas Hardy, is not the sudden disintegration of a traditional rural order but a change in literary bearings which brings into focus a persistent rural disturbance that had previously been excluded or blurred.

Thus *Adam Bede* is set by George Eliot in Jane Austen's period: at the turn of the eighteenth into the nineteenth century. What she sees is of course very different: not primarily because the country has changed, but because she has available to her a different social tradition. ⟨. . .⟩

Jane Austen ⟨. . .⟩ had been prying and analytic, but into a limited group of people in their relations with each other. The analysis is now brought to bear without the class limitation; the social and economic relationships, necessarily, are seen as elements, often determining elements, of conduct.

It is more important to stress this aspect of George Eliot's development of the novel than her inclusion of new social experience in a documentary sense. Certainly it is good to see the farmers and the craftsmen, and almost the labourers, as people present in the action in their own right. But there are difficulties here of a significant kind. It is often said about the Poysers in *Adam Bede*, as about the Gleggs and the Dodsons in *The Mill on the Floss*, that they are marvellously (or warmly, richly, charmingly) done. But what this points to is a recurring problem in the social consciousness of the writer. George Eliot's connections with the farmers and craftsmen—her connections as Mary Ann Evans—can be heard again and again in their language. Characteristically, she presents them mainly through speech. But while they are present audibly as a community, they have only to emerge in significant action to change in quality. What Adam or Dinah or Hetty say, when they are acting as individuals, is not particularly convincing. Into a novel still predicated on the analysis of individual conduct, the farmers and craftsmen can be included as 'country people' but much less significantly as the active bearers of personal experience. When Adam and Dinah and Hetty talk in what is supposed to be personal crisis—or later, in a more glaring case, when Felix Holt talks—we are shifted to the level of generalised attitudes or of declamation. Another way of putting this would be to say that though George Eliot restores the real inhabitants of rural England to their places in what had been a socially selective landscape, she does not get much further than restoring them *as a landscape*. They begin to talk, as it were collectively, in what middle-class critics still foolishly call a kind of chorus, a 'ballad-element'. But as themselves they are still only socially present, and can emerge into personal consciousness only through externally formulated attitudes and ideas.

I would not make this point bitterly, for the difficulty is acute. It is a contradiction in the form of the novel, as George Eliot received and developed it, that the moral emphasis on conduct—and therefore the technical strategy of unified narrative and analytic tones—must be at odds with any society—the 'knowable community' of the novel—in which moral bearings have been extended to substantial and conflicting social relationships. One would not willingly lose the Poysers, the Gleggs, and the Dodsons, but it is significant that we can talk to them in this way in the plural, while the emotional direction of the novel is towards separated individuals. A knowable community can be, as in Jane Austen, socially selected; what it then lacks in full social reference it gains in an available unity of language in all its main uses. But we have only to read a George Eliot novel to see the difficulty of the coexistence, within one form, of an analytically conscious observer of conduct with a developed analytic vocabulary, and of people represented as living and speaking in mainly customary ways; for it is not the precision of detailed observation but the inclusive, socially appealing, loose and repetitive manner that predominates. There is a new kind of break in the texture of the novel, an evident failure of continuity between the necessary language of the novelist and the recorded language of many of the characters. ⟨. . .⟩

As if overcome by the dead weight of the interests of a separated and propertied class, the formal plots of the later works are in a different social world. *Felix Holt* is made to turn on the inheritance of an estate, and this is a crucial surrender to that typical interest which preoccupied the nineteenth-century middle-class imagination. Of course Esther rejects the inheritance in the end; George Eliot's moral emphasis is too genuinely of an improving kind, of a self-making and self-made life, to permit Esther to accept the inheritance and find the fashionable way out. The corruption of that inheriting world, in which the price of security is intrigue, is powerfully shown in Mrs. Transome and Jermyn. But the emphasis of want is now specialised to Felix Holt: to the exposed, separated, potentially mobile individual. It is part of a crucial history in the development of the novel, in which the knowable community—the extended and emphatic world of an actual rural and then industrial England—comes to be known primarily as a problem of ambivalent relationship: of how the separated individual, with a divided consciousness of belonging and not belonging, makes his own moral history.

—Raymond Williams, "Knowable Communities," *The Country and the City* (1973), reprinted in *George Eliot*, ed. Harold Bloom (New York: Chelsea House Publishers, 1986), 82–85, 90

GEORGE LEVINE

The scientific texture of *Middlemarch* is even denser than the usual recognition of its many scientific metaphors might suggest. Henry James's general objection to Eliot that she worked too consistently from an idea to dramatic embodiment might seem, on the basis of *Middlemarch*, quite reasonable. The novel's most intense dramatic moments are recognizable as articulations of the same scientific vision that impelled G. H. Lewes's astonishingly ambitious, and uneven, *Problems of Life and Mind*, the first two volumes of which were being written at the same time. Yet to criticize George Eliot for such sweepingly intellectual structure is to miss the point of *Middlemarch*, almost to fail to read its subtexts. For among other things, that book, with *Daniel Deronda* after it, is a demonstration of the human and moral necessity of the scientific vision. Dorothea's recognition of her participation in the "involuntary, palpitating life" of mankind is dramatically powerful; but it is comprehensible in terms of the Victorian debate over evolution and the place of consciousness in nature. The ideas are dramatically central to Eliot's imagined universe, for her novels participate in a program like that of many writers on science: by virtue of rigorous secularity they attempt, in a way comparable to that of Feuerbach, to resacralize a world from which God has been dismissed.

Science stands to the text of *Middlemarch* as religion stands to that of *Paradise Lost*. It makes sense of an experience that threatens, to the perceptions of common sense, to disintegrate into meaninglessness. In his remarkable review of *Middlemarch* in 1873, Sidney Colvin sensitively noted the great ambition of the book and the integral part played in it by science. But he did not find the book "harmonious." The massive attempt to encompass everything was a grand failure. "Is it," he asks, "that a literature, which confronts all the problems of life and the world, and recognises all the springs of action, and all that clogs the springs, and all that comes from their smooth or impeded working, and all the importance of one life for the mass,—is it that such a literature must be like life itself, to leave us sad and hungry?" Colvin finds the consolation of mere meaning, as opposed to more direct satisfaction, inadequate. The tough-minded disenchantment implicit in much of the narrative, corresponding, of course, to George Eliot's belief in the "externality of fact," and as Lewes was to call it, the "physical basis of mind," provides the wrong *kind* of meaning.

By detecting so well the way science works in the book, Colvin demonstrates, however, that there is an "ideal" shape to the narrative of *Middlemarch*. We are now perfectly comfortable with criticism that shows us how intricately and minutely Eliot makes everything connect (as everything in science was believed to connect). It is worth briefly noting here the unprovable assumptions Huxley says underlie Victorian science: the "objective existence of a material world," the "universality of the law of causation," and the truth "for all time" of "any of the rules or so-called 'laws of Nature,' by which the relation of phenomena is truly defined." *Middlemarch*, through many devices that imply the coherence "assumed" by science, makes sense. But even these assumptions were under attack, and it was part of the enterprise of Lewes's intended magnum opus to provide a metaphysical ground for the assumptions of coherence on which science is based. In any case, Eliot gives us, in Dorothea's central act, the experience writ large of every human being. Dorothea chooses to do what is required of us all—not by God but by the evolution of our species. In the abstract, her absorption into an "involuntary, palpitating" life is grim and without warmth; in the dramatic experience, its incarnation, it is a remarkable and bracing moment.

Huxleyan science becomes a fully human, not merely an intellectual, possibility, and the novel here, the "nearest thing to life," or Lawrence's "one bright book of life," resists the abstraction for the incarnation. And the incarnation confirms the idea. Without the idea, ironically, the flesh would disintegrate, the real would become that corrupting horror that, as we shall see, Lewes observed in the world available to common sense, that Newman saw in the world without God, that Conrad's Kurtz was to see lurking in the mystery beyond the idea, beyond the Victorian faith that the mystery might be benign. ⟨. . .⟩

The adjustment of desire to external fact requires, in George Eliot's fiction, and in Victorian moral thought, the finest discernment, and is further complicated by the possibility that "external fact" does not deserve accommodation—as seems true in *Daniel Deronda*. One's own sensations complicated the "earnest study" Marian Evan sought, for disentangling objective reality from individual perception required nothing less than scientific rigor and seemed increasingly difficult the more science revealed about nature. Victorian astronomers, for example, had taken account of the fact that the reaction time of different observers varied by fractions of seconds, but sufficiently to throw off astronomical calculations vastly. There was introduced then into the earnest study of the heavens what was called the "personal equation," which would help correct for human differences. George Eliot's famous statement in *Adam Bede* already notes how the narrator will attempt to "give a faithful account of men and things as they have mirrored themselves in my mind." But the narrator knows that the mirror is "defective" and that "the outlines will sometimes be disturbed, the reflection faint or confused."

—George Levine, "The Scientific Texture of 'Middlemarch'," *The Realistic Imagination: English Fiction from Frankenstein to Lady Chatterley* (1981), reprinted in *George Eliot*, ed. Harold Bloom (New York: Chelsea House Publishers, 1986), 187–89, 192

BARRY V. QUALLS

Perhaps *Daniel Deronda* is so disturbing because it seems, *ab initio*, like none of George Eliot's earlier works. There is no Wordsworthian glow of memory to displace the fragmented present with a Hayslope, no invocation of a St. Theresa to cushion the reader by framing and elevating the often confused and blind doings of a woman and a rural community living in an England with no certain notion of what the signs of the time might portend. Instead, we are placed *"in medias res,"* in the readers' present. And the spiritual values of St. Ogg's, Stoniton, Lantern Yard, and Transome Court are combined and become horribly, because unmediatedly, present. A "scene of dull, gas-poisoned absorption," featuring men and women as drugged as any of the Veneering crowd, begins the novel; the Land of Goshen has become a casino. Yet it all ends with Manoa's elegy from the conclusion of *Samson Agonistes*—as if these Philistines had been destroyed and the children of light were quite triumphant in their cleansed Promised Land.

Which they in no way are. Yet we, as readers, have *seen* that land, and seen it in the most clearsighted way because George Eliot, after so many fictions alluding to the Judaic-Christian myth and Bunyan's use of it, constructs this final novel overtly around the chief situations and landscapes that had provided the texture of Puritan and evangelical biography and autobiography, and of Dinah Morris' sermons. The "children of light" are in bondage, to their own psychic heritage of slavery and to heathens "doing as they like" with more fervor than even Arnold's Philistines. And lest any casual reader miss the analogies—the Morality Play beneath the surface—the "children of light" in *Deronda* are not sensitive "Christians" like Maggie and Dorothea, but actual Jews. One is even a Moses as well ("an accomplished Egyptian"). The novel's formal construction insists on our recognition of its epic historical foundation: a beginning *in medias res*, constant allusions to Tasso's *Gerusalemme liberata*, to Handel's *Rinaldo* (itself based on a scene in the Tasso), to Dante's *Commedia*, and to the story of the Exodus and the Dispersion. Furthermore, the titular hero is himself identified as a savior-knight, as Moses and Prince Camaralzaman, at once the leader of history and a hero of romance. As in all romance, this hero does go off to found a newer world; as in the history, on the final page he stands like Moses glimpsing the promised land—although his sight is the vision and not Moses' reality. ⟨. . .⟩

And for George Eliot such a vision must be Jewish. Like Carlyle, she has no other "language" but the "nomenclature" of the Judeo-Christian religion to assert the paramount duty of fellow-feeling, and to illustrate the "pathway" towards freedom from slavery to the self and from the idolatry of a world which is alien to any better self and cares not to choose between right and wrong or anything beyond satisfying itself. In her final novel George Eliot ceases to be the historian or remembrancer we have known; memory and history have not been enough to keep vision free, unconstricted. In *Daniel Deronda* she is the sacred romancer, and baldly so. Tasso (with Handel) gives her the double plot structure to express the novel's key idea: "separateness and communication." And it gives her demons a-plenty to explore the inner life. The telling changes—indeed, reversals—she makes place the "Christians" of mid-Victorian England in the guise of Tasso's heathens, worshippers of self and of this world; and Tasso's saving Christians become in the modern retelling two Jews and one "Egyptian" whose words—"like the touch of a miraculous hand"—have something of Christ's power of love about them. The "sorceress," in both romance and novel, is converted; but beyond that we know nothing for both endings are alike. The sorceress' new life inscribes a tangent to the larger myth. Tasso's romance and Judaism show men a higher and a lower rather than a constant image of what lies about them in history's time. Romance originates in polarity, in the separation of the Hebrew from the heathen, the wheat from the chaff, the better self from the demon-empire. The Tasso and the history of the Jews together give life a vertical dimension, and man the possibility of transcendence. ⟨. . .⟩

We all—narrator, characters, readers—engage in constructing this book of life, "trying to make character clear before [us], and looking into the ways of destiny." For Gwendolen Harleth's inner life, as for Daniel Deronda's more outwardly connected story, we have seen that "tragic mark of kinship . . . such as has raised the pity and terror of men ever since they began to discern between will and destiny." For George Eliot, rewriting her book for the last time, only one structure was available in 1876 that she hoped would still give meaning to action and choice: that of the *Commedia*, *Pilgrim's Progress*, Israel in Egypt—epic, allegory, history: biblical romance. We discover our spiritual and better self only by seeing it in relation to a world larger than our own, only by breaking out of ourselves into that larger world, "above and below." As novelist—historian, seer, romancer—she offers us the parchment roll.

    —Barry V. Qualls, "Speaking through Parable: 'Daniel Deronda'," *The Secular Pilgrims of Victorian Fiction: The Novel as a Book of Life* (1982), reprinted in *George Eliot*, ed. Harold Bloom (New York: Chelsea House Publishers, 1986), 203–204, 219–21

F. R. LEAVIS

Adam Bede is unmistakably qualified to be a popular classic—which, in so far as there are such to-day, it still is. There is no need here to offer an appreciation of its attractions; they are as plain as they are genuine, and they have had full critical justice done them. Criticism, it seems to me, is faced with the ungrateful office of asking whether, much as *Adam Bede* deserves its currency as a classic (and of the classical English novels it has been among the most widely read), the implicit valuation it enjoys in general acceptance doesn't represent something more than justice. The point can perhaps be made by suggesting that the book is too much the sum of its specifiable attractions to be among the great novels—that it is too resolvable into the separate interests that we can see the author to have started with. Of these, a main one, clearly, is given in Mrs. Poyser and that mellow presentation of rustic life (as George Eliot recalled it from her childhood) for which Mrs. Poyser's kitchen is the centre. This deserves all the admiration it has received. And this is the moment to say that juxtaposition with George Eliot is a test that disposes finally of the 'Shakespearean' Hardy: if the adjective is to be used at all, it applies much more fitly to the rich creativeness of the art that seems truly to draw its sap from life and is free from all suspicion of Shakespeareanizing. George Eliot's rustic life is convincingly real even when most charming (and she doesn't always mellow her presentation of it with charm). ⟨. . .⟩

It is a related point that if 'charm' prevails in *Adam Bede* (and, as Henry James indicates, in *Silas Marner*), there should be another word for what we find in *The Mill on the Floss*. The fresh directness of a child's vision that we have there, in the autobiographical part, is something very different from the 'afternoon light' of reminiscence. This recaptured early vision, in its combination of clarity with rich 'significance,' is for us, no doubt, enchanting; but it doesn't idealize, or soften with a haze of sentiment (and it can't consort with 'art'). Instead of Mrs. Poyser and her setting we have the uncles and aunts. The bearing of the change is plain if we ask whether there could have been a Dinah in this company. Could there have been an Adam? They both belong to a different world. ⟨. . .⟩

That Maggie Tulliver is essentially identical with the young Mary Ann Evans we all know. She has the intellectual potentiality for which the environment into which she is born doesn't provide much encouragement; she has the desperate need for affection and intimate personal relations; and above all she has the need for an emotional exaltation, a religious enthusiasm, that shall transfigure the ordinariness of daily life and sweep her up in an inspired devotion of self to some ideal purpose. There is, however, a difference between Maggie Tulliver and Mary Ann Evans: Maggie is beautiful. She is triumphantly beautiful, after having been the ugly duckling. The experience of a sensitive child in this latter rôle among insensitive adults is evoked with great poignancy: George Eliot had only to remember. The glow that comes with imagining the duckling turned swan hardly needs analysing; it can be felt in every relevant page, and it is innocent enough. But it is intimately related to things in the book that common consent finds deplorable, and it is necessary to realize this in order to realize their nature and significance and see what the weaknesses of *The Mill on the Floss* really are. ⟨. . .⟩

One's criticism is that it is done too purely from the inside. Maggie's emotional and spiritual stresses, her exaltations and renunciations, exhibit, naturally, all the marks of immaturity; they involve confusions and immature valuations; they belong to a stage of development at which the capacity to make some essential distinctions has not yet been arrived at—at which the poised impersonality that is one of the conditions of being able to make them can't be achieved. There is nothing against George Eliot's presenting this immaturity with tender sympathy; but we ask, and ought to ask, of a great novelist something more. 'Sympathy and understanding' is the common formula of praise, but understanding, in any strict sense, is just what she doesn't show.

> —F. R. Leavis, "The Early Phase," *The Great Tradition* (1984), reprinted in *George Eliot*, ed.
> Harold Bloom (New York: Chelsea House Publishers, 1986), 15–20

ALEXANDER WELSH

Middlemarch is not only concerned with the limitations of knowledge but with the close bearing of motives of reputation on knowledge. In *Felix Holt* the juxtaposition of a positive public opinion and crude blackmail expresses this relation; in *Middlemarch* the relation of knowing to being known is persistently and finely drawn in each of the stories, so that the extreme case of blackmailing Bulstrode is but one of four relevant actions. Casaubon, Lydgate, Brooke, and Bulstrode are every one susceptible to threatening publicity. It is as if George Eliot were saying that the pursuit of knowledge, in modern society, is not separable from questions of publicity. If knowledge itself is remote, storable in "documents," exchangeable, publishable, and sometimes concealable, then the same effects of distance that govern its being govern also its practitioners, who are thereby subject to exposure in a way very different from Caleb Garth's experience. Garth is known personally for the work he does and can do; the seekers of knowledge have placed themselves at risk in a culture of information, a culture that can inform against them.

George Eliot makes abundantly clear that virtually the sole motive of Casaubon's scholarship is fame, and that this relation between his knowledge and his being known runs far deeper than mere vanity, his pleasure in sitting for the portrait of St. Thomas Aquinas and the like. Casaubon is both vain and "resolute in being a man of honour," a person "unimpeachable by any recognized opinion"; but he is subject to the deepest terror by authorship. He will be judged in absentia from his writings, and already is so judged, as he fears. ⟨. . .⟩

Blackmail is the stuff of sensation novels, and it is no wonder that students of George Eliot have had difficulty in accommodating the story of Bulstrode to their interpretations of *Middlemarch*, which is nothing like a sensation novel as a whole. The first requirement of such accommodation is to accept Bulstrode's close relation to Lydgate, and by contiguities and partial analogies to other characters in the novel as well. Still, the manifest ambition of the novel to become an epic of society might seem to preclude such crass irony as may be imported by a ruinous bit of information. Like Fielding before her, George Eliot aspired to an epic representation of contemporary life, but her model was finally Dante's epic rather than Homer's. The historical particularity of Dante's characters appealed to her nineteenth-century sense of past and present. The urgency of his dead heroes' longing to establish a link with this world she reinterpreted as a common experience of discontinuity within the world. Her Casaubon identifies himself almost complacently as a ghost: "I feed too much on the inward sources; I live too much with the dead. My mind is something like the ghost of an ancient" (chap. 2). Fame is no less a need for Casaubon than it was for one of Dante's characters, and his apparent complacency turns to anguish as George Eliot enlarges his story and makes it representative of a modern experience of writing in which she shared. But for a character with one life irrevocably fixed in the past and another life in the present, she chose Bulstrode, and arranged things so that the information threatening Bulstrode's career threatened Lydgate's as well.

The Dantean model first inspired Mrs. Transome in *Felix Holt*, a woman whose history actually anticipates Lydgate's modern experience. Like Lydgate, Mrs. Transome "had been thought wonderfully clever and accomplished, and had been rather ambitious of intellectual superiority" in her youth; and she has since experienced "crosses, mortifications, money-cares, conscious blameworthiness" (chap. 1). Yet the promise of her youth is never given a chance to impress the reader, as Lydgate's impresses. It is he whose stature and whose punishment are most Dantean of all—though his life is scarcely as divided as Bulstrode's. The stories of Lydgate and Bulstrode together combine the pursuit of knowledge with the constraint of public opinion, in the one case elaborating the novelist's most careful study of the action of circumstances and in the other melodramatically and metaphorically demonstrating the effect of discontinuity, and of "successive events inward and outward" as they obstinately return from the window of a lighted room.

—Alexander Welsh, "Knowledge in *Middlemarch*," *George Eliot and Blackmail* (1985), reprinted in *George Eliot's Middlemarch*, ed. Harold Bloom (New York: Chelsea House Publishers, 1987), 117, 138–39

GILLIAN BEER

Many Victorian commentators characterised George Eliot as a novelist preoccupied with passion. If we identify passion solely with sexual love between peers we shall find a dearth of any extended description of such love-sensation in her work. Henry James commented on the singular austerity with which George Eliot treated love, suggesting that *Middlemarch* and *Daniel Deronda* did

> seem to foreign readers, probably, like vast, cold, commodious,
> respectable rooms, through whose window-panes one sees a snow-
> covered landscape, and across whose acres of sober-hued carpet
> one looks in vain for a fireplace or a fire.

It is necessary to insist, in our culture, that passion does not describe solely heterosexual love-affairs. If her representations of sexual encounter are at the opposite extreme of reticence from *My Secret Life*, it is worth remembering Foucault's comment that that work is part of the Victorian process of transforming sex into discourse. But if we understand passion in relationships as vehement human need sustained past the accomplishment of moments of desire, we shall more exactly mark what it meant for her. ⟨. . .⟩

In Maggie, passion takes the form of vehement intellectual need experienced as emotion. Desire for knowledge, for "more instruments playing together," had traditionally been enregistered as the man's story. Faust and his wild passion for full possession of the world that knowledge may open, is saved by the innocent, stay-at-home, untutored Gretchen. Steadfast love is divided from the thirst for knowledge, polarised as female and male. George Eliot rejects that polarisation, first in Maggie, and then, more and more powerfully in the later novels by means of the polymathic narrative which, through learning, constantly discovers emotional connection. The writing ranges freely through and beyond such oppositions, but it also experiences them. In "Armgart" we are presented with the urgency of creative anger and need—an anger which is generated more by desire than by frustration, and a desire which is for the creative act itself:

> I carry my revenges in my throat;
> I love in singing, and am loved again.

Several feminist critics, notably Christ (1976) and Midler (1980), have pointed out the urgency of anger in George Eliot's creativity and her need, also, to reach beyond anger. In her anger, although there is often an edge of frustration and criticism of current social forms, there is frequently also a more Pythian "rage." Not all anger is social reformist nor seeking solution. ⟨. . .⟩

Elaine Showalter (1977) sees the story of Maggie Tulliver as George Eliot's concession to a particularly Victorian configuration of the female which produces a "passive, self-destructive heroine." This reading makes Maggie sound more renunciatory than she is portrayed as being in the book. As Nina Auerbach (1982) shows, Maggie is connected from the beginning of the story with the demonic.

> "Oh I'll tell you what that means. It's a dreadful picture, isn't it? But I can't help looking at it. That old woman in the water's a witch— they've put her in to find out whether she's a witch or no, and if she swims she's a witch, if she's drowned—and killed, you know—she's innocent, and not a witch, but only a poor silly old woman. But what good would it do her then, you know, when she was drowned? Only, I suppose, she'd go to heaven, and God would make it up to her."
>
> (bk. 1, chap. 3)

Maggie here cities the tale of the witch in Defoe's *History of the Devil*. The witch epitomises Maggie's bind. If she is innocent, she drowns. If she bobs up again, she is guilty. Is Maggie's drowning used in some half-magical way to prove her innocence? If so, such innocence is useless. Like the witch, Maggie is dead. Only the narrator can "make it up to her." The last chapter, indeed, is entitled "The Final Rescue," and that rescue is undertaken by the writer. Within the work, Maggie herself makes jokes about another such magical ordering in novels and fairy tales, that of the blond and the dark heroine. The blond represents restraint and social order, the dark, passion and disruption. The blond is bound to win, and Maggie resents that. So do we. ⟨. . .⟩

The work playfully draws attention to its own order and knowingly prognosticates what comes to seem inevitable: Maggie's defeat. Yet it presages, too, the paradoxical sense of Maggie's triumph and vengeance with which, despite her death, the book concludes. ⟨. . .⟩

The end of the book sets up double-binds of the kind that Maggie had observed much earlier when in her early childhood she read Defoe's *History of the Devil* and embarrassed her father with her improper knowledge of the way the world treats women whom it selects as deviants. At the end of *The Mill on the Floss*, Maggie drowns, and is innocent, and receives her reward momentously and in an unsustainable instant in this world. She has rowed safely back to the mill. Tom, seeing the "huge fragments, clinging together in fatal fellowship" approaching them, reacts thus: "'It is coming, Maggie!' Tom said, in a deep hoarse voice, loosing the oars, and clasping her."

The orgasmic reference is overwhelming, and overwhelms them: and so does the flood. The transgressions that George Eliot liberates at the end of the novel are in that same moment suppressed and done away with. Opposing forces appear not in the calm of enigma but in the vehemence of conclusion. Conclusion permits events without consequences and without social force.

—Gillian Beer, "'The Dark Woman Triumphs': Passion in *The Mill on the Floss*," *George Eliot* (1986), reprinted in *George Eliot's The Mill on the Floss*, ed. Harold Bloom (New York: Chelsea House Publishers, 1988), 125–28, 137–38

LAURIE LANGBAUER

Gender is important in a breakdown of the distinction between realism and romance in Eliot's fiction, and its importance turns on the duplicity of detail. Realism directly opposes itself to that alternative mode of presentation, romance, by claiming a special relation to visual data and privileging those data as the real. Realism supposedly presents an objective picture that displays common, everyday details in their proper light; romance sees either too much or too little, charting some illusory realm outside the ordinary. Yet, as Naomi Schor argues, any focus on ordinary or extraordinary detail relies on gender assumptions. "The detail is gendered and doubly gendered as feminine," she writes; it is "bounded on the one side by the *ornamental*, with its traditional connotations of effeminacy and decadence, and on the other, by the *everyday*, whose 'prosiness' is rooted in the domestic sphere of social life presided over by women." This gendering of detail as feminine is so insistent that the association of women and detail persists even in aspects of detail—the decadent, the everyday—that seem contradictory. ⟨. . .⟩

In the English tradition, George Eliot's works have become synonymous with classical realism, and the relation of realism to the authority of the visual is a consistent focus that they investigate as well as rely on. ⟨Like the other novelists I consider⟩ Eliot uses romance to define her own realistic novels; in her novels, the claim of realism to the precision and clarity of specularity contrasts with a rhetoric associating the dizzying profusion of details, or their indistinctness, with romance. Yet, as for other novelists, Eliot's realism cannot keep separate from what it casts as its opposite. In *The Mill on the Floss*, describing Maggie "battling with the old shadowy enemies that were forever slain and rising again" (*MF*.7.5.644), Eliot describes too the struggle between the realism of her novels and an undispatchable romance within them. Eliot locates the terms of the dynamic I have been charting a little differently from the other novelists I have considered: between what critics call modes, not genres, attitudes or presentation rather than types or forms. Eliot means for her dominant mode of presentation to ensure the primacy of her genre, the novel, but romance is a shadowy enemy, always rising again, because, in fighting it, realism is fighting its own shadow. ⟨. . .⟩

What seems the pessimism of George Eliot's fiction, and the real reason that feminists are often angry at her, may reflect the concentration of her fiction on the limits of the possibilities for directly willed feminist change. But rather than being antifeminist, her fiction enables our feminist struggle by highlighting that that struggle is necessarily interminable and that it must go on despite the absence of a clear goal or reward. The much-discussed loss of faith fueling Eliot's fiction may well be another version of the way the very issue of the doubtfulness of our endeavors provides the focus that fuels and justifies them. Eliot's peculiar double vision about feminism—that her works seem caught between a clarity of vision and a willful blindness when it comes to the cause of gender inequities—exposes the contradictions within feminism rather than dispensing with it. Her novels, in attempting both to establish and to question their own authority, interrogate the question of gender within the metaphor of vision that underwrites them—a metaphor that they, too, do not just adopt but investigate. Their examination provides a kind of admonitory vision, which suggests the necessity of keeping the limits on us as subjects from letting us as feminists settle for a complacent pessimism, of continuing instead the necessary process of self-examination. Like Dorothea, Eliot may yearn "after order and a perfect rule" (MM.9.98); with an "eagerness for a binding theory" (10.112), she may impatiently identify herself with the very authority she cannot escape, but she nowhere settles long for it, nor for easy answers.

—Laurie Langbauer, *Women and Romance: The Consolations of Gender in the English Novel* (Ithaca: Cornell University Press, 1990), 190, 200–201, 231–32

ALISON BOOTH

Eliot's fourth novel seems to grope for generic as well as aesthetic alternatives to the conventional embodiment and emplotment of women; its ending opens as many questions as it closes. This "heroine's text" defies the "either/or closure" of marriage or death that Nancy Miller has traced; such defiance in itself might account for a Victorian reader's distaste for the Epilogue, with its strange disposition of gender and other hierarchies. Recent readers, on the contrary, are more likely to construe the Epilogue as a forced concession to convention; if Eliot's heroine avoids marriage or death, she is nevertheless compelled to sit still, like a feminine idol reassembled after a bout of iconoclasm. Both resisting readings would find support in the text: *Romola* does violate novelistic closure, "writing beyond the ending" in its own feminist way, and yet it does appear to end with a technically polished illustration for a handbook of irreproachable advice. ⟨. . .⟩

⟨. . .⟩ If we read Romola's story as a contribution to Victorian discourse on woman's mission, we detect the activism in this quiet close. Romola has had her cake, and is now eating it without betraying any unseemly appetite. She has started a great feminist historical march while appearing to sit still and ask for nothing, complaining of no personal injustice. Few of Eliot's characters find the cure for egotism so miraculously easy. *Romola* suggests that narratives of feminine greatness—of heroines not necessarily famous who perfect an ethic of disinterested kindness—belong among the biographies of great men, and indeed that these suppressed narratives force a revaluation of masculine historical achievement.

Romola owes her success in challenging the monopoly of great men to the great Victorian reforming women, her true contemporaries. Hutton is right that Romola is modern, that is, a Victorian woman in search of a vocation (and she, of course, reflects in many ways George Eliot's own bid for greatness as a writer). She emulates certain prominent contemporary women, above all two famous cousins, Barbara Leigh Smith Bodichon and Florence Nightingale, both of whom in turn could be figured as female saints in art. Both women came of prosperous reforming stock and in different ways attacked laws and practices that confined women to domestic dependency and ignorance. Barbara, who looked remarkably like Romola, was a fearless champion of the oppressed; she was the close friend whom Eliot liked to picture as her "fresco of St. Barbara." A painter and writer, among other projects she exposed the property laws that subjected women, launched one of the first committees for women's suffrage, and helped found the first college for women at Cambridge. Several of Romola's experiences illustrate the wrongs Bodichon crusaded against, including the son-in-law's right to supplant the daughter as heir and the prohibition on the daughter's becoming a scholar in her own right.

Florence Nightingale, of course, was the lady with the lamp, who shared her name with her own and Romola's birthplace. Unlike Bodichon, Nightingale was resistant to feminism and antagonistic to most women, but she became the idol of millions as the female savior of the wounded soldiers in the Crimean War, much as Romola is worshipped by the starving Florentines and villagers dying of the plague. ⟨. . .⟩

Within the frame of an erudite and tasteful historical romance, Eliot masks contemporary conflicts, such as debates about prostitution and the double standard. Romola's husband Tito pretends to marry his mistress as he pretends to ally himself with two political parties and two foster fathers, but unlike his fellow politicians and his first foster father, who finally succeed in killing him, Romola the wronged wife never retaliates with the rage of the Bacchantes or Bardi. Rather, she comes to resemble the Victorian leader Josephine Butler, who established homes for prostitutes and crusaded against the Contagious

Diseases Acts (which policed all women in military districts to make prostitution safe for men). Implicitly revoking men's self-indulgent license, Romola rescues the "other," fallen woman in the name of a superior (feminine) altruism. Deflected into rescue work and charity, these women's sense of violation could be transformed into an image less disfiguring, not that of Medea but of an immaculate mother skilled in taking personal politics impersonally. ⟨. . .⟩

I have been suggesting that the conclusion of *Romola* supports the heroine's claim to moral ascendency in terms consonant with the Victorian women's movement, and that it reveals a mixture of loyalty and rebellion in its tension between a statuesque ideal and a promise of female action.

—Alison Booth, "The Silence of Great Men: Statuesque Femininity and the Ending of *Romola*," *Famous Last Words: Changes in Gender and Narrative Closure*, ed. Alison Booth (Charlottesville: University Press of Virginia, 1993), 111–12, 117–18, 121–23

BIBLIOGRAPHY

Scenes of Clerical Life (2 vols.). 1858.
Adam Bede (3 vols.). 1859.
The Mill on the Floss (3 vols.). 1860.
Silas Marner (2 vols.). 1861.
Romola (3 vols.). 1862–63.
Felix Holt, The Radical (3 vols.). 1866.
The Spanish Gypsy: A Poem. 1868.
How Lisa Loved the King. 1869.
Middlemarch (2 vols.). 1871–72.
The Legend of Jubal and Other Poems. 1874.
Daniel Deronda (2 vols.). 1876.
The Works of George Eliot (24 vols.). 1878–85.
Impressions of Theophrastus Such. 1879.
Early Essays (privately printed). 1919.
Quarry for Middlemarch. 1950.
The George Eliot Letters. 1954–55.
The Essays of George Eliot. 1963.

ELIZABETH GASKELL
1810-1865

ELIZABETH CLEGHORN GASKELL was born Elizabeth Stevenson on September 29, 1810, in the Chelsea section of London. Her father, William Stevenson, came from a naval family but became a Unitarian minister instead of going to sea. Gaskell's mother, the former Elizabeth Holland, died a year after her daughter's birth. The child was raised by her Aunt Lumb in Knutsford. The young Elizabeth Stevenson had an extremely happy childhood in Knutsford, where she was raised in her parents' faith of Unitarianism, which advocated equal education for both boys and girls. Elizabeth received an excellent education locally and also attended the enlightened Avonbank School in Stratford-Upon-Avon.

In 1828, she suffered a serious blow when her older brother John was lost at sea, and in 1829 she was called home to care for her dying father. After her father's death, she moved back to Knutsford, where she met William Gaskell, an assistant minister at the Cross Street Chapel in Manchester. William Gaskell and Elizabeth Stevenson were married in Knutsford in 1832 and went to live in Manchester. Although only sixteen miles from Knutsford, Manchester could not have been more different from that quiet, rural village. Nevertheless, the Gaskells were very happy together. As Unitarians, they had a more equal marriage than many of their contemporaries. During the early years of their life together, Mrs. Gaskell was occupied with domestic duties and with working for social reform.

In the midst of this activity she managed to publish occasional pieces in magazines and journals, including her poem, "Sketches Among the Poor" (1837). But it was after the death of her only son, Willie (he died in 1845, shortly before his first birthday), that Gaskell tried her hand at the novel. Writing helped Mrs. Gaskell manage her grief, and the result was her first novel, *Mary Barton* (1848). The novel was an enormous success and aroused the interest of Charles Dickens, who invited Mrs. Gaskell to contribute to his weekly periodical, *Household Words*. Several of Gaskell's stories, including the first sketch of what would become *Cranford*, were published in Dickens's periodical. In her next full-length novel, *Ruth* (1853), Gaskell explored the problem of the fallen woman. *North and South*, which explores the relationship between a middle-class girl from the south and a northern mill owner, was serialized in *Household Words* between 1854 and 1855.

In 1857, Gaskell published her only biography, *The Life of Charlotte Brontë*. Although it is considered to be one of the best biographies of the period, it angered several people who had been involved with the Brontë family. John Stuart Mill demanded a retraction over a note written about his wife, Harriet Taylor Mill, and the Reverend Carus Wilson of Cowan Bridge School also protested against the biagragra-phy's portrayal of his school. Despite these problems, Gaskell was earning a considerable amount of money as a writer. Her later works retreated from the social problems with which she had concerned her-self early in her career. And although she continued to publish her work in Dickens's periodical, her last important works were published by Smith Elder & Co. Gaskell attempted historical fiction in *Sylvia's Lovers* (1863) and returned to the idyllic scenes of her early years at Knutsford in *Cousin Phyllis* (1864) and *Wives and Daughters* (1864–65), both of which were serialized in *The Cornhill*. Gaskell died suddenly of a heart attack in 1865, just before the expected completion of *Wives and Daughters*. Mrs. Gaskell's intentions for the novel's conclusion were described by Frederick Greenwood, who had assumed *The Cornhill's* editorial duties after Thackeray retired in 1862.

CRITICAL EXTRACTS

GEORGE BARNETT SMITH

The several stages of our author's career may be said to be marked by three of her works, though the lines of demarcation in her case are not so apparent as in most writers; for she appears in her first widely-known work to have attained a power of expression very rarely witnessed in the maturest efforts of those of her order. Still, were we expected to define clearly the various stages of progress which she has attained—or rather to note the influence of time in ripening her gifts—we should direct attention to the first, the middle, and the final stage of her genius—into each of which divisions we should be able, we imagine, to classify her work. The novel which first fixed public attention, and which belongs to the first stage, was *Mary Barton*; that which marks the second is *Sylvia's Lovers*; and that illustrative of the third is *Wives and Daughters*. Each of these works presents considerable points of difference, while they are all at the same time stamped by the genuine impress of genius. Several others could be cited, which for particular qualities may even be superior to those named; but they do not so decisively show Mrs. Gaskell at her best, or her pen animated

by the varied charms which these books individually and indisputably discover. The charge has been made that Mrs. Gaskell was but a member of "that
school of novelists which her friend Charlotte Brontë inaugurated," but after a
careful study, and possessing a somewhat intimate acquaintance with all that
the two have accomplished, we are bound to say that the charge appears to us
to have no foundation. In fact, there is a considerable difference in method, as
there was a considerable difference in gifts, between the two. The only
grounds for the comparison which has been made are these—that the two
have successfully dealt with certain phases of Northern English life, and that
both, perhaps, have been most successful in their delineation of female character. ⟨. . .⟩

In stating the qualities for which, as a novelist, Mrs. Gaskell is most conspicuous, we should enumerate them in the following order:—individuality,
force, truthfulness, and purity. As regards the first-named quality no one
would be inclined to dispute her possession of it after reading *Mary Barton*,
Ruth, or *Wives and Daughters*. The power of detaching a human unit, with all its
special thoughts, griefs, hopes, and fears, from the rest of its kind, is in full
force in all the works we have named. Indeed, there is scarcely any contemporary author who has excelled her in this respect. But upon that quality, and
also upon her force or power, we have sufficiently enlarged already.
Concerning the truthfulness of Mrs. Gaskell there is room for genuine
approval. Into whatever sphere of life she conveys her readers, they are conscious that there is no exaggeration, no undue exaltation of this person, and
no undue depression of the other. Upon this estimable quality we should be
inclined to build most fearlessly for her assurance of immortality. Yet while
there is no quality which should singly so well ensure it, if any work is to live
and have a constant impression upon successive generations it must be combined with qualities which may seem humbler, but which in reality have more
vitality in them from the fact that however the world changes their special
power remains the same. Let Mrs. Gaskell's novels be read after the lapse of a
hundred years, and one feels that the verdict delivered then would be that
they were penned by the hand of a true observer—one who not only studied
human nature with a desire, but a capacity, to comprehend it. This is one of
the great motive powers which will ever keep the name of the author green in
the public remembrance. The other principal quality to assist this consumma-
tion is purity. We were struck in reading her various volumes with this fact—
that there is really less in them than there is in most other authors which she
herself could wish to be altered. In fact, there is no purer author in modern
times. And what has she lost by being pure? Has she failed to give a fair
representation of any class of human beings whom she professes to depict?
Not one; and her work stands now as an excellent model for those who would

avoid the tendencies of the sensuous school, and would seek another basis upon which to acquire a reputation which should have some chances of durability.

—George Barnett Smith, "Mrs. Gaskell and Her Novels," *Cornhill Magazine* (February 1874), excerpted in *The New Moulton's Library of Literary Criticism*, Vol. 8, ed. Harold Bloom (New York: Chelsea House Publishers, 1989), 4801, 4804

WILLIAM MINTO

To promote a better understanding between different sections of society, to remove prejudices, to enlarge the limits of tolerance and charity, to dispel that ignorance of ways of life different from our own, which is so fruitful a source of injustice in the smaller as well as the weightier matters of social intercourse, may be said to have been the central purpose of all Mrs. Gaskell's earlier novels. As if afraid lest in *Mary Barton* she had produced too unfavourable an impression of the manufacturers as a class by describing the life of the manufacturing towns too exclusively from the workmen's point of view, she wrote *North and South* from the point of view of the masters. She did not hold a brief for the masters in this novel, any more than she held a brief for the men in *Mary Barton*. Shakespeare himself was not more dramatically impartial in his presentation of character; but by choosing her hero from the manufacturing class she centred the interest of the reader in their life, and enabled us, as it were, to look out upon the world from their windows, and justify their conduct as they were in the habit of justifying it to themselves. Mr. Thornton is not a type of the whole manufacturing class, any more than John Barton is a type of the whole artisan class, but he is a type of many, and his faults are explained and his virtues illustrated with the same penetrating insight into the play of lifelong circumstances upon character, and we are taught in the same way how natural it was that two such men should be in antagonism, and how much more smoothly they might work together for their common interest, if their relations had a little of the oil of mutual understanding. In *North and South* also Mrs. Gaskell had another unprejudicing mission to perform,—to remove from the whole industrial system of the North the coarse and savage aspect which it wore in the eyes of populations among whom the ways of life were smoother and the struggle for existence less strenuous and fierce. She shows that the higher elements in man are not all trodden down and extinguished in the sordid race for wealth, that there is opportunity in the manufacturer's life for loftier sentiments than the mere pride of money-getting; nobler visions than bank notes and stock. As her manner is, she does not undertake this apology in her own person, but puts it into the mouth of one of her characters. ⟨. . .⟩

Mrs. Gaskell, in several of her shorter stories, as well as in *North and South*, seeks favour for the men of the North as hiding warm hearts and bold imaginations under hard, inelegant, unceremonious manners. Everywhere in her novels we come upon traces of this persistent desire to break down prejudices and open the way to harmony. It is very prominent in her tragic story of *Ruth*, where she pleads the cause of a class more in need of intercession with society and more likely to be grateful for it than the sturdy manufacturers of "Milton." Even in *Cranford*, brimming over as it is with humorous satire, we are conscious of a kindly underlying moral. The makeshifts and affectations of decayed gentility have long been a favourite subject for ridicule, but Mrs. Gaskell, while she is not inferior to Miss Austen herself in the power of making us laugh at the foibles of her old ladies, takes care to give emphasis to their good qualities. Miss Jenkyns, with all her "Dragon o' Wantley" notions of dress and genteel discipline, does say, when a certain gentleman is seen sitting in the drawing-room with his arm round Miss Jessie Brown's waist, that "it is the most proper place for his arm to be in;" and the prying, man-hunting, tart Miss Pole takes the lead in the "movement" for contributing the mites of the coterie "in a secret and concealed manner" to impoverished Miss Matty. We are disposed to think more amiably of gossiping old women after reading *Cranford*. ⟨. . .⟩

Although pre-eminently a moralist in the sense of being a writer whose works touch the heart rather than the imagination or the philosophical intellect, Mrs. Gaskell is not to be numbered among the preachers. No one, however impatient of reproof and correction, need be frightened away from her novels by the fear of having to listen to didactic homilies. She prefixed a little sermon, pithy and well timed, by way of preface to *Mary Barton*, extracting from it a lesson for the day; but the lesson is not formulated and expounded in the novel, which is, what it professes to be, a tale—a representation of life. It is shaped and coloured by the author's good-natured wisdom, but it is not stiffened and distorted as a work of art by any hard specific moral purpose. Mrs. Gaskell was, indeed, a born story-teller, charged through and through with the story-teller's peculiar element, a something which may be called suppressed gipsiness, a restless instinct which impelled her to be constantly making trial in imagination of various modes of life. Her imagination was perpetually busy with the vicissitudes which days and years brought round to others; she entered into their lives, laughed with them, wept with them, speculated on the cardinal incidents and circumstances, the good qualities and the "vicious moles of nature" which had made them what they were, schemed how they might have been different, and lived through the windings and turnings of their destinies the excitement of looking forward to the unknown. ⟨. . .⟩

No one would dream of ranking Mrs. Gaskell as a novelist beside Dickens or Thackeray, but she deserves a very high place among those who are comparatively unambitious in their efforts, and who, having a just measure of their own powers, succeed perfectly in what they undertake.

—William Minto, "Mrs. Gaskell's Novels," *Fortnightly Review* (September 1878), excerpted in *The New Moulton's Library of Literary Criticism*, Vol. 8, ed. Harold Bloom (New York: Chelsea House Publishers, 1989), 4806–807

MAT HOMPES

Ruth, her second great work in order of publication, is, as regards style and power, inferior to *Mary Barton*, perhaps to all her sustained effort. But it stands out from the rest, as the handling by a woman of a side of life which is unfortunately too often either ignored in real life and in fiction, or treated in a light, flippant manner. It is the story of an innocent young girl, led into sin by a profligate, who afterwards heartlessly deserts her. She is left in that position where, if a woman once reaches it, nearly all virtuous women seem to consider it their duty to keep her, by treating her with utter contempt, debarring her all respectable society and any decent means of earning a livelihood. We will not say all women: there are a few at least among Christian women who can more truly interpret their Master's words when he said, "Neither do I condemn thee; go and sin no more." Mrs. Gaskell bids us consider this problem. She shows us how this poor, erring girl is brought through the kindness extended to her to lead a good life, bringing up her boy in honour and virtue as any mother might be proud to do. It is a tale of tears, most pathetic and pitiful throughout; but it was given us for a high purpose, and we must admire Mrs. Gaskell's womanly courage as well as her talent. The world should be careful to distinguish, in its zeal for honour and morality, between those who court sin and those who are sorely tempted, and in their weakness fall. Let us be watchful lest we thrust mere weakness into wickedness, by barring the doors for ever against those who are anxious to return where once they stood. ⟨. . .⟩

North and South may be called a companion book to *Mary Barton*, since, like its predecessor, it deals with the labour question in Lancashire. Here Mrs. Gaskell defends the masters' side. But the interest of the book does not centre there, but rather in Mr. Hale's resignation of the ministry for conscience' sake. This subject would have a peculiar interest for Mrs. Gaskell, for her father's sake. The scene is laid in the South of England, and Mrs. Gaskell takes this opportunity of contrasting Hampshire with Lancashire men, greatly to the advantage of the latter. These she knew with a fuller and truer knowledge, and it is plain to see where her heart lies.

There is one weak point in this book, a blemish for which there surely was no need. Margaret Hale, the heroine, is made to tell a lie in order to screen her brother—save his life, indeed—instead of daring to speak the truth. There is no doubt that most people would have done the same, but I like my heroes to be of sterling metal, to stand head and shoulders above the crowd. Such men and women exist, if only rarely; let us take our heroes from the chosen few. Sir Walter Scott thought so when he gave us his Jeanie Deans, and we all know the effect.

In 1857 Mrs. Gaskell published *The Life of Charlotte Brontë*, a biography which has been compared with Boswell's *Life of Johnson*. It brings the little Yorkshire lady, who possessed such great genius, most vividly before us. No one could have been found so well fitted to write her life, and we feel grateful to Mrs. Gaskell for having undertaken the task. She knew Charlotte Brontë as few could know, and she loved her most truly and tenderly. A tender, loving hand was needed to lay bare the records of that sad, lonely life amid the Yorkshire hills. And yet had they not been told how much we should have lost! Not only should we want the key to the books which, coming from the lonely parsonage at Haworth, took the world by surprise, but we should have missed what is of greater value still—namely, the lesson how this woman bore up against the keenest trials and became thereby not hardened, but only more and more refined to the end. Some later authorities think that Mrs. Gaskell put in the dark lines of the picture rather too thickly; but her book remains on the whole tender and true, and will be prized as one of the best biographies in the English language.

—Mat Hompes, "Mrs. Gaskell," *Gentlemen's Magazine* (August 1895), excerpted in *The New Moulton's Library of Literary Criticism*, Vol. 8, ed. Harold Bloom (New York: Chelsea House Publishers, 1989), 4808–809

KATHLEEN TILLOTSON

It is partly because it is a novel which starts from 'individuals' that *Mary Barton* stands out from the run of 'novels with a purpose'. It is not less truthful than others of its kind, nor less passionate; but it is also, as befits a woman's novel, more purely compassionate; 'the poetry is in the pity'. But there is no patronage or condescension towards suffering. The denizens of the 'other nation' are neither harrowing victims nor heroic martyrs; they are shown in their natural human dignity, as Wordsworth might have shown them had he fulfilled his promise to make 'authentic comment' on 'sorrow barricadoed evermore within the walls of cities'.

It was that sorrow which effectively awoke the writer in the Unitarian minister's wife. That is not to say that we directly owe to it her later masterpieces, such as *Cousin Phillis* and *Wives and Daughters*; but *Mary Barton* was the novel she felt compelled to write, whose instant popularity smoothed her whole subsequent literary career, and the work which set free her powers. Not itself a great novel, it is the first novel of a great novelist; and the progress is an understandable one, if we agree with the young Henry James that we have here to deal with a novelist whose 'genius' was 'so obviously the offspring of her affections, her feelings, her associations . . . so little of an intellectual matter . . . little else than a peculiar play of her personal character'. ⟨. . .⟩

Mary Barton is a tale of Manchester life, of the Manchester that Engels saw, in whose poorer quarters the infant mortality was sixty per cent; it was also the Manchester of the opening chapters of *Past and Present*—

sooty Manchester, it too is built upon the infinite abysses!

'It too'; 'Birmingham people have souls'. Manchester life is the life of men and women stirred by the primary human affections, and made in the divine image. On this simple intuition the novel is built. ⟨. . .⟩

It is the diversity and density of Manchester life, and the figure of John Barton rising craglike above it, that is built up before our eyes in the slow-moving expository opening chapters. They needed to be slow, because of the novelty of the material; they needed also to be reassuring. The author had to enlist the reader's sympathy for her hero; she could not abruptly introduce him as a Trades Union man, a Chartist, an advocate and perpetrator of violence; and it would indeed be foreign to her purpose, which is not to demand approval or condemnation, but interest and understanding. ⟨. . .⟩

Courage to give utterance to unfamiliar points of view—that of the workman driven to violence; of the stern self-made factory-owner; of the seduced girl and the parson who protects her; but always with the purpose, unconscious perhaps, of promoting sympathy, not sharpening antagonisms; between regions, classes, sexes, generations; on the quiet assumption that to know is to understand, to forgive, and even to respect.

Not even George Eliot shows such reverence for average human nature as Mrs. Gaskell; and this is evident from her earliest work. It helped to teach her the art which her later novels perfected; helped to guide her instinctive tact in avoiding the overemphases of sentimentality and sensationalism, even in situations that tempt towards them. For she accepts, and not ruefully, the ordinariness of people and the dailiness of life. Already in her first novel the minor characters (such as the boy Charley, Mrs. Wilson, Sally Leadbitter) are solid and distinct; each character, however small, has its scale of moral values, and its social medium; all are closely associated with the domestic detail of their surroundings. (Her explicit descriptions are mainly of what people use or make themselves at home in.) This unheightened truthfulness establishes confidence, so that we are ready to accept her 'big scenes'—the chase down the Mersey, the murder trial; like the bank failure in *Cranford*, they seem simply emergencies which must occasionally arise in ordinary life and which test character. And more: this almost pedestrian truthfulness is already accompanied by something spacious: her common flowers of human nature are rooted in earth, but over them arches 'the divine blue of the summer sky'.

—Kathleen Tillotson, "Mary Barton," *Novels of the Eighteen-Forties* (Oxford: Clarendon Press, 1954), 202–203, 210, 214, 221–22

MARTIN DODSWORTH

Most readers seem to feel that the spirit of *Cranford* is most aptly expressed in the delicate—not to say charming—illustrations of Hugh Thomson. The world of *Cranford* is faded, full of small snobbery and great kindness; it is a feminine novel, not only as all the important characters are women, but as preeminently the work of a woman, ever held by the details of a room's arrangement or a bonnet's trimming. This familiar view is usually accompanied by a subsidiary judgement: that the book has no structure. The short story that now forms the two opening chapters was originally all that there was to be of *Cranford*: the rest is a happy accident. The fiction is tender and reminiscential, and depends not on plot but on character. Its want of structure is no fault, since only the vestige of plot is required to present the characters, whose descent from the eighteenth-century sentimental comic novel is obvious. Miss Matty is, like the rest of her friends, as Lord David Cecil has observed, 'the childlike, saintly innocent, full of harmless foibles,' easily found in Sterne or Goldsmith. For readers who take this view of the book, the summit of Mrs. Gaskell's literary achievement will probably be the chapter entitled 'Visiting', the simple description of a Cranford tea-party at which nothing occurs that is not to be expected. They would attribute the success of this scene, in Lord David's words, to the 'play of Mrs. Gaskell's microscopic, incessant, ironical observation'—in other words, to her sympathetic record of a life of innocent triviality.

This is just the sort of delightful insipidity to which the novels of Jane Austen have often been reduced (she too has suffered the fate of Thomson illustrations), and it is this fact that may put us on our guard. For many people the reading of Jane Austen has become so conventionalised that they are incapable of tasting the acid in her lemon-drops; the same could be true of Mrs. Gaskell. Charlotte Brontë wrote to the author of *Cranford* that her book was 'graphic, pithy, penetrating, shrewd', besides being 'kind and indulgent'; it is time that the penetration of her art was given fuller attention. If *Cranford* is a novel of escape—Mrs. Gaskell's escape from the confining world of Manchester to pastoral Knutsford, the reader's escape from a depressing reality—then its psychological accuracy is strangely out of place in a genre noted for evasion and lack of observation in this direction (compare, for example, the work of a contemporary novelist like Monica Dickens). There is more to be said about Mrs. Gaskell; the fundamentally serious concerns of her book have been neglected for a belle-lettriste study of incidental detail. The force of the novel lies in plot, however, not in character. ⟨. . .⟩

It is well known, and may be easily deduced in the reading, that its author never intended that there should be more of *Cranford* than this story, which was first published as 'Our Society at Cranford' in *Household Words* for December 13, 1851. The story was so successful that Dickens persuaded Mrs. Gaskell to write more, and a further seven episodes of Cranford life appeared at irregular intervals in his magazine between 1851 and May 1853. In June of that year the stories were reprinted in a barely altered text under the title of *Cranford*.

How far do the stories form an artistic whole? Most readers seem to think of *Cranford* as a series of disconnected lavender-and-lace sketches, and yet there are signs that Mrs. Gaskell consciously set out to make her book a formal unity as soon as she had begun its second instalment, 'A Love Affair at Cranford', which comprises Chapters 3 and 4 of the finished work, and which first appeared on January 3, 1852. ⟨. . .⟩

The difficulty by which the critic is here faced, that is, of discovering the book's effective principle of unity, can surely be solved by a simple change of approach. Instead of treating *Cranford* as the literal representation of a series of actions that might really have taken place, he must rid his mind altogether of the knowledge that some of them did in fact take place, and treat the novel as symbolic of a conflict within the mind of the author. *Cranford* is a kind of trimmed and tidied dream, in which Mrs. Gaskell's unconscious hostility to the male struggles with her awareness of the pointlessness of such hostility in the predominantly masculine society of her day. ⟨. . .⟩

There are faults; to be completely satisfied, one would prefer, I think, an action that was also adequately motivated at a conscious level. Peter's return is certainly not managed with the greatest dexterity, but this cannot damage the book's central theme of adjustment to the reality-principle. It may be said that, in acquiescing to the masculine predominance of her day, Mrs. Gaskell is a quietist; but this is to misunderstand the novel, which has to do, not with the wrongs of the female at the hands of the male, but with the consequence of attempting to repress sexual needs under the cover of feminism. This may seem a very cumbersome exegesis of a simple fiction. While we acknowledge *Cranford*'s wit and good humour, however, it is not out of place to consider that these are the fruits of its author's own sanity and adjustment to the masculine world about her.

—Martin Dodsworth, "Women without Men at Cranford," *Essays in Criticism* (April 1963), excerpted in *The Critical Perspective*, Vol. 8, ed. Harold Bloom (New York: Chelsea House Publishers, 1989), 4527–28, 4531

EDGAR WHITE

Mrs. Gaskell had been writing for eight years, from 1847 to 1855, when *North and South* was published. Her remaining fiction was written in another eight-year period from 1858 to 1865, when the best of her work with the exception of *Cranford* was produced. It was a period when her writing carried steadily fewer traces of being written with a sense of obligation towards ideals of moral or public duty, and this freedom to write to suit herself is reflected in the range and tone of what she produced. The industrial world, with which she had never been really in sympathy, disappears from her work, and with it a good deal of the earnestness which had accompanied it; a disappearance reflected technically by the way in which the amount of direct comment lessens as well as in the nature of the authorial comment that remains. She can still be serious enough, but humour and pleasantness preponderate at the end, a reflection of the more relaxed attitude and the congenial world she treats of as she returns once again to describe the manners and idiosyncrasies of Cranford, or of a way of life closely related to its tradition and principles. There is an evident relish of delight as she observes the behaviour of her characters and their individual responses to convention within the social setting in which she was happiest, that of the small country community. Three of the important stories of this period, *My Lady Ludlow*, *Cousin Phillis* and *Wives and Daughters*, have both the humour and the setting. But the serious side of her nature, with its awareness of a darker side to life, finds expression in two others, 'Lois the Witch' and *Sylvia's Lovers*, and in them, something of the old earnestness of the moral sense demands attention. With the disappearance of the social description of the industrial contemporary scene her interest in historical and old-fashioned social life also becomes more apparent. ⟨. . .⟩

She concentrates on exploring with the full insight of her sensibility and experience the motives and feelings of her characters. While she remains the social historian of the small community, these novels and stories develop, without the pressure of ulterior issues, that interest in personal relationships which is at the heart of all her work; it is round the natural interplay of these relationships, unhampered by artificial manipulations of plot to suit a thesis, that they unfold. The underlying values and standards of conduct are still there but more and more assimilated within the behaviour and speech of the characters; *Cousin Phillis* and *Wives and Daughters* are surely two of the most convincingly natural novels in the English language. ⟨. . .⟩

Mrs. Gaskell's retreat from contemporary themes was thorough and permanent ⟨. . .⟩ Yet the idea of change and the concern for stability and continuity still remained with her. She concentrated now on the individual and the small community, giving full rein at last to her interest in the psychology of character and conduct, and noting, generally with quiet satire, the inconsistencies and self-deceptions which people bring to the business of living, as well as their oddities of behaviour. Social change and stability are considered first from their effect on the individual. But because they still occupy her, the past she deals with gradually moves toward the present again, while the social range extends until contrasts between sections and broad classes become as important as those between individuals and types. So it is that much of the work of this period has for its setting a more or a less immediate past, in which the transition from an older generation through the fictional 'present' can be explored in terms of social comedy, with the conclusion looking forward to a future which was in fact Mrs. Gaskell's own present.

    —Edgar White, "Manchester Abandoned: *The Life of Charlotte Brontë, My Lady Ludlow*," *Mrs. Gaskell: The Basis for Reassessment* (1965), excerpted in *The Critical Perspective*, Vol. 8, ed. Harold Bloom (New York: Chelsea House Publishers, 1989), 4531, 4533

CORAL LANSBURY

It has become fashionable in recent literary criticism to regard *Wives and Daughters* as a comedy of manners, a work set apart in style and content from the rest of Elizabeth Gaskell's novels. *Mary Barton, Ruth* and *North and South* are considered to be social problem novels, while *Wives and Daughters* is seen as a pleasant excursion by Elizabeth Gaskell to the faraway world of her childhood with Jane Austen as her travelling companion. And yet this novel embodies the crisis in English life that endures to the present day. Industry still functions in a fashion reminiscent of a country estate, as though Melton Mowbray had quietly imposed its standards upon a city like Manchester. Nothing would have seemed more absurd to the Victorian observer than to state that the industrial city was being run like a rural village, but this was the case. What worked inefficiently in the country failed to work at all in the city. Industrial managers thought of themselves as country squires in a landscape of machines instead of cows, and while poets mourned the loss of rural values, it was precisely these values, translated to the city, that were to shackle the new society to the past. It was a process assisted by the long tradition of finding peace in the country and problems in the town. Men who had forgotten the Rebecca Riots and Captain Swing now felt that if only the methods of the farm could be applied to the factory then concord and harmony would prevail. Only recently have social historians stated that the Manchester of Victorian England can only be properly defined when it is seen as part of an agricultural community belonging to the eighteenth century. ⟨. . .⟩

    Far from being a romantic breezy novel of the countryside, *Wives and Daughters* never looks at scenery without seeing economic value. Nature does not provide a sense of release but entails responsibilities and financial rewards. Squire Hamley loves the old trees under which he played as a boy, but he never forgets their worth as timber. There is a sense of constriction in the novel as great as that of the narrow streets of Manchester. Those who live in the country and by it, never cease to be aware of its worth in cash terms. ⟨. . .⟩

Unlike the romantic's vision of the country where people live untroubled by the pettifogging cares of commerce, Elizabeth Gaskell sees a town like Hollingford and the countryside around it presided over by a spirit that is more mercenary than arcadian. Lady Cumnor and old Mrs Thornton had more in common than they would ever have cared to acknowledge, and the standards of Hollingford were not so alien to the attitudes of the Manchester manufacturers as men might imagine.

It is true there are romantics in the novel who see the land primarily as an inspiration for poetry. Mrs Hamley has taught Osborne to be oblivious to the material aspects of the countryside and to devote himself to its aesthetic qualities. The result is an enfeebled sense of reality and quantities of flaccid verse that Molly, as a young girl, finds most affecting. Osborne professes to care nothing for the pursuit of agriculture, but he cannot support himself without the allowance derived from the estate. In many ways his attitude to the country is less appealing than that of Sheepshanks and Preston, who make no pretence of despising the source of their income.

There is one man who sees the country around him in quite a different fashion from the farmers and country gentry. Roger Hamley is a scientist, a naturalist bent on exploring a world in which his fellows stumble like blind and deaf cripples. ⟨. . .⟩

Nature existed in its own right for Roger Hamley and he saw it without the acquisitive and predatory gaze of country folk. It was an attitude that bemused his father and convinced others of his inherent stupidity or lack of sensitivity. For romantics, nature existed to complement or arouse human emotions; for farmers, it was a source of income. The scientist is the intruder into this settled rural society, disturbing customary values, and subtly changing people's vision of the world, just as Roger teaches Molly to see a different landscape. Roger Hamley, in appearance and vocation, was Elizabeth Gaskell's close friend and relative Charles Darwin. Like Darwin, who used to come home at dawn with the foxes from his long nocturnal rambles, Roger neither exploits nor abuses nature. His greatest joy is to explore it. ⟨. . .⟩

Mrs. Gibson and Squire Hamley remain as unconscious as ever to the force of change that Roger Hamley represents in science and society. But the Cumnors are more astute and Lord Hollingford, the Cumnor heir, is already a friend and associate of Roger Hamley. Unlike Osborne who dies dreaming of making a name for himself as a lyric poet, Hollingford contemplates leaving politics for science. It is a question of survival, and there is little doubt in the novel that the process of natural selection has operated in favour of Hollingford and Roger Hamley. Evolutionary theories are implicit in *Wives and Daughters* as heredity and individual will struggle to produce a human being with the strength to survive in society and ultimately change it.

> —Coral Lansbury, "Wives and Daughters: The Economic Landscape," *Elizabeth Gaskell: The Novel of Social Crisis* (1975), excerpted in *The Critical Perspective*, Vol. 8, ed. Harold Bloom (New York: Chelsea House Publishers, 1989), 4536, 4539–40

JOHN LUCAS

Like most of her contemporaries, Mrs. Gaskell is obsessed with the past. In particular she broods over that which recedes and becomes remote, ways of life from which we feel ourselves to be cut off. Memory alone preserves such ways and there is no doubt that for nineteenth-century writers memory takes on a radically new significance. It is the only means by which some kind of continuity or link with the past can be established and, as a result of which, identity (familial, personal, social) can be grounded in more than simple assertion. Memory is activated by an entirely new awareness of what change *is*: disruptive, likely to fracture and destroy any sense of connection and continuity. ⟨. . .⟩

As with Wordsworth and Dickens, Mrs Gaskell is keenly aware of the frailty of the present's connection with the past, its inheritances and continuities. ⟨. . . T⟩hroughout *Sylvia's Lovers* Mrs Gaskell makes great use of dialect words and phrases, often pausing somewhat awkwardly to explain their meaning. More deeply, though, there is a sense in which she sees certain lifestyles as hopelessly at odds with social pressures which are inferior to them in worth and yet defeat them. And against that, the primly complacent official Mrs Gaskell occasionally bestirs herself. One recognizes her entry by a brisk no-nonsense air that comes over the prose, an insistence that the past is after all merely quaint and that we ought to give thanks for living in the present. 'It is astonishing to look back and find how differently constituted were the minds of most people fifty or sixty years ago; they felt, they understood, without going through reasoning or analytic processes, and if this was the case among the more educated people, of course it was still more so in the class to which Sylvia belonged' (ch. 28). No irony there.

Such a passage reveals of course that Mrs Gaskell was very conscious of George Elliot's approach to history and of her positivistically derived belief in social evolution. But though such an approach can sometimes be detected in *Sylvia's Lovers* it isn't at all part of Mrs Gaskell's historical imagination. In short that passage—and others are scattered among the novel's pages—feels very much at odds with the novel's prevailing tone. *Sylvia's Lovers* is set on the north

Yorkshire coast. The time is the 1790s and much of the action of the novel has to do with repeated attempts of a press-gang to take away local men for the war against France. The action serves a purpose: it dramatizes the ways in which values of town and rural communities, of law and freedom, collide, interlock, do battle; and how the battle ends in defeat for some, victory for others. ⟨. . .⟩

But the finest of the works under present consideration is without doubt *Cousin Phillis*. Indeed, having read and reread it some half-dozen times I am fairly sure that it is the most perfect story in the language. And, as with *Sylvia's Lovers*, so here, one is struck by the astonishingly tactful and truthful way in which Mrs Gaskell deals with inevitabilities of social change. But there is no interposed view in this lovely story, no allowance made for that liberal, conciliatory, account of conflict which occasionally threatens the achievement of the full-length novel. ⟨. . .⟩

Much of its perfection rests on Mrs Gaskell's wonderfully preserved neutrality, her scrupulous regard for the inevitability of what she has to record. There are no villains in this tale, nobody is to blame for the sadness and feeling of defeat that provide its dominant tone. Time, one might perhaps say, is the real villain. And yet we have to note that nobody in this tale is merely the victim of time. People exist in and through time, change and are changed. From the very beginning our attention is drawn to the fact and nature of change.

—John Lucas, "Mrs. Gaskell and the Nature of Social Change," *The Literature of Change: Studies in the Nineteenth-Century Provincial Novel* (New York: Barnes & Noble, 1977), 15, 17–18, 26–28

CATHERINE GALLAGHER

In one important respect, ⟨. . .⟩ Elizabeth Gaskell must be considered Harriet Martineau's heir: she intended John Barton's story, the story of a working man, to be a tragedy. "I had so long felt," she wrote in a letter, "that the bewildered life of an ignorant thoughtful man of strong power of sympathy, dwelling in a town so full of striking contrasts as this is, was a tragic poem, that in writing he was my 'hero.'" In several ways John Barton is a more successful working-class character than Martineau's William Allen, for many of Allen's characteristics seem inappropriate to a worker. His heroism relies, for example, on an elevated style of speaking, while Barton's tragic heroism gains poignancy from his working-class dialect. Adhering closely to classical models, Martineau presents Allen as far superior to other members of his class: she stresses how unusual his forbearance and intelligence are, and even makes him the victim of the striking workers. Barton, on the other hand, is presented as a typical worker. Indeed, his typicality is precisely what makes his story an important one to tell: "There are many such whose lives are tragic poems," Gaskell wrote, "which cannot take formal language." Moreover, Gaskell did not adopt the reversed chronology of Martineau's fiction, her tendency to reveal the ending at the beginning of the story, destroying suspense and precluding catharsis. In fact, Gaskell believed that the ordering of events was a major flaw in Martineau's work; she complained about one of Martineau's books that "The story is too like a history—one knows all along how it must end." Gaskell's own story, although it makes John Barton's decline seem inevitable, is not "like a history": she maintains suspense and seeks an intense emotional reaction from the reader. Barton has neither of Allen's defenses against suffering; he lacks both foreknowledge and stoicism. Barton thus seems more unequivocally victimized than did Allen.

Yet when the book came out, Gaskell complained that no one seemed to see her idea of a tragedy. She concluded that she had failed but could not identify the source of her failure. Her confusion is not surprising, for there are many ways in which Gaskell undercut her own intended tragic effects. One of these, a relatively minor one, reminds us again of the religious kinship between Gaskell and Harriet Martineau: the providential resolution of John Barton's story partly mitigates his tragedy. Although moral freedom was an increasingly important idea in Unitarian theology in the 1840s, Gaskell was still writing within a teleological tradition. John Barton feels responsible for his crime, but in the end the very intensity of his remorse leads to both his own and his enemy's spiritual regeneration. There is not even a hint of possible damnation in the novel; evil is eventually self-effacing and productive of good, although sin is not explicitly ordained by God. The close of Barton's life, therefore, hardly appears to be tragic; his life veers from its tragic course in the final episode, and readers are apt to agree with an early reviewer who complained that the ending was a religious homily, "twisted out of shape, to serve the didactic purpose of the author." ⟨. . .⟩

Unlike Harriet Martineau, Gaskell is not able to rest comfortably with the determinism she traces. Two obstacles present themselves: first, her idea of heroism entails moral freedom; and second, Gaskell's and Martineau's determinisms are of very different kinds. Martineau's does not explain the development of the protagonist's character. William Allen is a fully formed hero at the story's outset; the development of his character is unexplored and irrelevant to the story. He is a heroic, working-class *homo economicus* whose actions may be explained by his character, but whose character is not itself tragically determined. Gaskell's tragic vision, on the other hand, encompasses the formation and deformation of John Barton's character. Her social determinism is, in this sense, closer to Charlotte Elizabeth Tonna's than to Harriet Martineau's. Both use Robert Owen's brand of social theory, showing how the worker's environment and experiences shape his moral being. But unlike Tonna, Gaskell wishes to show us a worker who is a hero, not a monster; she wishes to give us a tragedy, not a freak show. As she traces Barton's inescapable decline, a decline that entails moral degeneration, she risks reducing him to a character without a will. In the words James Martineau used to describe the effects of Necessarianism, she almost "crushes" him "into a mere creature" with her causation. ⟨. . .⟩

The conclusion of John Barton's story points to narrative as an instrument of God's Providence without having to sort out the tangle of its own narrative threads. In the few episodes that remain, the characters settle in Canada, and the domestic tale is finally protected by distance from the tragedy caused by industrial vicissitudes. But the final episodes fail to settle the question that the novel repeatedly raises: the question of an appropriate narrative form. It is not surprising that, in Gaskell's words, no one "saw" her "idea of a tragic poem," for the tragedy is even more obscured by antagonistic interpretations at the end of the novel than in the early chapters. We must therefore agree with the author's judgment that she failed to express perfectly her tragic intentions. But we must also remember that her tragic purpose contained its own contradiction, which had definite historical roots in the Unitarianism of the 1840s and in certain features of the tradition of industrial social criticism that Gaskell inherited. We should also remember that her failure is the foundation of the book's formal significance, for its very generic eclecticism points toward the formal self-consciousness of later British realism.

—Catherine Gallagher, "Causality Versus Conscience: The Problem of Form in *Mary Barton*," *The Industrial Reformation of English Fiction: Social Discourse and Narrative Form 1832–1867* (1985), reprinted in *Victorian Fiction*, ed. Harold Bloom (New York: Chelsea House Publishers, 1989), 84–85, 91, 103–104

CHRISTINE L. KRUEGER

Recently, feminist and poststructuralist reading practices have enabled us to see the structural nonconformity of Gaskell's narratives, not as lapses of control or aesthetic failures, but as strategies for eluding and disrupting patriarchal plots. The result has been new appreciation for such eccentric fictions as "The Grey Woman" and "My Lady Ludlow." But it can also be argued that in those novels with apparently overdetermined plots and trite closures Gaskell likewise resists the myth of the harmonious social structures that these literary devices typically imply. Nowhere does she manage this disruption with greater vehemence and toward more radical ends than in her only historical novel, *Sylvia's Lovers* (1863). ⟨. . .⟩

The novel in fact points up the cost of its own aesthetic integrity. The last word on *Sylvia's Lovers*, I will argue, is precisely the wrench in the works for all attempts to make women's lives and stories conform with apparent ease to patriarchal plots. For one thing, what I take to be the last word, a speech spoken by Sylvia, comes, not at the novel's end, but six chapters earlier. This speech of defiance resonates throughout the novel, contorting its linear structure, resisting, contradicting its closure. Sylvia's version of her story ("I'm a woman as been wronged," as she puts it) does not admit of resolution—neither tragic nor comic closure. It becomes a tale of unremitting, unchanging pain and resentment. *Sylvia's Lovers* thereby resists the reigning Victorian definition of the novel, a definition that Nancy Armstrong has characterized as valorizing "fiction that authorized a particular form of domestic relations." Just as Sylvia's story cannot be pressed into the service of romance closure, it must be excluded from history—the legend of Sylvia with which the novel closes. In order for the romance plot of history to be resolved, the wrongs of woman must be ignored. The effect is to present the wronged woman, and thereby more sweepingly the "wrongs of woman," in inexorable opposition to any ideology or discourse that would figure women as willing or dutiful participants in their own subjection.

Moreover, the strategy of *Sylvia's Lovers* as a historical novel demands not only that we view its romantic closure with skepticism but that we apply the same critique to history itself. ⟨. . .⟩

Sylvia's Lovers suggests that such historical narratives had been characterized by an overriding imperative: to consolidate male power. What failed to serve this purpose was not history—could not be represented as having happened. What is more, women had been taught to relish their own obscurity. Gaskell's narrator remarks that Mrs. Robson felt "as if she would rather have had her child passed by in silence than so much noticed. Bell's opinion was, that it was creditable to a woman to go through life in the shadow of obscurity,—never named except in connexion with good housewifery, husband, or children." To be an object of public admiration, as Sylvia is, does not earn a woman the right to be represented as a historical agent, as it might for a man. Rather, as Nancy Armstrong comments regarding women's participation in the public sphere, such admiration always causes a woman to lose "her value as a subject." In fact, historical narratives are among the means by which women's sexuality is simultaneously constructed and covered over, as the wife is legally concealed in the identity of her husband. ⟨. . .⟩

The continuity of history ⟨. . .⟩ reminds us that in one tragic sense, women's history from the time of Wollstonecraft and her circle to Gaskell and such contemporaries as Caroline Norton, had changed little. The 1832

Reform Bill, from which novelists and historians alike dated the gradual, but ineluctable, progress of British society, did little to ameliorate women's lot. Caroline Norton's court battles with her husband in the 1830s, and again in the 1860s, equaled the persecutions experienced by eighteenth-century women seeking divorce, such as Wollstonecraft's *Maria* had dramatized. As Mary Poovey has argued, Norton could finally make sense of her own futile legal battles by turning them into romance. In *English Laws for Women in the Nineteenth Century* (1854), Norton achieved an imaginary happy ending by narrating her trial as a melodrama, wherein she could assume the power of the male judge and jury. Women's history certainly had continuity then, but unfortunately, outside fictionalized accounts, it did not have much in the way of plot development. Instead, the same disappointments, injustices, subjugations, were repeated with a dismal regularity. So, to write history—to write historical novels as Disraeli, Dickens, Newman, or George Eliot did—with faith in some force of rational, ameliorating change was to write history *as* romance, at least as far as women's history was concerned. In Gaskell's novelistic version of history, by contrast, an unrepentant woman, Sylvia, would have the last word. ⟨. . .⟩

In Gaskell's novel, there is no evidence that Sylvia's strategy brings about political change. The romance narrative resumes, apparently unimpeded, after Sylvia's speech, suggesting Gaskell's awareness that at this historical moment there is yet no real base from which to attack patriarchy. Writing at a similar historical moment, Gaskell may place Sylvia's speech six chapters from the novel's close as a way of declaring, "and now I said my last [openly radical] word." Nevertheless, if, as I suggested above, Gaskell hoped that future readers would be compelled to read beyond the ending, she has succeeded. Now that a feminist movement has begun to transform both narrative and political realities, Sylvia's speech obviously pervades and disrupts the novel's overdetermined patriarchal closure.

—Christine L. Krueger, "'Speaking Like a Woman': How to Have the Last Word on *Sylvia's Lovers*," *Famous Last Words: Changes in Gender and Narrative Closure*, ed. Alison Booth (Charlottesville: University Press of Virginia, 1993), 136, 138, 140, 143–44, 150

RAE ROSENTHAL

In her landmark essay, "Feminist Criticism in the Wilderness," Elaine Showalter explains that outside of the dominant male culture the muted women's culture has a space, a "wild zone," that "stands for the aspects of the female life-style which are outside of and unlike those of men" (262). According to Showalter, in an attempt to enlarge and endorse such spaces, "women writers have often imagined Amazon Utopias, cities or countries situated in the wild zone or on its border" (263). In a subsequent list of examples, Showalter cites first, "Gaskell's gentle *Cranford*" (263). And indeed, when read as an exploration of Showalter's wild zone, Elizabeth Gaskell's *Cranford* suddenly explodes with resounding power. This text, seemingly so innocent, now presents the most stirring of visions; it creates the possibility that the muted culture might accept its marginal space, reject the dominant culture, and establish itself as an alternate community—a feminist utopia—a separate and better world in which women live pacifically and where "good-will reigns among them to a considerable degree" (*Cranford* 40). ⟨. . .⟩

When establishing a definition of feminist literary utopias, scholars note, repeatedly, three distinguishing traits: emphasis on feminine values and issues, commitment to communalism, and an ability to overcome male intruders through either expulsion or conversion. ⟨. . .⟩

Clearly, the community of Cranford, as it has evolved by the end of the novel, corresponds closely to this appropriately collective definition of a feminist utopia. In Miss Matty, the most influential of the Cranfordians, we see the blend of the "marketplace and the humane hearth" of which Pearson speaks, and radiating from Miss Matty, we see the way in which the entire society gradually becomes immersed in feminine values, including generosity, connection, and above all, harmony. This desire of the Cranfordians for harmony, combined with their commitment to egalitarianism, leads to a communal system of governance whereby, in moments of crisis, they utilize a "politics of consensus" in order to resolve their difficulties collectively. The development and implementation of such a system proves them to be truly, what Kessler describes as "responsibly communitarian" (*Daring to Dream* 6). Cranford proves adept too at self-defense, in that it manages both to reject those males who cannot be co-opted and to convert to "mother consciousness" those outsiders, both male and female, who can. ⟨. . .⟩

As the text begins to foreground Matty, her femininity is brought into sharper focus by its constant differentiation from that of her late sister Deborah, and it quickly becomes clear that Matty possesses in abundance precisely what Deborah lacked most—a feminine soul, one that attaches itself readily and communes well with others. ⟨. . .⟩

Significantly, the characteristics that distinguish Matty from her sister—support of feminine values, commitment to communalism, and the ability to influence others in the adoption of feminine values—are precisely those that scholars associate with feminist utopias in general. Yet Matty shows little evidence of being a feminist if we accept the nineteenth-century definition of feminism, as outlined by Mary Wollstonecraft in *Vindication of the Rights of*

Woman: according to Wollstonecraft, feminism is "a REVOLUTION in female manners" that devotes itself to the pursuit of "the rights which women in common with men ought to contend for" and the belief that "the sexual distinction which men have so warmly insisted upon, is arbitrary" (318–19). Matty actually evinces little interest in political issues, choosing rather to concern herself with matters relating directly to her small, homogeneous society. Nonetheless, by so thoroughly exemplifying and advocating feminine values and by contributing to the development of a female community based on those values, Matty does, albeit perhaps unconsciously, lead Cranford into an era of feminist utopianism and does thereby help to further the cause of feminism in general.

—Rae Rosenthal, "Gaskell's Feminist Utopia: The Cranfordians and the Reign of Goodwill," *Utopian and Science Fiction by Women: Worlds of Difference*, ed. Jane L. Donawerth and Carol A. Kolmerten (Syracuse, NY: Syracuse University Press, 1994), 73–74, 76, 79, 82–83

BIBLIOGRAPHY

Mary Barton, A Tale of Manchester Life (2 vols.). 1848.
The Moorland Cottage. 1850.
Libbie Marsh's Three Eras: A Lancashire Tale. 1850.
Cranford. 1853.
Ruth: A Novel (3 vols.). 1853.
North and South (2 vols.). 1855.
Hands and Heart and Bessy's Troubles at Home. 1855.
Lizzie Leigh and Other Tales. 1855.
The Life of Charlotte Brontë (2 vols.). 1857.
My Lady Ludlow: A Novel. 1855.
Round the Sofa (2 vols.). 1859.
Right at Last and Other Tales. 1860.
Lois the Witch and Other Tales. 1861.
A Dark Night's Work. 1863.
Sylvia's Lovers (3 vols.). 1863.
Cousin Phillis: A Tale. 1864.
The Grey Woman and Other Tales. 1865.
Wives and Daughters: An Every-Day Story (2 vols.). 1866.
The Novels and Tales of Mrs. Gaskell (8 vols.). 1872–73.
The Works of Mrs. Gaskell (8 vols.). 1897.

The Novels and Tales of Mrs. Gaskell (11 vols.). 1906–19.

My Diary: The Early Years of my Daughter Marianne. (Privately printed by Clement Shorter). 1923.

The Letters of Mrs. Gaskell. 1966.

Mrs. Gaskell's Observation and Invention. 1970.

HARRIET MARTINEAU
1802-1876

HARRIET MARTINEAU was born on June 12, 1802, in Norwich, Norfolk. She was the sixth child of Thomas and Elizabeth Martineau. The Martineaus were Hugeunots who had emigrated to England to escape religious persecution. Martineau's father departed from the family profession of medicine and became a manufacturer of textiles, particularly bombazine. Harriet Martineau's early life was full of neglect and unhappiness. Shortly after her birth, she was sent to a wet nurse, where she suffered from semistarvation. As a girl, she was convinced that her parents did not love her. Her relationship with her mother was especially difficult, particularly since her mother appeared to prefer Harriet's sister Rachel. Harriet sought consolation in religion and literature—reading Milton at age seven and a few years later absorbing the works of Shakespeare. The deafness that was to mar her happiness (although she went to great lengths to accept it with equanimity) began around age 12, and in her early twenties her family's financial situation began to look bleak. Around that time, Martineau became engaged to John Worthington, apparently with some reluctance. She was spared marriage, however, when her fiancé died of "brain fever" in 1825.

After successfully publishing an article in the Unitarian periodical *The Monthly Repository*, Martineau hoped to earn her living as a writer. By 1829, her family's financial ruin was complete, and Martineau moved to London, where she attempted to find a market for her work. She was recalled home by her mother, who felt her daughter would do better to earn money from needlework. But after winning all three essay prizes in the *Repository* in 1830, she decided on a life of authorship. She had her first success with her *Illustrations of Political Economy* in 1832. Despite being savagely attacked by John Wilson Croker in the *Quarterly Review* in 1833, her *Illustrations* were extremely successful and established her reputation. Over the next few years, Martineau led an exhausting life. She was constantly writing and was also busy meeting many of the important writers of her day. She escaped the London scene by travelling in America from 1833–36. After publishing *Society in America* in 1837, Martineau demonstrated her great versatility as a writer in 1838 by publishing a novel, *Deerbrook*, and two works of nonfiction: *The Guide to Service* and *Retrospect of Western Travel*.

In 1839, she became ill and began a long period of invalidism at Tynemouth. Nevertheless, 1841 saw the publication of *The Hour and the*

Man, her fictionalized account of the career of Haitian revolutionary Toussaint L'Overture, and *The Playfellow*, her stories for children that are often considered her best fiction. After publishing *Life in the Sickroom* in 1844, Martineau was persuaded to try a mesmeric cure. She regained her health, but her public enthusiasm for mesmerism created something of a scandal and further strained her relations with her family. In 1846, she moved to the Knoll, at Ambleside in the Lake District, where she had built a house. That same year, she travelled to Egypt, which resulted in the publication of *Eastern Life, Past and Present* in 1848. While enjoying this period of good health, she wrote continually, took long walks, and supervised the workings of her farm. In 1854, however, Martineau once again began to experience symptoms of serious illness. Convinced that she did not have long to live, she began to write her autobiography. Since she had already asked her correspondents to destroy all her letters, the autobiography would be her only opportunity, she felt, to record her life for posterity. Although she was never to be truly well after this, her health did not prevent her from writing over the next decade. One effort was her collaboration with fellow invalid Florence Nightingale and Josephine Butler, "An Appeal to the Women of England" denouncing the Contagious Diseases Acts. In 1864 Martineau suffered a blow when Maria, her niece and companion, died from typhoid. The last work to be published in Martineau's lifetime was *Biographical Sketeches* (1869). Martineau died on June 27, 1876, having lived, despite her many infirmities, a long and full life. Her autobiography was published posthumously in 1877.

CRITICAL EXTRACTS

W. R. GREG

Her character was easy to read, for in one sense it was consistent enough and presented no mysteries or depths; and her faults, which were neither few nor small, were readily forgiven her, for she loved much and laboured hard for the happiness of others. In an unusual degree it was to be said of Harriet Martineau *qu'elle avait les défauts de ses qualités*. It would indeed have been difficult for her to have had the mental and moral gifts which distinguished her so signally without the analogous errors, in the way of deficiency or excess, which impaired their perfection and detracted from their value. "Authors," says

Southey, "may be divided into two classes, spiders and silk-worms—those who spin because they are empty, and those who spin because they are full." Miss Martineau was one of the latter. She never, after her very youthful years, wrote either for money or for fame. She wrote because the matter was borne in upon her, because the idea or the subject had taken possession of her, because the thing in her conception "wanted saying," and it was in her to say it, and was not open to her to withhold it. With the promptitude and force of irresistible conviction the work assumed in her mind the position of a duty to be done— almost of an inspired utterance that *must* be given forth. Hence the curious arrogance with which she resented the slightest approaches towards sugges- tion, remonstrance, or advice, the *noli me tangere* vehemence with which she insisted that no other mind should ever be permitted to interfere with the operations or visions of her own. Hence also the extraordinarily rapid imagi- nations she poured out, and the unhesitating confidence with which, when once written, she hurried them to the press. She not only would not alter at the suggestion of others; she would rarely if ever revise or correct in conse- quence of any caution or misgiving of her own. Misgiving seems, indeed, to have been a sensation that was alien to her constitution. Like Balaam, the word that the Lord put into her mouth, that she must speak. Her marvellous pro- ductiveness, the unequalled rapidity with which she turned out her admirable stories, might well cultivate her self-confidence to an extravagant degree. No one who worked so quickly or so hard ever worked so well. It seemed almost—quite so to herself—"as if it were given her in that same hour what she should say." There was no long brooding, no meditation, no slow process of hatching inchoate germs, no painful collection of ample and carefully sifted materials; the plan and the table of contents of her books, as it were, flashed upon her like the intuitions of a poet; the executive efficiency of her intelli- gence was absolutely unrivalled; her style was always, nearly from the outset, clear, lucid, vigorous, and simple, without a trace of effort, and never, as far as we remember, betraying the faintest lapse into those faults of fine or ambitious writing which are the besetting sin of youth. ⟨. . .⟩

Given, then, a mind of really almost unrivalled innate powers, and, as was inevitable, a strong consciousness of those powers and an irrepressible impulse to use them, a vivid imagination incessantly at work, and—owning partly to deafness and partly to the early want of exuberant sympathies around her— working usually in solitude; courage, fortitude, and pertinacity of something like the Stoic stamp, a force of conviction akin to that of the fanatic and the martyr, an impatience of temperament amounting to a sort of incapacity for doubt, and rendering suspension of judgment an unnatural frame of mind— and the fair analyst of character is driven to pronounce that Harriet Martineau could not easily have been less dogmatic, less hasty, or less imperious than she was. One grievous mistake—the parent of countless errors and injustices—she might indeed have escaped, and it is strange that so clear an intelligence as hers should have become so habitually its victim; for the rock was staringly above water. Her deafness absolutely disqualified her either for accurate observation or positive judgments of men—yet she never appears to have dreamed of the disqualification. In society she heard only what was directly intended for her, and moreover only what was specially designed to pass down her trumpet; and comments, sentiments, and statements that must go through this ordeal are inevitably manufactured, or at least modified for export. A hundred things are *dropped* or whispered which are never shouted, or pronounced *ore rotundo* or oracularly—and these former are precisely the things which betray character and suggest true conclusions. As Sydney Smith remarked in reference to her, 'she took *au sérieux* half the sayings I meant as mystifications.' Moreover, not only was she not on her guard against this obviously fertile source of blunders—not only did it inspire no sense of misgiving—but she aggravated its unavoidable mischief by a practice, which grew upon her as life went on, of laying down the trumpet before the sentence or the paragraph of her interlocutor was complete, or sometimes, we must add, when she had decided that it would not be worth listening to, or when it was apparently tending in an unwelcome direction. Thus the information or impression conveyed to her by a conversation was often altogether inaccurate or imperfect, but never on that account for one instant mistrusted. Those who knew her were fully aware of this peculiarity, and those of her readers who remember the times, and scenes, and people of whom she writes can trace innumerable instances of it, and will be on their guard against too absolute a reliance on narratives and statements written down twenty years after date, then printed and laid up in lavender for another twenty years, and now in many cases out of reach of authoritative correction.

—W. R. Greg, "Harriet Martineau" (1877), *Miscellaneous Essays* (1882), excerpted in *The New Moulton's Library of Literary Criticism*, Vol. 9, ed. Harold Bloom (New York: Chelsea House Publishers, 1989), 5009–10

Margaret Oliphant

Deerbrook is a much more worthy production as a work of art than the Political Economy series; yet but for the Political Economy series it would have lasted its year or two, as many a work as deserving has done, and then dropped into the limbo where a great many works of art, good, but not great, are *sospesi*, like the great heathen world in the *Inferno*. It has not a single feature of greatness in it. The character of the hero, Miss Martineau herself informs us, was "drawn from" an American friend—which is of itself an infallible guarantee of mediocrity; and the story is that of another friend. It is the history of one of those mistakes occurring rarely in life, and every disagreeable to meet with in fiction, which, however, are tempting enough to some imaginations. The hero of a village circle, a young doctor, falls in love with the younger of two sisters who come suddenly into the little place; but by force of representation on the part of friends, and certain signs of preference shown by the young lady herself, proposes to, and marries the elder, while still passionately attached to her sister, who, however, knows nothing of this, and continues to live with the married pair. This situation, however, affords but little of the play of the story, being too evidently dangerous ground for the treatment of a writer so little experienced in passion. And the chief dramatic action is occasioned by a perfectly causeless persecution got up against the doctor, who, there being no possible foundation for it, lives through it triumphantly, learns to love his wife, and becomes eventually as happy as so high-principled and well-balanced a man has a right to expect to be. The curious unnecessariness of the whole, the feebleness of the arguments which induce Hope to run the risk of breaking his own heart to make Hester happy, and the mere nothings which move the other lover to wring the heart of the exemplary Margaret, are quite remarkable evidences of the weakness of fiction when it is, as in this case, an elaborate manufacture—the only *raison d'être* of the party of people thus exhibited being that Miss Martineau wished to write a novel, not that her imagination naturally framed itself into those everlasting variations of the story of human life which genius has in its own heart. The novel called the *Man and the Hour*, and embodying the story of Toussaint l'Ouverture, the black hero of St Domingo, we have not read—and the author herself seems to have considered it the better of the two; but it made less impression upon the public. Infinitely better and finer is the little story which was written after Miss Martineau fell ill, and which is, in our judgment, the only one of her productions which specially deserves to live, the beautiful little idyll of the north, called *Feats on the Fiord*. It adds, of course, to the wonder of this little book that its author never was in the country which she describes with so much freshness and power; but this is but a vulgar wonder after all, and the book itself requires no such adventitious recommendation. It has its "object," for it was impossible for Miss Martineau to write without one; but as this is the vaporous object of discouraging superstition, it does no particular harm to the tale, which, with its salt fiords and grassy mountains, the breath of the cows, and the glimmer of the sea, is really beautiful. The other works of the same little series, which was called the "Playfellow," are very inferior, though children still like *The Crofton Boys* and the *Settlers at Home*. For the first and only time in her life, a spark of genius seems by some charm of wandering reflection to have communicated itself to the steady good workmanship and well-selected material, lighting up this one little volume as nothing else from the same hand had ever been lighted up; but the author seems completely unaware of the difference. She is pleased that people were so much impressed by it as to wonder and hold up their hands in amazement when they heard she had never been in Norway; but of the other wonder, which seems to us so much greater, she knows nothing at all.

— Margaret Oliphant, "Harriet Martineau," *Blackwood's Edinburgh Magazine* (April 1877), excerpted in *The New Moulton's Library of Literary Criticism*, Vol. 9, ed. Harold Bloom (New York: Chelsea House Pulishers, 1989), 5011–12

R. BRIMLEY JOHNSON

Miss Martineau was herself, indeed, in no sense of the word a scholar. In the strangely frank biography of herself, which she prepared for the *Daily News*, she confessed that "her original power was nothing more than was due to earnestness and intellectual clearness within a certain range. With small imaginative and suggestive powers, and therefore nothing approaching to genius, she could see clearly what she did see, and give a clear expression to what she had to say. In short, she could popularise, while she could neither discover nor invent. She could sympathise with other people's views, and was too facile in doing so; and she could obtain and keep a firm grasp of her own, and, moreover, she could make them understood." Her talents were those of a first-class journalist and, without obtaining a thorough grasp or profound knowledge of any subject, she completely satisfied the demand for information at any price just then so prevalent.

She could tell her readers what they ought to think and know without troubling them to go through any process of reasoning for themselves, and thus it was that philosophers welcomed her abstracts or illustrative tales, that politicians requested her to write up their projected measures, that newspaper editors continually "asked for more," and that nations entreated her to justify them in the eyes of the English people. She had a phenomenal capacity for hard work, and a marvellous power of rapidly assimilating impressions; so that her most hasty digests have an air of lucidity and completeness. Her style is admirable of its kind, clear, rapid, and concise; the phrases pithy and suggestive, the sentences well modulated, the thoughts definite and sincere. Her facility increased with practice, and the *Biographical Sketches* have been justly called "masterpieces in the style of the vignette." They are, indeed, telling portraits of character, but it must be admitted that, in manner at least, Miss Martineau's judgments are sometimes over-confident and pugnacious, partly perhaps because she knew herself to be, as a woman, in advance of her contemporaries, and had suffered from the fact.

The Hour and the Man is a clever historical romance, some of the characters in *Deerbrook* are well drawn, and all right-minded children must love the

Playfellow series, but, as she herself admits, "the artistic aim and qualifications were absent; she had no power of dramatic construction; nor the poetic inspiration on the one hand, nor critical calculation on the other, without which no work of the imagination can live . . . none of her novels or tales have, or ever had, in the eyes of good judges or in her own, any character of permanence." Her gift to literature was for her own generation. She is the exponent of the infant century in many branches of thought:—its eager and sanguine philanthropy, its awakening interest in history and science, its rigid and prosaic philosophy.

But her genuine humanity and real moral earnestness give a value to her more personal utterances, which do not lose their charm with the lapse of time. After stating that we have no right to crave for personal immortality, she adds:—"The real and justifiable and honourable subject of interest to human beings, living or dying, is the welfare of their fellows, surrounding them or surviving them. About this I do care and supremely." Her care for men included a care for "faith, the noblest of human faculties." However persistently she might run counter to the orthodoxies of her day, the most striking characteristics of that admirable book of travel, *Eastern Life: Past and Present*, for instance, is its reverence—its reverence for what has made men noble in the past, and is therefore, to her mind, permanently worthy of honour. Her hatred of slavery and of other social evils nearer home enabled her to join hands with some whom the world called fanatics, while her "own idea of an innocent and happy life was a home of her own among poor improvable neighbours, with young servants whom she might train and attach to herself." The postman who scribbled "try Miss Martineau" on an envelope addressed to "The Queen of modern Philanthropists" was not deceived in his estimate.

—R. Brimley Johnson, "Harriet Martineau," *English Prose* (1895), excerpted in *The New Moulton's Library of Literary Criticism*, Vol. 9, ed. Harold Bloom (New York: Chelsea House Pulishers, 1989), 5006

LOUIS CAZAMIAN

When Miss Martineau's first stories were published in 1832, informed opinions stood thus: the masses suffer because they do not understand the laws regulating society; all their misery springs from these inexorable socio-economic laws, and if they really want to attack the social order they must first understand it. Therefore it would be a useful and noble work to show them where their mistakes lie. ⟨. . .⟩

To read one of Miss Martineau's stories is to know them all. The same artistic inadequacy runs throughout the series. The style is prosy; the characters are pedantic assemblages of parts; the incidents are unconvincing; the whole effect is lifeless. These failings were inevitable, and Miss Martineau actually deserves respect for having kept them to a minimum. Her language is clear, her structure logical, and the abstract ideas she handles are deftly simplified. Indeed, in this last respect she worked miracles: Ricardo's entire theory of rent is expounded and summarised through two simple, ignorant inhabitants of the Orkneys. And among all the poor writing there are some interesting passages which carry a universal message and explain the success of the series. ⟨. . .⟩

The bourgeois mind's practical energy had a challenging vigour whose very strength made it beautiful. But it was also a mind containing pettiness and cruelty, and this too can be deduced from Miss Martineau's work. We might conclude from 'Life in the Wilds' that the following characteristics were typical of her class: a smug acquiescence in established conventions, including social inequality; a tacit admission that material values are the only ones that count; an utter lack of idealism. Stone, the chaplain to the colonists, thanks Providence for the fact that 'we know we have only to work . . . to provide ourselves and our child with all that is necessary now, and with comforts and luxuries by and by.' A child dies of snakebite, and 'it was an affecting thing to observe how George was missed by everybody,' comments the author; 'a sure sign what a valuable member of society he had been.' The little band's efforts are ultimately rewarded by material prosperity: their storehouses are filled and their possessions replaced, and Adams, their leader, sums up the moral:

> Let us still be united, let us still be industrious. . . . Let us be tolerant of mere folly, and honour wisdom and reverence virtue, and we shall be sure of enjoying all the happiness a benignant Providence thinks good for us. Let us try whether it be not true of societies as well as of individuals, that Providence places their best happiness within their own reach.

This happiness consists of security: a roof overhead, a reserve for the future. It constitutes a decent, orderly society, but has no place for purely spiritual values or the dedicated pursuit of social justice. ⟨. . .⟩

All the evidence is that she was accepted instantly. Each monthly part of the *Illustrations* sold more than 10,000 copies. The author was unknown one day, and the celebrity of the moment the next. Polite society talked about her; politicians wanted to meet her. Hallam, Sydney Smith, Malthus, Bulwer, and the Mills, the leaders of the liberal coalition, became her friends. Lord Brougham supplied documents in support of her plans for stories on the Poor Law; Malthus paid a special visit to thank her for her work. Even Robert Owen tried hopefully to win the brilliant writer to his cause. ⟨. . .⟩

So she was widely read. But did she persuade any readers who were not already convinced political economists? Charles Knight, the liberal historian, wrote thirty years later that her literary skill 'excited the admiration of thousands of readers, who rose from the perusal of her monthly volumes without the "Principles" having taken the slightest hold upon their minds.' On the other hand, he conceded that the *Illustrations* influenced the development of the social novel:

> Nevertheless, we hold these remarkable little books to have, in a
> considerable degree, led the way in the growing tendency of all
> novel-writing to extend the area of its search for materials upon
> which to build a story, and to keep in view the characteristic relations
> of rich and poor, of educated and uneducated, of virtuous and vicious,
> in our complicated state of society.

Miss Martineau had unwittingly prepared the ground for Dickens and Kingsley.
    —Louis Cazamian, *The Social Novel in England 1830–1850: Dickens, Disraeli, Mrs. Gaskell, Kingsley*, translated by Martin Fido (Boston: Routledge & Kegan Paul, 1973), 51, 55–56, 58–59

VALERIE KOSSEW PICHANICK

The Hour and the Man, though lacking depth as a novel, succeeded in capturing the impassioned spirit of late eighteenth-century French colonial Haiti. The story was about the island's struggle for independence from white domination, and in it Martineau probably came closer to endorsing revolution than at any other time. Toussaint was the symbol of black liberty. He knew that for his people the choice was either "slavery or self-defence," and that by his own eventual overthrow only the trunk "of the tree of negro liberty is laid low. . . . It will shoot again from the roots, they are many and deep." But although she sympathized with the problem of black bondage, Martineau was not personally familiar with black Haitians, and her characters lacked ethnic authenticity. She was interested primarily in promoting the cause of emancipation and racial equality, and if her urbane, philosophical Toussaint more than slightly resembled Shakespeare's noble Moor, it was probably because she wanted to convince her white readers of the essential dignity of the black man. ⟨. . .⟩

Much more popular than the Haitian novel was Martineau's *Playfellow* series of four children's books published between 1841 and 1843. To the modern reader the stores seem morbid and moralistic, but Martineau's contemporaries of all ages enjoyed the *Playfellow* stories enormously. These were not her first venture into children's literature; her earliest children's fiction—the obscure *Principle and Practice; or, the Orphan Family*—having been published in 1827 anonymously. In this early novella, five orphaned children survived heroically under the guidance and influence of the eldest who "has had so much to do and bear, that she has learned not to look from side to side in hope and fear, but to go on, straight forwards, in the road to duty, whether an easy one or not." This same sentiment pervaded all the *Playfellow* stories except *The Prince* which was based on the tragic life of the young dauphin of revolutionary France and which was the only nonfictional tale of the four. The other three stories were all about children who succeeded in overcoming enormous odds without any significant adult assistance. The Robinson Crusoe element—so popular in the nineteenth century, especially with the middle class—was especially strong in *Settlers at Home* and to a lesser extent in *Feats on the Fiord*, where resourceful children were pitted against the elements and forced to cope with hazards which threatened their very survival. *The Crofton Boys*, the most popular of the tales, was much closer to the experience of the average middle-class Victorian child. It was one of the earliest of English boarding-school stories, predating *Tom Brown's Schooldays*, which was not published until 1857.

Martineau had been driven to write her *Illustrations of Political Economy* by conviction as well as necessity, but her *Playfellow* stories seem to have been inspired mainly by necessity. Although at the time she regarded them as her final contribution to literature, she did not use them for any significant final radical gesture. In fact, it was probably because she was relying upon the income which she would derive from them that she chose to write in the conventional genre of the children's story and to express the conventional sentiments. In spite of her earnest social consciousness she did not choose, as Dickens was doing, to write about the underprivileged or abused child. Though she was concerned about the rearing of children and abhorred the still prevailing eighteenth-century convention of treating children like little adults, it was precisely as little adults that she depicted her boys and girls. Her small heroes and heroines bore premature responsibilities, were expected to act with the propriety of their elders, and were made to mouth proper and pious cant. Her necessarian logic and embryonic skepticism did not prevent her from expressing the usual religious dogmas and the belief in traditional prayer. Nor did her concern about the unequal role of women effect any concessions toward the conventional depiction of her little girls. The boys were the real heroes of her stories; the girls were simply passive bystanders or at best helpmeets. It was almost as if she went out of her way to avoid controversy and to give the public what it liked and expected.

—Valerie Kossew Pichanick, *Harriet Martineau: The Woman and Her Work, 1802–76* (Ann Arbor: University of Michigan Press, 1980), 125–27

GILLIAN THOMAS

Although the vast majority of Martineau's fiction is of interest to the modern reader because of the light it sheds on the history of the period rather than because of its literary merit, her novels and tales are chequered with episodes and passages which suggest that she narrowly missed becoming a Victorian novelist of some significance. Certainly her main preoccupations as a novelist and many of the characteristics of her fiction parallel those of other nineteenth-century writers with more significant achievements in fiction. Like Mrs. Gaskell, Dickens, and Charlotte Brontë she writes of unions, strikes, and the earlier machine-breaking phase of the industrial revolution. Like Scott, Bulwer Lytton, and other popular novelists of the period, she was attracted to historical subjects. The sense of place and the precise observation of social life in a small community in *Deerbrook* has much in common both with Gaskell's *Cranford* (1853) and the larger canvas of George Eliot's *Middlemarch* (1871–72). 〈. . .〉

Perhaps Martineau's greatest weakness as a writer of fiction is her indulgence in exposition where dramatization would have served her purpose better. Although direct addresses to the reader occur frequently in nineteenth-century novels, in the hands of a George Eliot or a Mrs. Gaskell, they exist as an integral part of the novel's structure since they spring from a narrative voice that is a fully realized persona in the novel. Martineau, on the other hand, often volunteers what sounds like an idiosyncratic personal opinion on the action. While she does not indulge in frequent authorial interventions of the "Dear reader" variety, she has a tendency to tell rather than show what she wants the reader to know about the characters. The action of the novels and tales only rarely fully embodies the ideas she wishes to incorporate and she is thus compelled to frame the action within passages of exposition to guarantee the reader's comprehension. 〈. . .〉

Martineau wrote in what many consider to be the Golden Age of novel writing, and we are therefore compelled to judge her fiction according to somewhat rigorous standards. The nineteenth-century novelists who are currently ranked highest in the critical pantheon are probably those who, like Dickens, provide a huge cast of characters, or, like George Eliot or Mrs. Gaskell, delineate a comprehensive relief map of the social landscape of the time. Martineau's fiction never aspires to this sort of scope. The election scenes in Deerbrook might, at times, be mistaken for the work of a writer like Mrs. Gaskell, but the dramatic realization frequently falters and drops into crude melodrama because she is so uncertain about the effect she is creating. Martineau lacks the sustained fictional power required to paint a large social canvas, nor, on the other hand, do we find in her fiction the passionate intensity of a Charlotte or Emily Brontë. Indeed Martineau, like many of her contemporaries, was strongly repulsed by Charlotte Brontë's most ambitious novel, *Villette*, precisely because its intensity seemed to her to come perilously close to morbidity. Her vision is essentially a cool and rational one, but one that lacks the comprehensiveness of a George Eliot or the intricate patterning of a Jane Austen.

Despite these shortcomings, her fiction is still of considerable interest to the serious student of nineteenth-century history and literature. While the modern general reader is usually impatient with obvious didactic or illustrative works, the serious student of the period will find a good deal to admire even in such works as *Illustrations of Political Economy*. *Deerbrook*, despite its unevenness, is of much greater interest and gives clear indications of a genuine and significant fictional gift. Martineau's only fully achieved works of fiction that can still be read for their strictly literary merit rather than their historical significance are *The Playfellow* stories and especially *The Crofton Boys*, which, alone among her fictional works, allows us to see the operation of a highly original intelligence on a vividly imagined fictional world.

—Gillian Thomas, "Martineau as a Fiction Writer: The Power and Scope of Her Fiction," *Harriet Martineau* (1985), excerpted in *The Critical Perspective*, Vol. 8, ed. Harold Bloom (New York: Chelsea House Publishers, 1989), 4693–95

GAYLE GRAHAM YATES

Martineau's position as a model for today's feminists or as an inspiration for female achievers is important. Alice S. Rossi's inclusion of Martineau's chapter on women from *Society in America* in her selection of classic feminist statements, *The Feminist Papers* (1973), indicates the current value of Martineau's thought. In presenting her chapter from Martineau, Rossi especially represents Martineau as a forerunner of the discipline of sociology.

Others could make such a claim for her relation to economics, though Martineau was a popularizer in that field, not an original thinker. Although it would be much too extravagant to claim a significant place for her as a fiction writer—her didactic tales, children's stories, and novel *Deerbrook* having small current readership—it is, nevertheless, important to note that she wrote a considerable amount of fiction. The most comprehensive "first" that Martineau accomplished as a woman was as a journalist, for besides earning her living from her early thirties by writing numerous popular books and many articles for major journals, she contributed, as mentioned, over 1,600 editorials to the London *Daily News* on an enormous range of political and social topics during the 1850s and 1860s.

The historian Janet Courtney, writing in the 1930s about the British women's movement in the 1830s, believed Harriet Martineau to be the leading feminist of the period. Courtney wrote, "And when I found Harriet Martineau, the ablest of them all, announcing that the best advocates of women's rights would be the successful professional women and the 'substantially successful authoresses,' I recognized that she had put in a nutshell the whole truth about the women's movement."

Courtney believed that in the 1830s women and women's rights made great advances only to fall back under the influence of Queen Victoria and the Victorians. Though Martineau did not write the passage Courtney selected until she wrote her *Autobiography* in 1855, faith in individual women's accomplishments was a central point of Martineau's feminism from the beginning.

The female role model idea is significant in Martineau's first published piece, "Female Writers of Practical Divinity," published in the Unitarian journal *Monthly Repository* in 1822. ⟨. . .⟩

In contradiction to her theme, however, she signed the article, "Discipulus," implying a male author, a practice she followed in pseudonym or textual voice off and on throughout her career in spite of the fame she gained in the 1830s writing in her own name. ⟨. . .⟩

Education for women was another theme Martineau pursued all her life. Her second published piece was on that topic. She was well aware early that intellectual occupation was not considered fitting for a girl, writing that "when I was young, it was not thought proper for young ladies to study very conspicuously; and especially with pen in hand. . . . and thus my first studies in philosophy were carried on with great care and reserve." Martineau's youthful writings suggested that women should be educated in order to enhance their companionship with men and improve their teaching of their own children, although she always advocated a rigorous course of study for girls, physical exercise for girls as well as boys, and domestic arts for women in addition to the program followed by males. Her feminist consciousness grew, and in later life, she encouraged the idea of education of women for its own sake and recommended a full program of advanced subjects. As a public figure in the press, she supported the establishment of the colleges for women in London, Queens College in Harley Street and the Ladies College in Bedford Square, of the first professional school of nursing at St. Thomas' Hospital in London, and of women's medical education.

Work for women was also a frequent theme. Martineau made a strong argument—amazing for the time—in favor of equal pay for equal work. Hers was not the literal argument still heard today that women should be paid the same amount of money for exactly the same jobs as men but was much stronger, insisting that equivalent labor deserves equal pay. ⟨. . .⟩

When Harriet Martineau was fifty-two, she wrote to all her correspondents asking them to address her henceforth as "Mrs.," but her request had nothing to do with marriage. It was an acknowledgment that greater respect was carried by the title "Mrs." than "Miss" and an assertion that she was entitled to such respect. This was resonant with the original meaning of the word "mistress," of which "Mrs." was first an abbreviation, a word that meant female authority in the household and had nothing to do with marital status. That meaning was largely gone by the end of the eighteenth century, but a few distinguished nineteenth-century single women like Martineau attempted to renew it, showing a sensitivity to the dignity conveyed by a title. Their attempts came from the same impulse that pressed feminists of the 1970s to introduce "Ms." as a general title by which a woman might be addressed whatever her marital status.

Martineau was outspoken about the degradation and limits imposed on women by marriage, but she was understandably ambivalent in some of her statements and contradictory in some of her behavior having to do with marriage. In her time and place where marriage was so definitively normative for women, the wonder is that she was at times so piercingly critical of marriage in general, not that most of the time she fostered and approved of specific marriages between people she knew. This too is more consistent with contemporary feminists' views of the disabilities of marriage than with those of Martineau's own time.

—Gayle Graham Yates, "Introduction: Harriet Martineau's Feminism," *Harriet Martineau on Women* (1985), excerpted in *The Critical Perspective*, Vol. 8, ed. Harold Bloom (New York: Chelsea House Publishers, 1989), 4696–97

VALERIE SANDERS

'I have read Miss Martineau on Sick rooms, but I cannot understand it, it is too sublime for me,' reported Sydney Smith. Appropriately, her next group of heroes are prisoners and invalids, weak children, and victims of revolutions, accidents, or natural disaster. Herself confined on two rooms, she described the misery of Toussaint L'Ouverture in his dungeon, a schoolboy whose foot has to be amputated, and the French Dauphin, imprisoned with his family. At the same time, her sickbed vision transcended barriers of place and age, floating her back into history, and out into unfamiliar regions of the world; to revolutionary Haiti and France, seventeenth-century England and eighteenth-century Norway. Her characters fought, navigated, scaled mountains, defended passes, and rescued each other from floods, while she herself lay marooned at Tynemouth, expecting death. Each story seemed to combine, even to reconcile, the opposite notions of activity and passivity, quiet patience and vigorous resistance, which were all aspects of her illness. Her brother-in-law, Thomas Greenhow, who was also her doctor, felt that her illness perhaps served 'in some degree to explain some of the peculiarities of character which were apparent during her remarkable career.' Certainly her experience of protracted invalidism, which she shared with many contemporaries, including Florence Nightingale and Elizabeth Barrett Browning, profoundly influenced her view of literature and life, compensating for physical weakness and imprisonment with a sense of newly-acquired moral and spiritual potency. The narrowing of her immediate vision to ladylike lodgings in Tynemouth only intensified her creative sympathy for the real and fictitious heroes of history; though as before, she offers no mitigating hand, no unexpected reprieve for those who emerge untainted. ⟨. . .⟩

Harriet Martineau's preoccupation with deformed, blind and deaf characters is worth comparing with later examples in the work of Charlotte Brontë, George Eliot, and Elizabeth Barrett Browning, who burned, blinded and maimed their heroes to complete their moral education. Partly punitive, these maimings may be a way of reducing arrogant heroes to a state of dependence akin to the heroine's, and by extension, to the woman writer's. Hugh, for example, has to abandon his ambition to be a soldier or sailor. He leaves the masculine atmosphere of school to be nursed, for a time, by his mother and sister, and depends on callers for news of the outside world. As Sally Mitchell puts it, in an article on women's leisure-reading in the 1860s, 'the victim-hero, though nominally masculine, often represents an essentially feminine predicament': exclusion from physical activity, dangers, adventures. Harriet Martineau usually plays down the punitive element that we find in *Jane Eyre* or *Aurora Leigh*, since she wanted to show how accidents inflicted by providence for the sufferer's good may test, educate and strengthen him. ⟨. . .⟩

Her sickroom experiences seemed to offer her a fresh and powerful insight into human problems; a heightened perception both of private and public affairs. She told Monckton Milnes about 'the advantage of the havock [sic] made among one's small complacencies,' 'the thorough reduction to essentials,' which she supposed few situations except sick solitude could offer as an experience. This serves in some way to explain the presence of another recurrent theme in *The Playfellow*: the test of sudden adversity, which snatches children from a familiar environment, and makes them struggle for survival, often through a literal 'reduction to essentials'. Unlike her first group of children's tales, from *Principle and Practice* to *Five Years of Youth*, which kept to plain, largely domestic settings (apart from Mr. Byerley's stay in a French prison), *The Playfellow* belies its happy-go-lucky title by subjecting its child-heroes to the most gruelling tests of religious faith and practical ingenuity in a hostile environment. Her *Settlers at Home* and *Feats on the Fiord* are child-sized *Robinson Crusoes*, relying for much of their interest on detailed accounts of meals eaten in rough conditions, snatched sleep and the discovery of new practical schemes. Above all, both tales emphasise the latent heroism of children who find themselves equal to Herculean calls on their self-reliance. ⟨. . .⟩

However debilitating, Harriet Martineau's illness became a valuable part of her experience, another aspect of her Carlylean reverence for heroism though her heroes, in fiction, as in history and present life, were often weak men forced, by circumstances, into positions of command and responsibility. Confinement had become a means of increasing her understanding, as she acknowledged in *Life in the Sick-Room*:

> When I think of what I have seen with my own eyes from one back window, in the few years of my illness; of how indescribably clear to me are many truths of life from my observation of the doings of the tenants of a single row of houses; it seems to me scarcely necessary to see more than the smallest sample, in order to analyse life in its entireness. (p. 85)

The 'one back window' lets her 'analyse life in its entireness': this passage neatly summarises the contradictions of her invalid state. But she had seen more than 'the smallest sample': she had been to America, and she was to visit Egypt and Palestine; she was to view miles of dramatic landscape from the tops of pyramids and mountains. Yet the freshly-discovered consciousness of her own insight and wisdom in relation to world-wide human problems seems to belong peculiarly to her chrysalis years at Tynemouth.

—Valerie Sanders, "A 'Pioneer in the Regions of Pain'," *Reason over Passion: Harriet Martineau and the Victorian Novel* (1986), excerpted in *The Critical Perspective*, Vol. 8, ed. Harold Bloom (New York: Chelsea House Publishers, 1989), 4698–701, 4704

LINDA H. PETERSON

Martineau sought to make it possible for women to write as sages by demonstrating their competence in masculine rhetoric, then by breaking down common (mis)assumptions about "masculine" versus "feminine" capacities. Her attempts frequently brought her up short against the problem that feminist theorists today debate about women's writing: whether women (inevitably or essentially) write differently or whether writing is (or can or should be) genderless. ⟨. . .⟩

Martineau's commitment to a genderless ideal for writing is evident in virtually all of her books, in the structure, style, and theoretical models she assumes. Her *Autobiography* takes the (genderless) form of a Comtean progression from theological to metaphysical to positivistic enlightenment. In the version of Comte's *Positive Philosophy* she translated two years before writing the *Autobiography*, she had argued the applicability of Comtean patterns to all human experience: ⟨. . .⟩

Similarly, in *Household Education* Martineau's advice implies a theory of developmental psychology that posits a sexless model of the human mind. This volume, intended to break from the practice of treating female education as a subject separate from male education, argues that the aim of all education should be "to bring out and strengthen and exercise all the powers given to every human being" (19). She acknowledges no differences between the "powers" of the two sexes and attacks older patriarchal schemes in which "women— half the race—were slighted" (19–20). Style reinforces theory. Examples featuring both girls and boys illustrate Martineau's commentary on the development of the powers (will, hope, fear, patience, love, veneration, truthfulness, conscientiousness). Anecdotes using men and women, or girls and boys, make points about intellectual training (of the perceptive, conceptive, reasoning, and imaginative faculties) and about the development of good habits. Throughout the text Martineau uses the now-common feminist technique of alternating masculine and feminine nouns and pronouns: a boy this, a girl that; she this, he that. The very fabric of this work makes differences between male and female, masculine and feminine, difficult to discern. ⟨. . .⟩

In reasoned prose and carefully balanced clauses, Martineau argues for— and simultaneously displays—the powers of the female mind. Her syllogisms cut through the irrationality of her opponents' position and show the superiority of her own logic.

The emphasis on logos, with a parallel deemphasis of pathos, contributes to a peculiarly unfeminine prose style. All is calm, rational, authoritative. In Martineau there are no outbursts, as there are in Charlotte Brontë's *Jane Eyre*, that rebel against the narrow lot of women—no pacing of attic halls in suppressed anger, no impassioned cries that "women feel just as men feel," that "they need exercise for their faculties, and a field for their efforts as much as their brothers do." So, too, in Martineau the depersonalization of examples contributes to a deliberately masculine (or defeminized) style. Many of the cases that illustrate arguments in *Household Education*, like the capacity of girls for abstract studies or their faithfulness to domestic chores, originate in Martineau's own experience as a female learner. Yet the personal knowledge that underlies the examples and syllogisms has been transformed into generalized principles and universal cases—into what might be called genderless rhetorical material.

Martineau's purpose, of course, is to gain access to traditionally masculine domains and to prove that women can master those domains, both in style and content. Her prose seeks to unsex the "masculine" and make it the perogative of both sexes. Thus in *Household Education*, as in many other of her works, she herself becomes a "masculine" female sage—but masculine only because the forms of discourse she uses traditionally have been associated with men, not because men possess any inherent or essential capacity to engage in logical, reasoned argument. That capacity surpasses biological sex or social gender.

> —Linda H. Peterson, "Harriet Martineau: Masculine Discourse, Famale Sage," *Victorian Sages and Cultural Discourse*, ed. Thais E. Morgan (New Brunswick: Rutgers University Press, 1990), 175–76, 178

SHELAGH HUNTER

Harriet Martineau's remarkable life forms a part of many overarching stories told and retold about the nineteenth century. Her name crops up in the collected letters of the famous, in accounts of the spread of phrenology and mesmerism, the early roots of sociology, the diffusion of popular education and the rise of the social novel. However interpreted, her story must be part of any history of nineteenth-century women and the growth of feminism. ⟨. . .⟩

Modern readers know her voluminous work from quoted snippets on a wide range of familiar and mid-century preoccupations, not to mention crazes. Slavery, taxation, religious toleration, the Corn Laws, the Poor laws, India, the Crimean war, the Civil War, the conditions of labour, the woman question— she took a stand on all these issues, was listened to by the uneducated and consulted by the powerful. Her life was conducted well within the norms of society, without a Scutari on the one hand, nor long-term adultery on the other. The gradual but determined independence she achieved in her role as daughter was celebrated by establishing her own domesticity in a house she built for herself, surrounding herself with surrogate daughters among her nieces and servants. Her life and work open a window onto the Victorian past we have inherited, but which in many of its aspects is as foreign as the remotest culture. Recognizing her journalist's finger on the pulse of the time, we may, for instance, be deterred by the seriousness of her concerns from dismissing as a mere comic fad a vociferous mid-life enthusiasm for mesmerism. Nevertheless, questions persist. What are we to think of a pioneer who prized both respectability and domesticity? Of a self-aware woman who listened to the 'Stern daughter of the Voice of God' before the dictates of passion? Of a free-thinker whose work advanced, above all else, Christian morality? Of an embryonic sociologist who expounded her theory in stories? The apparent anomalies must be accepted in their own terms if they are to be understood for what they were—a part of the revolutionary moment. ⟨. . .⟩

The woman who made her name popularizing the 'science' of Political Economy and found a philosophic home in a pragmatic Positivism may seem one of the odder manifestations of Romantic sensibility. But her 1851 declaration of apostasy, *Letters on the Laws of Man's Nature and Development*, has recently received its due as a representative document of its time in Diana Postlethwaite's *Making it Whole*, where it is shown to belong to the century-long Coleridgean search for organic unity. Among contemporaries, Carlyle shrewdly saw the motivating force in her personality when he first met her in the years of her London celebrity. He describes her with characteristic vigour, in a letter to Emerson (dated 1 June 1837), as 'one of the strangest phenomena to me . . . a genuine little Poetess, buckrammed, swathed like a mummy into Socinian and Political-Economy formulas; and yet verily alive inside of that'. 'Poetry', in this Victorian sense of an active unity of thought and feeling, is central to the mixture of the self-reflective and the performative in Harriet Martineau's characteristic work. ⟨. . .⟩

Written by an educated person for popular consumption, Harriet Martineau's works represent what Carlo Ginzburg calls a lost 'form of knowledge or understanding of the world' (Muir, p. xxi and n. 35). They share the culture of greater works, and while, lacking the 'plurality of significances' which Frank Kermode says makes a classic endlessly reinterpretable, they are most illuminating when embedded in the values of her time, they repay close reading with the evocation of that historical moment. ⟨. . .⟩

Precisely because this woman identified a waiting audience so accurately, we can see her simultaneously engaged in the variety of forms then available to occasional writing, with her own needs and the circumstances of her time. Actively inventing a self as she struggles to make a living and fulfil a self-appointed role, she necessarily alters the circumstances she finds, thus truly fulfilling, if without conscious intention, the role of a social pioneer.

—Shelagh Hunter, *Harriet Martineau: The Poetics of Moralism* (Aldershot, UK: Scolar Press, 1995), 7–8, 22, 24–25

BIBLIOGRAPHY

Devotional Exercises Consisting of Reflections and Prayers for the use of Young Persons: to which is added a Treatise on the Lord's Supper. By a Lady. 1823.

Addresses with Prayers and Original Hymns for the use of Families . . . By a Lady. 1826.

Principle and Practice; or, the Orphan Family: A Tale. 1827.

The Turn Out; or, Patience the Best Policy. 1829.

Traditions of Palestine. 1830.

Five Years of Youth; or, Sense and Sentiment! A Tale. 1831.

Poor Laws and Paupers (4 vols.). 1833–34.

Illustrations of Political Economy (9 vols.). 1834.

Christmas Day; or, The Friends. 1834.

Illustrations of Taxation (5 vols.). 1834.

The Hamlets. 1836.

Miscellanies. 1836.

Society in America (3 vols.). 1837.

Retrospect of Western Travel (3 vols.). 1838.

How to Observe: Morals and Manners. 1838.

Guide to Service. 1838.

My Servant Rachel. 1838.

Deerbrook: A Novel (3 vols.). 1839.

The Martyr Age in the United States. 1840.

The Playfellow (4 vols.). 1841.

The Hour and the Man (3 vols.). 1841.

Life in the Sickroom: Essays by an Invalid. 1844.

Dawn Island: A Tale. 1845.

Letters on Mesmerism. 1845.

Forest and Game Law Tales (3 vols.). 1845–46.

The Billow and the Rock. 1846.

Eastern Life, Present and Past (3 vols.). 1848.

Household Education. 1849.

History of England during the Thirty Year's Peace 1816–46 (4 vols.). 1849–50.

Two Letters on Cow-Keeping. 1850.

Half a Century of the British Empire: A History of the Kingdom of the People from 1800 to 1850, Part I. 1851.

Introduction to the History of the Peace from 1800 to 1815. 1851.

Letters on the Laws of Man's Nature and Development. 1851.

Merdhen, the Manor of the Eyrie, and Old Landmarks and Old Laws. 1852.

The Positive Philosophy of August Comte (2 vols.). 1853.

Letters from Ireland. 1853.

Guide to Windermere, with Tours to Neighbouring Lakes and Other Interesting Places. 1854.

A Complete Guide to the Eastern Lakes. 1855.

The Factory of Controversy: A Warning against Meddling Legislation. 1855.

Sketches from Life. 1856.

A History of the American Compromises. 1856.

Corporate Traditions and National Rights. 1857.

The "Manifest Destiny" of the American Union. 1857.

British Rule in India: A Historical Sketch. 1857.

Suggestions Towards the Future Government of India. 1858.

Endowed Schools. 1859.

England and Her Soldiers. 1859.

Health, Husbandry and Handicraft. 1861.

Biographical Sketches. 1869.

Harriet Martineau's Autobiography: With Memorials by Maria Weston Chapman (3 vols.). 1877.

The Hampdens: A Historette. 1880.

MARGARET OLIPHANT
1828-1897

MARGARET OLIPHANT was born Margaret Oliphant Wilson on April 1, 1828, at Wallyford, Scotland, near Edinburgh. Her father, Frances Wilson, was a civil servant whose work required the family to move frequently. Because he was both ineffectual and bad-tempered, Margaret looked to her mother for guidance. Margaret Wilson, a well-read and interesting conversationalist, was her daughter's most important influence during her early years. Though the family was Presbyterian, Margaret converted to the Anglican Church. She remained proud of her Scottish heritage, even though she lived in London for most of her life.

Margaret was a precocious child and her mother made sure she received a solid education. She wrote from a young age and when her brother Willie took her novel, *Margaret Maitland*, to Henry Coburn, it was accepted immediately. The work went into three editions, and at the age of twenty-one Margaret Wilson was off and running on a literary career that would span fifty years. In 1852 she married her cousin, Frank Oliphant, a painter and stained glass artist. In that same year, she also began her long association with the Blackwoods with the serialization of her novel, *Katie Stewart*. Over the years, she would contribute 267 articles, reviews, and pieces of fiction to *Blackwood's Magazine*.

For the next few years, Oliphant wrote novel after novel, earning about $400 for each. This was fortunate since her husband was proving to be a poor provider and Oliphant's brother William turned to her to help fund his drinking problem. The Oliphants' marriage was not a particularly happy one, yet it was preferable to what ensued after Frank Oliphant became terminally ill with tuberculosis. After taking the entire family on an ill-fated trip to Italy with the hope that the climate would improve his health, Frank died, leaving Margaret stranded, penniless, and seven months pregnant with their third child. To make matters worse, when Oliphant returned to London, she discovered that her fiction was no longer in demand. Her next work was rejected by *Blackwood's Magazine*, and she went home and wrote "The Executor," the first story of her *Chronicles of Carlingford*, which would prove to be her most lasting work.

In addition to reviews, articles, and non-Carlingford fiction, Oliphant wrote *Salem Chapel* (1863), *The Rector and the Doctor's Family* (1863), *The Perpetual Curate* (1864), and *Miss Marjoribanks* (1864). Over the next few years *Phoebe, Junior* (1876) would complete the Carlingford series. Around this time, Oliphant also published her biography of the Presbyterian minister Edward Irving (1862), which would be a standard of the genre. Indeed, Mrs. Oliphant was one of the most proflific of all Victorian novelists, publishing twice as many books as Anthony Trollope. She produced about two novels, ten articles (including her incisive reviews), and a story or nonfiction work each year, and somehow managed to maintain high artistic standards.

Despite her public successes, however, Oliphant continued to suffer private losses. In 1864, her daughter, Maggie, died in Rome. Her brother, Frank, was chronically ill and when his wife died he suffered a nervous collapse. From that point, he and his children were Oliphant's responsiblity. Oliphant's two remaining children, her sons Cyril and Cecco, disappointed their busy mother with their indolence. They died in 1890 and 1894 respectively, predeceasing their mother. Yet even though her family situation forced her to write continually out of financial necessity, Oliphant appears to have enjoyed her last years. She was a frequent traveler, and she enjoyed the company of many friends. During her final illness, she worked on her three-volume *Annals of a Publishing House: William Blackwood and His Sons*, which she never completed. She died of cancer on June 25, 1897. "Mrs. Oliphant," remarked one contemporary after her death, "is to the English world of letters what Victoria is to England."

CRITICAL EXTRACTS

W. ROBERTSON NICHOLL

It is of course as a novelist that Mrs. Oliphant did her work and earned her reputation. When one begins to specify particular books, it is easy to see that Mrs. Oliphant never wrote anything conspicuously above or conspicuously below her standard. In our judgment—a judgment which it must be confessed fluctuates on this point—*Phœbe Junior* is on the whole the best and most perfect of Mrs. Oliphant's works. It is the story of the clever daughter of a dissenting minister whose chapel, by the way, is evidently meant to be Regent's Park Baptist Chapel. There is very little padding in it, and the writer is almost at her best throughout. *Salem Chapel*, though very good in parts, is melodramatic and far from true to the phase of life described. Mrs. Oliphant became more and more Conservative as her days went on, and she had a certain contempt for dissent in every form. Perhaps the ablest of all her books is the powerful and painful story, *Agnes,* a story distinguished by one of those rare prefaces in which Mrs. Oliphant give us her own conception of her art. The writer in the *Times* specifies some of the Scotch novels, and picks out *Mrs. Margaret Maitland* as the best. *Katie Stewart* was a great favourite with Mr. John Blackwood, and for long in the Blackwood inner circle Mrs. Oliphant was affectionately known as "Katie." ⟨. . .⟩

Mrs. Oliphant's theory of life is consistent throughout. Her aspirations were after peace and quietness, but she persuaded herself, after long trail, that such things could not be. She delighted in picturing the life of leisurely ladies in the country, ladies with pleasant surroundings and ample means, with no spots upon their conscience, abiding in a soft established order that promised to endure, and in showing how into such haunts of rest trouble inevitably came—trouble from pecuniary loss, from wicked relatives, from the appearance of cancer, even, perhaps, from the impulses which arose strangely amid the hush and gentleness, and brought their bitter pangs. To one faith, however, she was unswervingly true—the faith that it is better to live in the full sense than to vegetate. Sorrow, pain, conflict, labour—she understood what these things were, but she deliberately elected to have them instead of a monotonous, imperturbed, solitary existence. For to suffer was to live. We hope that some one fit for the task will collect and digest from her books her excellent wisdom upon the conduct of life.

Mrs. Oliphant was much more than a novelist. She was an ambitious and, on the whole, not unsuccessful biographer. Her first biography was that of Edward Irving. As to its great interest, there can be no dispute. Many who knew Irving, however, do not think it rendered his career fairly. The writing and publication of the book brought her into close contact with leaders of the Church of Scotland, and among her subsequent productions in this line was the biography of Principal Tulloch, a biography which contained many charming passages, but which it is no secret some of those closest to Tulloch passionately disliked and disavowed. The very worst of all her biographies is that of Count Montalembert, but in fairness it has to be remembered that she was greatly restricted in her treatment. She was truly religious, but shrank from the more intimate expressions of her religious feeling. Perhaps her heart never opened itself so fully as in that beautiful book, *The Beleaguered City,* a book which had several companions not unworthy to stand beside it. She wrote toward the end of her life a rather poor little biography of her early hero, Dr. Chalmers. Of course, it could hardly be expected that she should treat ecclesiastical questions either with knowledge or with fairness; and she did not. Her personal associations with many ministers, especially with the late Dr. James Hamilton, were very close.

She was also a very great journalist and critic. Perhaps we should say magazinist rather than journalist. When she lived at Englefield Green, she formed a friendship with her neighbour, Mr. R. Hutton, of the *Spectator*, and the result was that she contributed many articles to his journal. When she had a concrete subject like Principal Tulloch, for example, she wrote very well, but in an evil hour she commenced a weekly *causerie*, called "A Commentary from an Easy Chair," which was a conspicuous failure, and had to be discontinued. In the *St. James's Gazette*, under Mr. Frederick Greenwood, she wrote similar articles with similar results. But when she took her pen in hand for *Blackwood*, she was at her greatest. She vivified the magazine by innumerable articles on men and books which had no parallel in any other periodical. In her, as the conductors of *Blackwood* observe in the just and generous notice which appears in the July number, they found one who more than any other maintained unimpaired the traditions of the magazine, and she will be sorely missed. She had an honourable pride in *Blackwood*, the only one of the great periodicals now left to us which has disdained to lower its standard, and to which we can still point as maintaining all the excellence of its brightest past.

—W. Robertson Nicholl, "Mrs. Oliphant," *Bookman* (August 1897), excerpted in *The New Moulton's Library of Literary Criticism*, Vol. 10, ed. Harold Bloom (New York: Chelsea House Publishers, 1989), 5925

GERTRUDE SLATER

Mrs. Oliphant is so exactly truthful that she has hardly had full praise given her for her truthfulness; her men and women are so absolutely the men and women of real life that it almost seems as if no art need have gone to their making: they are so very real that we have forgotten to call their creator a realist. Yet if by realism we mean, not a particular mannerism nor the acceptance of any particular catchword, but what it ought to mean, the habit of depicting men and women exactly as they are—a sight free from illusion, a hand inapt at exaggeration or suppression, and a disposition to use these gifts freely and simply—then there has never been a more uncompromising realist than Mrs. Oliphant.

No one is further than is she from making, or from trying to make, a flattering picture of life. She does not underline her sombre passages, or draw her readers' attention to the fact that in this or that personage she has ventured to draw an undilutedly bad character; but she is equally far from obeying the dictates of those very pessimistic readers who require their authors to look through frankly optimistic spectacles, paying human nature the very bad compliment of holding that it must be falsified to be made endurable. Mrs. Oliphant has never denied the shadows, and has introduced them into her pictures in due proportion; and when, now and then, she is in the mood to draw a bad character, how relentlessly truthful she can be! In all our fiction there is scarcely a more odious picture of unlovely old age than is given in *Old Mr. Tredgold*, published last year; and it is not the physical or mental weaknesses, the accidents of senility, that disgusts us, but the utter sordidness of the man's soul. And who, except Mrs. Oliphant, would have ventured on such a conclusion to this story, a conclusion so entirely at variance with the requirements of poetic justice? The old wretch has one daughter fully worthy of him, who, being offered a bribe to give up her lover, takes that bribe in order to elope with him more comfortably, and then, with a stupidity born of intense selfishness, cannot be made to believe that she is to be disinherited: nor indeed is she, for in the end the father dies with his long-planned piece of shameless injustice unrevoked, and the daughter who has stayed with him gets a pittance, while his wealth goes to her whom to mention in his presence was to provoke a string of curses. The family lawyer in the story wonders whether it was mere forgetfulness, or utter cynicism, that kept the old man from altering his will; at any rate, the conclusion is entirely in keeping with a book which, had it come from another author, would probably have provoked some protest for its sombreness. ⟨. . .⟩

Who but an immensely patient woman could have described with such minuteness, yet with never the merest suspicion of unkindness in her tone, that petty domestic tyranny, the tyranny of the weak over the strong, which is exemplified in *The Doctor's Family* and many a succeeding novel? She knows so well the futility of the sacrifices which the energetic little Nettie is so absorbed in making, and how hopeless is the struggle against the irremediable selfishness of Fred and his wife; yet no harshness creeps into her treatment of these poor creatures. Perhaps, had this story come late instead of early in her string of novels, the good fortune which relieves Nettie from her self-imposed burden might not have chanced so satisfactorily; but the general attitude, from first to last, remains unchanged. *Tout comprendre, c'est tout pardonner* is the noblest of mottoes; and this attitude of unwearied kindliness gives to Mrs. Oliphant as a novelist her most enduring claim on our faithful remembrance. ⟨. . .⟩

What a wonderfully full portrait-gallery hers is! If there are few portraits in it of very exceptional physiognomy, it embraces every variety of our everyday folk in their ordinary habit, and no artist has given these with more fidelity and minuteness. It might have been thought that this art, so unflinchingly truthful, yet so completely free from the spice of truth, satire, would not be sufficiently appreciated; but Mrs. Oliphant's early recognition by the reading public and her enduring popularity are happy tokens, and prove again, if further proof were necessary, that nothing in literature is so sure of success as honesty of workmanship. Mrs. Oliphant has followed the natural bent of her talent, making no concessions to the supposed demands of the public either on the point of sensation or of sentiment, and the result has shown her wisdom. Whether many generations will continue to hold her in remembrance, and, better still, to read her, is a matter on which it is idle to speculate; we ourselves allow so many novelists of so varied talent to lie forgotten on their shelves. But here again there seems to be no better merit in which to trust than this one of truthfulness. Where anything of the false has been allowed to creep in, though an author's contemporaries may like him the better for it, the flaw is bound to show in time; and it is just on these two sides, of sensation and sentiment, that the novelist is likely to be led into falsity. Dickens' wonderful exaggerations, full of genius as they are, already are turning that enchanted country of his into too much of a fairyland; and how unreadable is the stale sentiment of a Lytton! To put too much of even absolutely genuine sentiment into a book is a somewhat dangerous proceeding, and there are many fine passages in George Eliot's novels which one is half inclined to wish away for that reason. But Mrs. Oliphant has steered very clear of these two dangers; and while people continue to be interested in reading about men and women there seems to be no reason why they should not continue to read the books in which her men and women are so well described.

—Gertrude Slater, "Mrs. Oliphant as a Realist," *Westminster Review* (December 1897), excerpted in *The New Moulton's Library of Literary Criticism*, Vol. 10, ed. Harold Bloom (New York: Chelsea House Publishers, 1989), 5927–29

VINETA AND ROBERT A. COLBY

Mrs. Oliphant's Carlingford, like Barchester and Middlemarch, is a country of the mind. It lacks the breadth and depth of Middlemarch and the minute particularity of Barchester. On the one hand it is not, as is George Eliot's imagined community, a microcosm, a universalization of the whole pattern of Victorian provincial life. On the other, neither does it have a local habitation, as Trollope's community had in Salisbury, nor its precise geographical detail. It would be impossible to draw a map of Carlingford and difficult to illustrate the scenes and characters of the Carlingford novels. Yet the scenes are described with sufficient vividness so that Carlingford emerges as a place with an identity of its own. ⟨. . .⟩

Seven works of fiction comprise the Chronicles of Carlingford. Three, *The Executor*, *The Rector*, and *The Doctor's Family*, are long short stories. Indeed, *The Executor* and *The Doctor's Family* may claim to be part of the series only because they are set in Carlingford, but they form no real part of the Carlingford scheme. The longer novels are two which center mainly on clerical life, *Salem Chapel* (1863) and *The Perpetual Curate* (1864) with clergymen as their leading characters, and two which center mainly on social life in the community, *Miss Marjoribanks* (1866) and *Phoebe, Junior* (1876), with young women as their leading characters. With the exception of the last-named novel, they were all written within the five years 1861 to 1866, a period crowded with other literary activity (including two serious long novels, *Agnes* and *A Son of the Soil*, the biography of Edward Irving, the translation of Montalembert's *Monks of the West*, and a flood of contributions to *Maga* and other periodicals), with travel, personal triumph and tragedy. All, with the exception of *Phoebe, Junior*, were published by Blackwood, first serially in *Maga* and subsequently in book form. They were written in haste—from the first all-night vigil in which Mrs. Oliphant dashed off *The Executor* through the witty installments of *Miss Marjoribanks*, which she wrote during the months of restless travel in Europe in 1864 following the sudden death of her daughter Maggie. Haste of composition is apparent everywhere—repetition, minor inaccuracies of detail, looseness and diffuseness of structure, clumsy padding and stretching. Nevertheless, with all their faults the Carlingford novels reveal Mrs. Oliphant at her best. They are lively, clever, humorous, sharply observed. At times they rise to social comedy worthy of comparison with Trollope's. In their more serious aspects they treat of family life and religious vocation with dignity and insight. ⟨. . .⟩

The major theme which unites the three principal religious stories of the series is vocation for the priesthood. It is a subject so serious that one wonders at Mrs. Oliphant's daring to treat it at all. On closer examination one finds she was peculiarly well suited by background and by sympathy for the subject. Because of the popular success of *Salem Chapel* and the relative obscurity into which the other novels fell soon after their publication, it is generally assumed that the Carlingford series was about Dissenters and the Dissenting Church only. Mrs. Oliphant was not a Dissenter herself. Only *Salem Chapel* and *Phoebe, Junior* actually treat of the Dissenting movement. The Rector, in the story of that name, is a staunch member of the Church of England, as is the hero of *The Perpetual Curate;* and while some Low Church members figure amusingly in the latter novel, Dissent has no place in it. Indeed, it is the question of how High a man may go short of conversion to Roman Catholicism which is central in this work.

Still it is true that her picture of the Dissenting congregation of Salem Chapel was the great attraction of that novel for Victorian readers. This gave the book its ring of truth and of originality—an inside view of an independent congregation presented with candor and humor and with just enough snobbish condescension to appeal to a predominantly Church of England reading public for whom the popular image of the Dissenter was still a vulgar, hymn-singing tradesman. ⟨. . .⟩

By 1876 when *Phoebe, Junior* was published, Mrs. Oliphant herself had come a long way from her humble origins in Scotland, the dingy Scotch church in Liverpool where she had worshipped as a young girl, and the sententious moralizing of her first heroine, Mistress Margaret Maitland. Religion was and remained a serious issue with her. Indeed, her faith was so firm that she could view it critically and even satirically without risk. *Phoebe, Junior* concludes the Carlingford series with a slightly mocking laugh at Dissent. It is not a "religious novel" in the sense that *The Rector, Salem Chapel,* and *The Perpetual Curate* are religious novels, having clergymen and their spiritual problems at their centers. Instead, it reduces sectarianism to social comedy. What interested Mrs. Oliphant, and her readers, in *Phoebe, Junior* is no matter of church doctrine but of human behavior. If Mrs. Oliphant sees Dissent with cynical eyes, it is only because she is looking at society in the same way. And Carlingford, in its modest way, has made its contribution to the Victorian human comedy.

—Vineta and Robert A. Colby, *The Equivocal Virtue: Mrs. Oliphant and the Victorian Literary Market Place* (Archon Books, 1966), 41–46, 74

JOHN STOCK CLARKE

There may be some excuse for the neglect of Mrs. Oliphant; she was probably the most prolific novelist of the nineteenth century, publishing about ninety-six works of fiction besides many uncollected shorter stories; and to make a serious study of such a writer must seem an act of mere masochism. Could anybody who wrote so much maintain any literary standards at all? In fact Mrs. Oliphant does fully warrant close study; she did maintain high standards throughout her career, and in spite of what critics have said of her she never degenerated into a hack writer. She is very much within the great tradition of the nineteenth-century novel, and when she is in the right vein she handles this tradition—in particular, the tradition of ironic social observation inherited from Jane Austen—with intelligence, accepting and yet modifying it, as important writers always do.

Mostly histories of the novel ignore her or dismiss her with contempt. But lately Lucy Stebbins and Vineta and Robert Colby in America and Q. D. Leavis in this country have done some work on her; and her name has begun to appear in recent books on the novel. Lucy Stebbins has said of Mrs. Oliphant that she was 'the most inventive and the most versatile novelist of the century' and that 'her power of invention was probably greater than that of any other woman novelist of the century'. If these views are even partly true, then Mrs. Oliphant is grossly overdue for rediscovery; her place is not with Mrs. Henry Wood and Mrs. Craik and Charlotte Younge, but with Jane Austen, Mrs. Gaskell, George Eliot and the Brontës. ⟨. . .⟩

As a Scotswoman living for most of her creative life in England, Mrs. Oliphant took an ironically amused view of the class-obsessed world of the English. There is always a great affection in her view of English society, of which in her later books she shows a shrewd and accurate understanding; but the tone is usually that of an ironic observer, especially when she writes of the new aristocracy of money, trade and industry. Many of her books are set partly or wholly in Scotland and these are notable for their zest and their authenticity (especially in the dialogue); but they are not usually her best books, being too inclined to self-indulgence, full of descriptions of scenery aimed seemingly at the tourist market. Her series of novels set in English provincial life, starting with the Carlingford series (1863–1866 with a final book in 1876), constitute her main claim to fame—a fame which she has so far notably failed to achieve.

The best Oliphant novels have a distinctive pattern and 'flavour' of their own. She worked to no theory of the novel and made no conscious innovations, and when at the end of her life theories—such as those of Henry James—about the novel began to appear in print she was doubtful of their value, though very respectful. Yet in the Carlingford novels she used a method of interlocking the characters of the various books resembling Trollope's method in the Barchester and Palliser novels; but much more sophisticated. Indeed in a rudimentary way she anticipated Bennett's use of parallel actions in *Clayhanger* and *Hilda Lessways*. She experimented with the first-person narrator—and very strikingly in *The Days of My Life* (1857) she chose a narrator meant to seem insufferably arrogant and egotistical. But this book is not a complete success, being written before she was ready for such ironic objectivity. She adopted the Victorian system of serializing novels in literary periodicals (*Blackwood's Magazine, Good Words, The Cornhill* and others) and this tended to favour the traditional 'strong' plot line with mysteries, coincidences, surprises and prolonged tension. Indeed her worst weakness was a disastrous taste for melodramatic characters and situations which she was unable to handle imaginatively. But elsewhere her tone is coolly ironic and her characterization remarkably free from stereotypes. ⟨. . .⟩

Mrs. Oliphant has a particular gift for the analysis of motivation, often complex and ambivalent motivation. She understands the perverse thought-processes of the self-deceiver, and the dishonesty that may underlie the best of intentions. Though she does tend to sentimentalize the soft-hearted young and (a special weakness, this) the affectionate elderly spinster, she softens the impact of her characters (at least in her best work) far less often than Trollope, who is also noted for his analysis of self-deception. This is because in spite of her willingness to supply on occasion the obligatory 'happy ending' she was temperamentally inclined to an anti-romantic view of life, which led her to challenge orthodox views, for example, of romantic love, and the ideal hero.

—John Stock Clarke, "Mrs. Oliphant: A Case for Reconsideration," *English* (Summer 1979), excerpted in *The Critical Perspective*, Vol. 9, ed. Harold Bloom (New York: Chelsea House Publishers, 1989), 5695, 5697–98

D. J. TRELA

Oliphant simply is a better writer than she is generally given credit for; many recent critics having unhesitatingly called her "great." In this sense, her actual work subverts the common scholarly impression of it, which is reasonably well expressed by the dismissive tone of Trevor Royle in *Precipitous City*. Oliphant, he says, "soon found that hack writing was a reasonable means of financial independence. From her house in Fettes Row [in Edinburgh] articles, biographies, novels, and reviews flowed from her pen, mostly for the formidable John Blackwood . . . . Today most of Mrs. Oliphant's work is forgotten. She wrote too much too quickly and with too little intellectual equipment to do her work justice." To this is added her success in supporting her family. The "hack" status accorded her is still a sadly typical epithet. ⟨. . .⟩

A second area where Oliphant has run into trouble from modern readers comes in her apparent opposition to women's rights, in part expressed in a comment in a private letter noting John Stuart Mill's "mad notion" about the vote for women and her early essays in opposition to suffrage. Marion Shaw, in "Victorian Women Prose Writers" in *The Victorians*, baldly asserts that "Margaret Oliphant . . . was no supporter of women's suffrage or the women's movement at all, as her articles for *Blackwood's Magazine* in the late 1850s and 1860s testify." While Shaw limits this observation to the 1860s, she does not document the evolution Oliphant's thought underwent in succeeding decades. By 1880, when she published "The Grievances of Women" in the radical *Westminster Review* she openly acknowledged the patriarchal devaluation of women's work and "women's sphere," had grown increasingly frustrated at her inability to find regular, salaried work as an editor in a male-dominated profession, and had more than twenty years' painful experience of the incapacity of most of the men in her own family. This article, and later letters support votes for women, property rights, professional and university education, female doctors and the like. ⟨. . .⟩

This clear evolution in her political and social attitudes toward the role of women in society is also evident in her fiction. Indeed, it has been a frequent observation among Oliphant's more thoughtful critics that her fictional representation of women was more radical than her public political views. While there is no question that Oliphant represents women primarily in the domestic sphere, she often very sensitively suggests the physical and psychological toll they endured and equally often shows women operating in an empowered and emboldened domestic space, and, less often, as empowered in a man's world.

A third general assumption about Oliphant is somewhat more complex. It grows out of the image of the long-suffering, hardworking mother writing primarily to support her children and extended family. It grows out of the common gloss on her fiction as "wholesome"—one of the more frequent and mis-guided of nineteenth century reviewers' characterizations. This image—for which Oliphant herself is partly responsible—is presented most clearly in the *Autobiography and Letters* published by her niece and cousin the year after her death. As Elisabeth Jay has shown in the complete text of the *Autobiography* published in 1990, this document's first editors consciously chose to fore-ground the mothering, nurturing, self-denying side of Oliphant. They chose to represent, in their own words, her "exquisite womanliness" whatever the tragedies of her life might be (A: ix). They chose, rather ironically, to repre-sent Oliphant as the unempowered center of a domestic sphere, and not as the accomplished famous novelist, critic, traveler, historian, and biographer that she was. ⟨. . .⟩

What does all this have to do with the presumed "wholesomeness" of Oliphant's fiction? Like the mistaken gloss given to her *Autobiography*, the fic-tion also has generally been misrepresented. Because it is primarily set in the domestic sphere and because it often appears to be resolved with a wedding, it seems to "fit" with conventional patterns so often used at that time. The truth again is considerably more complex. In general, while Oliphant worked within societal conventions, she was constantly testing the limits of those con-ventions, pointing out the hidden, unseemly side of the domestic role women were forced into and the abuses of power that men frequently engaged in. While readers can have little or no doubt about the "perfect happiness" of the unions with which Jane Austen's novels conclude, Oliphant leaves much greater room for doubt. ⟨. . .⟩

There is no disputing that her work is uneven in quality. However, there is also an integrity and consistency to much of her work, as well as a level of experimentation with form and theorizing about genre that mark her as a gen-uine artist.

—D. J. Trela, "Introduction: Discovering the Gentle Subversive," *Margaret Oliphant: Critical Essays on a Gentle Subversive*, ed. D. J. Trela (Selinsgrove: Susquehanna University Press, 1995), 12–17

MARGARETE RUBIK

One would normally expect in a nineteenth-century novel to find a submissive heroine or at least one who, like Charlotte Bronte's Shirley, for all her talk of emancipation in fact dreams of a man who will be her "master" and "break [her] in." Mercenary marriages are generally denounced as immoral in Victorian fic-tion and lead to unhappiness and lifelong remorse. The mention of an orphan was sure to conjure up pathetic images of helpless children at the mercy of unfeeling relatives. Poetic justice demanded "good" and "bad" characters to be rewarded at the end of a novel according to their deserts. Whatever the char-

acter qualities of a person in life, decorum required after his death that the
widow show proper signs of grief and affliction; any display of satisfaction and
relief would have been considered highly improper, even scandalous, since a
woman was expected to learn to love even a seemingly repulsive husband.

Most Victorian authors comply with such rules. In the novels of Margaret
Oliphant, however, clichés are often turned upside down. Although until
recently dismissed as little more than a conventional writer of trite love stories, Oliphant is, in fact, a much more vigorous and unconventional novelist
than most critics allow. Her treatment of the traditional themes of the domestic novel is often highly unusual and quite "un-Victorian." Much more uncom-
promisingly than many famous authors of the time she disappoints
stereotyped expectations, ridicules maudlin Victorian values and denounces
the false pathos and sentimentality of her contemporaries.

To be sure, many of her stories seem, on the surface, to be constructed
according to stereotypes, but John Stock Clarke has pointed out that, while
"she accepts the conventions in one part of the book, ... the pattern or plot
development of the book will suggest a very different view." Indeed, the challenging of traditional attitudes and beliefs is one of the characteristics of
Oliphant's writing. In her novels she questions and reassesses many Victorian
precepts and clichés—the role of women and the relationship of the sexes, the
convention of the happy ending and the concept of poetic justice, the treatment of death, and, quite generally, the Victorian moral code of behavior.

Her remarkable originality of tone and attitude can be illustrated by a
comparison of some of her novels with various famous literary works that she
obviously uses as foils; for she sometimes takes as a starting point for her novels well-known motifs and literary models, but views them from unconventional angles and develops solutions diametrically opposed to precedent. The
effect of her new version is almost always to counterpoint a heroic view of life
with a prosaic one and to oppose a realistic assessment to an idealized conception.

A telling example of this method is *Phoebe Junior, A Last Chronicle of
Carlingford*, which in its subtitle pays conscious tribute to Trollope's Barchester
series and indeed uses some of Trollope's plot elements, in particular the incident of the check that the Reverend Crawley, in *The Last Chronicle of Barset*, is
accused of stealing. In Trollope's novel the ladies in Barchester know all along
"that an ordained clergyman could not become a thief," and at the end of the
book Crawley is vindicated as the victim of a misunderstanding. In Oliphant's
version, however, the clergyman May actually does forge a bill. In her more
disturbing view, class is no guarantee for impeccable behavior; for all his
refined veneer a gentleman can be as irresponsible and unscrupulous as any
common criminal—an idea she also develops in *A Son of His Father*, a novel that
will be treated more extensively later.

Considering the conspicuousness of many of these inversions it is surprising how thoroughly both her contemporaries and many later critics managed to overlook the subversive aspects of her writing. Her novels were rendered harmless and recommended as "wholesome" reading for women and children, even though it is quite obvious that many of her characters, evaluations, and views do not conform to Victorian ideals. Some contemporary reviewers, indeed, were confused at what they considered to be an unnatural and untrue reversal of gender roles in her novels, as, for example, when one clearly exasperated critic in the *Spectator* complained: "We cannot recall among all her books one picture of a thoroughly competent man who is also good, or one . . . whom a male reader thoroughly likes." ⟨. . .⟩

Oliphant's view of marriage is obviously not idealized, but down to earth and unsentimental. On occasion, she can paint savagely disillusioning pictures of married life, as, for instance, the sketch of the frustrated wife who makes her husband roar with laughter at her witticisms, yet "all the time . . . would have liked to throw him down and trample on him, or put pins into him, or scratch his beaming, jovial countenance" (*Miss Marjoribanks*, 244). As a rule, however, she concentrates on average marriages with their daily frictions and trivial irritations. Indolent and self-indulgent, the men in her novels, under various pretenses, withdraw from all domestic responsibilities and leave their wives to solve the problems of daily life.

— Margarete Rubik, "The Subversion of Literary Cliches in Oliphant's Fiction," *Margaret Oliphant: Critical Essays on a Gentle Subversive*, ed. D. J. Trela (Selinsgrove: Susquehanna University Press, 1995), 49–51, 53

LINDA PETERSON

After working out the limitations of the female *bildungsroman* in the Carlingford series, Oliphant later experimented with what might be called a "masculine heroine"—the female protagonist who adopts masculine patterns of action. Thus in *Hester* (1883) Oliphant turns away from a *bildungsroman* that locates a woman's career within the domestic sphere and toward a masculine narrative that propels the heroine into the public realm. Hester, the heroine, never quite makes it into that realm. Like Lucilla Marjoribanks and Phoebe Beecham before her, she must remain a lady and "consent," as the narrator puts it, "to be bound by other people's rules, and to put her hand to nothing that was unbecoming" (77). The frustration that ensues from such consenting—especially if a girl has, like Hester, a capacity for business—preoccupies Oliphant for much of the novel. Yet despite her attack on social conventions that restrict women's actions, Oliphant seems unable (or unwilling) to devise a literary solution that would break with the traditional focus of the female *bildungsroman* and move her heroine into the world of work. ⟨. . .⟩

Catherine's achievement is masculine in a more subtle sense, moreover: It deals with power, power that originates in money and extends its grasp over the lives of other characters. That the male *bildungsroman* deals in money and power is no new insight—as Dickens registered in *Great Expectations*. What Oliphant seems to fear is the introduction of these terms into the female *bildungsroman*. Catherine is philanthropic, generous, even benevolent, but her knowledge of power seems to result in a loss of feminine virtues. Characters critical of her public achievements voice their criticism in terms of this loss. Mrs. Merridew notes that Catherine's business engagements have given her "an unfeminine turn of mind" (313). Hester interprets Catherine's manipulation of Edward as an unfortunate example of what happens when woman attains power: "Oh, how true it must be after all," she thinks, "the picture of the tyrannical, narrow despot, exacting, remorseless, descending to the lowest details, which a woman, when endued with irresponsible power, was understood to make" (303–304). Captain Morgan, a gentler and more subtle judge, discusses Catherine's loss in terms of "innocence."

In a speech to Hester about the importance of "soft, innocent creatures" like his wife and Mrs. John, the Captain articulates what I take to be Oliphant's fear:

> You are tempted to despise [them], you clever ones, but it is a great mistake. . . . It is such souls as these that keep the world steady. We should all tumble to pieces if the race was made up of people like Catherine Vernon and you. (93)

The danger of the masculine heroine, this passage implies, is that she threatens the extinction of the race—not simply because she remains single and produces no children, but because she fails to reproduce the values associated with the feminine: kindness, faithfulness, patience, forgiveness. A modern psychologist like Nancy Chodorow would call this "the reproduction of mothering." In *Hester* it is Mrs. Morgan who expresses these feminine values most concretely when she argues for a continuing relationship with her children and grandchildren, even though it means the end of "peace and quiet"; "I like to see the children come and go—one here, one there. One in need of your sympathy, another of your help, another . . . of your pardon" (169). Hers are selfless values, rooted in the woman's "relational" understanding of her place in the community.

By presenting Catherine's plot as a possible model and then preventing Hester from following it fully, Oliphant is able to experiment with a mixture of masculine and feminine values. Catherine's values are predominately masculine: public achievement, family (paternal) name, self-respect. But, exposed to masculine knowledge, she loses feminine innocence and becomes "cynical," laughing at human foibles that a woman might better weep over or try to reform (184). This cynicism has devastating effects on Edward's life and, almost, on Hester's. Oliphant intends, I think, for Hester to witness the defects of Catherine's life but avoid its extremes, to balance masculine and feminine. And the novel succeeds in that it shows Hester gaining a masculine knowledge of the self and others, while maintaining certain feminine values associated with the family. (Hester can reason out, for example, the psychological motivations of male characters like Roland and Edward, but she is appalled when Captain Morgan uses reason to argue for breaking ties with his adult children.)

—Linda Peterson, "The Female *Bildungsroman*: Tradition and Revision in Oliphant's Fiction," *Margaret Oliphant: Critical Essays on a Gentle Subversive*, ed. D. J. Trela (Selinsgrove: Susquehanna University Press, 1995), 78–80

ESTHER H. SCHOR

Readers of Oliphant's supernatural fiction can be grateful to feminist critics such as Ellen Moers and Ann Douglas, who have replaced monolithic accounts of a minor genre with varied testimonies as to how supernatural fictions and their predominantly female readership have accommodated a wide range of literary experimentation. Upon closer inspection, Oliphant's chosen rubric, "Stories of the Seen and the Unseen," suggests the flexibility and subtlety with which she too, experimented with the supernatural mode. "Earthbound," for example, is concerned with eruptions of the Unseen in the seen, mundane world; the "Little Pilgrim" series and "The Land of Darkness" reveal events and characters occurring in unseen realms, both heavenly and hellish; and "Old Lady Mary," shifts the setting from the Seen to the Unseen and back. In several stories, even the difference between the Seen and the Unseen proves critical, not essential. Oliphant's placement of such diverse writings under a single rubric is easily attributed to her reliable, if not unfailing, instincts for the market. She at times published mediocre sequels to her more popular works, and the supernatural fictions of the early 1880s were nothing if not popular. *A Beleaguered City* (1880), for example, was reprinted four times by 1897; in 1882, Macmillan printed over twenty thousand copies of the hugely successful *Little Pilgrim in the Unseen*. It would only have been reasonable for Oliphant, who never held a salaried position, to wish her readers to identify her later supernatural fictions with these early successes. ⟨. . .⟩

In both "Earthbound" and *A Beleaguered City*, the encroachment of the Unseen on the Seen causes an interpretive crisis. While Oliphant's haunted interpreters enact our task as readers by confronting an uninterpreted "text," they also interrogate Oliphant's own authority as an interpreter of literature. As John Blackwood's "general utility woman" (her own phrase), Oliphant had published nearly ninety critical essays on literature, art, and history by the late

1870s. Merryn Williams's bibliography reveals that in the 1870s Oliphant published essays on an extraordinarily varied group of English and Continental writers, in addition to seventeen books of fiction. By the end of this decade, Oliphant was writing fictions in which the meanings of signs and figures are radically indeterminate. Creating apparitions that stubbornly resist definitive interpretation, Oliphant foregrounds the interpretive strategies of the haunted. In "Earthbound," a hermeneutic romance worthy of late Borges, she demonstrates a congruence between interpretive and sexual mastery. In *A Beleaguered City*, Oliphant presents a public crisis of interpretation, considering how both gender and class are implicated in authorizing interpretations. Allegorizing the interpretation of texts as an affair between persons, Oliphant deftly conflates the discourses of interpretation and social relations. For Oliphant's haunted interpreters, confronting the unexplained figure often leads to an uncanny exchange of roles: as the ghostly figure assumes authority, the interpreters take on the aura of the irrational. By means of such transfigurations, these fictions reconfigure—surprisingly, and even subversively—familiar relations between interpreters and texts, interpreters and other interpreters, and interpreters and themselves. ⟨. . .⟩

Having lived so much of her life as a reader on the public pages of *Blackwood's* and other literary journals, Oliphant was keenly aware of her own authority as an arbiter of literary fates and fortunes. A published writer of fiction since her twenties, Oliphant had realized early that such critical pronouncements as she was paid to deliver had consequences for writers and their books. But by the late 1870s, she had come to reckon with her own power as a critic to shape the tastes and expectations of a nation's readers. In the mode of supernatural fiction, Oliphant explored her ambivalence about her own critical professionalism. What does it mean, these fictions ask, to use a rhetoric of distinctions, decisions, and determinations to account for a literary text? to assimilate one's mixed and perhaps irreconcilable responses to a single, morally viable and socially responsible position? to authorize and canonize the reading of a single reader? In "Earthbound" and *A Beleaguered City*, Oliphant provisionally views the burden of interpreting literary texts—those linguistic apparitions that resist explanation—as a shared burden. In "Earthbound," Edmund's close reading—an attempt to possess meaning by transforming a text into private property—renders illegitimate his claims as reader. In *A Beleaguered City*, on the other hand, Dupin's political authority is legitimated only because his interpretive authority is dialectical. If, as these fictions suggest, the way we love and the way we govern are crucially linked to the way we read, we can see why Oliphant found the task of being a critic formidable.

 —Esther H. Schor, "The Haunted Interpreter in Oliphant's Supernatural Fiction," *Margaret Oliphant: Critical Essays on a Gentle Subversive*, ed. D. J. Trela (Selinsgrove: Susquehanna University Press, 1995), 90–92, 107

LAURIE LANGBAUER

Margaret Oliphant, perhaps still most familiar to us from her autobiography, was herself always interested in autobiography. In her insightful and self-questioning way, she was also intrigued by her own interest: just what was it about autobiography, she asked herself, that made it so interesting? Between 1881 and 1883, in *Blackwood's*, she published a series of essays on the form, a series that directly poses this question. In those essays, she reviews a range of autobiographical texts, written by figures including the obscure Alice Thornton, who lived in the time of the Commonwealth, as well as the more renowned Madame Roland and Edward Gibbon. Within the writings of such disparately everyday and extraordinary figures, she finds a common interest: they are all, to some extent, engaged in "thrusting their own little tale of events between [themselves] and the history of the world, finding their infant or their apple-tree of more importance than the convulsions of nations." No matter their own status or part in the world's extraordinary affairs, what interests all these writers, she finds, are the most absolute commonplaces.

It is just such moments of engagement in these texts that engage Oliphant. She goes on to suggest that such self-consuming interest (common to us all) is more than foolish vanity. Oliphant implies that we are unthinkingly intrigued by such unimportant details in part because they are crucial to what we consider important; she makes a connection between commonplace details and the realm of politics, between the everyday lives of individuals and the momentous lives of nations. "Even an apple-tree," she writes, ". . . is of use in its way as revealing that undercurrent of peaceable life which streams serenely on, whatever storms may convulse the air, and which is the real secret of national continuance." The supposedly trivial concerns of private history are the stuff of history itself, and are what draw us to it. Oliphant feels that "the gentle calm of ordinary life" that we find in "the narrowest domestic record" is "as interesting and instructive as any other part of the perennial drama" of social relations that make up what we call history proper. Such commonplace details are useful in their own way, crucial in their very unimportance. The nation continues itself through them—through a calm bereft of signal import, an undercurrent secret if only because of its very obviousness: it is made up of everything that does not stand out. We find our interest in such an undercurrent, and, in it, we may really find our history. ⟨. . .⟩

The relation of the everyday to the historical record—of how the lives of institutions such as nations are inscribed in and carried by the quotidian, which we ignore as trivial—has been the focus of recent attention by theorists of social history, such as historians of the *Annales* school, whose general influence is perhaps best known in literary criticism through the works of Michel de Certeau or Michel Foucault; it is as well an abiding concern of feminist theorists, who investigate the ways women have traditionally been kept out of the privileged sphere of great public events and relegated to the mundane. For such critics, as for Oliphant, the relation of the banal to history revolves around the question of the creation of the subject—of the intimate connection between the everyday and how human beings turn themselves into subjects, turn themselves into that which is subject to such institutions and nations. Oliphant's attention to the commonplace in her writing of and about autobiography reveals too how the lives of nations are conducted at the level of our daily lives; our private and mundane moments, rather than being exempted from such history, actually carry it. But Oliphant's writing does not just record the connection of the public and private: it tells us something about that connection. By locating the emergence of the subject in its everyday record, she does not so much shift the ground of history's truth, as put that ground—and that truth—into question. The absolute commonplaces of our private and public histories make those histories—and history itself—ultimately unreadable. ⟨. . .⟩

By recognizing the importance of the commonplace in her own, and others' autobiographies, Oliphant has formed a theory of history to herself, one that adds to the most recent debate on the subject. Oliphant's emphasis that the everyday is exactly what we are unable to recognize or make out suggests that shifting our larger historical record to the subjects' relation to their daily lives will give us no more access to historical truth than our earlier attention to great events. The vast fretwork of the everyday, simply because it is everyday, remains ephemeral, meaningless, unplumbable. The self that emerges in recognition of its construction out of such a record is one that must ultimately give up claim to privilege, sense, to our usual notion of self at all. The close of Oliphant's own autobiography ("I cannot write any more" [A 154]) might be seen as the record of her own such recognition of her place as a subject in history, her invisibility in its record ("I am in very little danger of having my life written, . . . and that is all the better in this point of view—for what could be said of me?" [A 17]). It might be seen too, like the check to her attempts to read beyond the surface of the heavens, not as a frustration of her endeavors, but the very end toward which she writes. As she tells us of the rather commonplace private history left by the historian Edward Gibbon, "autobiography can go no further" because history cannot.

—Laurie Langbauer, "Absolute Commonplaces: Oliphant's Theory of Autobiography," *Margaret Oliphant: Critical Essays on a Gentle Subversive*, ed. D. J. Trela (Selinsgrove: Susquehanna University Press, 1995), 124–27, 132–33

MERRYN WILLIAMS

"The woman question" was debated with great intensity during the second half of the nineteenth century. Briefly, in the years while Oliphant was growing up, women had no votes and few rights. Their education was poor (except in her birthplace Scotland); the professions were closed to them; married women could not own property or claim custody of children. It was almost impossible to leave a bad husband or father. A double standard of morality existed. Women were trained to think that their aim in life was to get a husband, and be despised if they did not.

Several things changed in her lifetime. The Infants' Custody and Married Women's Property Acts passed; some women got the municipal vote and others succeeded in becoming doctors; good schools for girls opened as did women's colleges at Oxford and Cambridge. The demand for the vote, which would not succeed until after World War I, was heard more often in respectable circles. The "women's movement" became a real force. ⟨. . .⟩

Oliphant took an interest in women's issues from an early stage—indeed, before most English people could have heard of it. Writing in *Merkland* (1850), only two years after the Women's Rights Association was founded in the United States, the twenty-two year old author made her heroine say: "We are one-half the world—we have our work to do, like the other half—let us do our work as honourably and wisely as we can, but for pity's sake, do not let us make this mighty bustle and noise about it . . . no one gains respect by claiming it" (2:40).

The three articles that she wrote on this subject for *Blackwood's* during the 1850s and 1860s are all critical of the women's movement, although she made it clear that she did not want to defend injustice or thwart anyone's aspirations. "This idea, that the two portions of humankind are natural antagonists to each other, is, to our thinking . . . a monstrous and unnatural idea." Yet only a few pages later she refers ironically to the cherished belief that men had better brains. "Let us not enter upon the tender question of mental inferiority. Every individual woman, we presume, is perfectly easy on her own account that she at least is not remarkably behind her masculine companions." ⟨. . .⟩

Kirsteen is probably Oliphant's masterpiece. Here, most unusually, the heroine remains a spinster, although that does not free her from family ties. She has a fiance who dies in India; her feeling for him is the "golden thread" running through her life. But this relationship is not studied in detail. Her real links are with her sisters and the women who help her break away from home and become independent; her real fulfillment is in being a dressmaker and creating "beautiful manufactured things . . . with much of the genuine enjoyment which attends an artist in all crafts" (165). When the author looks closely at marriage relationships, her picture is much darker. Kirsteen's father, a former slave trader and future murderer treats his wife and daughters with thorough contempt, which proves intolerable for Kirsteen with her "quick temper and high spirit and lively imagination." She will "make a story for" herself (36).

It is Kirsteen who makes the family's fortune, fulfilling the pattern of success normally reserved for men, as Linda Peterson demonstrates. Yet it is done at a price, and, like her creator, she ends up a breadwinner, but also celibate with many poor relations needing her help and others upset with her because she has worked for a living. Thus Oliphant treats, not only Kirsteen, but the several spinsters in the novel, with respect and dignity. ⟨. . .⟩

She would not have liked modern feminists. Their attitudes to sex and children would have been deeply alien to her, as would be their stridency and frequent self-pity. It is more helpful and fairer to see her as one of a long and honorable line of women who were known in England between the wars as the Old Feminists. They did not concentrate on women's "special" or biological problems, although of course they were aware of them (and might even write about them as Margaret did). Ultimately all they asked was that men and women be equal before the law and that no persons should be forbidden to make their contribution because they were the "wrong" sex. Above all, they were aware, as was Oliphant, that the world "is round, and contains everything."

—Merryn Williams, "Feminist or Antifeminist? Oliphant and the Woman Question," *Margaret Oliphant: Critical Essays on a Gentle Subversive*, ed. D. J. Trela (Selinsgrove: Susquehanna University Press, 1995), 166–67, 175–76, 179

Bibliography

Passages in the Life of Mrs. Margaret Maitland of Sunnyside, written by Herself (3 vols.). 1849.

Caleb Field. 1851.

John: A Love Story (2 vols.). 1851.

Merkland: A Story of Scottish Life (3 vols.). 1851.

Memoirs and Resolutions of Adam Graeme of Mossgray (3 vols.). 1852.

Katie Stewart, A True Story. 1852.

Harry Muir: A Story of a Scottish Life (3 vols.). 1853.

Quiet Heart: A Story. 1854.

Magdalen Hepburn, A Story of the Scottish Reformation (3 vols.). 1854.

Lilliesleaf. Being a Concluding Series of Passages in the Life of Mrs. Margart Maitland (3 vols.). 1855.

Zaidee, A Romance (3 vols.). 1856.

The Days of My Life (3 vols.). 1857.

The Athelings: or, The Three Gifts (3 vols.). 1857.

Sundays. 1858.

The Laird of Norlaw, A Scottish Story (8 vols.). 1858.

Agnes Hopetown's Schools and Holidays. 1859.

Lucy Crafton. 1860.

The Last of the Mortimers, A Story in Two Voices (3 vols.). 1862.

The Life of Edward Irving, Minister of the National Scotch Church, London. Illustrated by his Journals and Correspondence (2 vols.). 1862.

The House on the Moor (3 vols.). 1862.

The Rector, and The Doctor's Family (3 vols.). 1863.

Heart and Cross. 1863.

Salem Chapel (2 vols.). 1863.

The Perpetual Curate (3 vols.). 1864.

Agnes (3 vols.). 1866.

Madonna Mary (3 vols.). 1866.

Miss Marjoribanks (3 vols.). 1866.

A Son of the Soil (2 vols.). 1866.

Francis of Assisi. 1868.

The Brownlows (3 vols.). 1868.

The Makers of Florence: Dante, Giotto, Savonarola, and Their City. 1868.

Historical Sketches of the Reign of George II (2 vols.). 1869.

The Minister's Wife (3 vols.). 1869.

The Three Brothers (3 vols.). 1870.

Squire Arden (3 vols.). 1871.

At His Gates (3 vols.). 1872.

Ombra (3 vols.). 1872.

May (3 vols.). 1873.

Innocent, A Tale of Modern Life (3 vols.). 1873.

A Rose in June (2 vols.). 1874.

For Love and Life (3 vols.). 1875.

The Story of Valentine and His Brothers (3 vols.). 1875.

The Curate in Charge (2 vols.). 1876.

Pheobe, Junior, A Last Chronicle of Carlingford (3 vols.). 1876.

Young Musgrave (3 vols.). 1877.

Carita (3 vols.). 1877.

Dante. 1877.

Mrs. Arthur (3 vols.). 1877.

Dress. 1878.

The Primrose Path (3 vols.). 1878.

Molière. 1879.

Within the Precincts (3 vols.). 1879.

The Greatest Heiress in England (3 vols.). 1879.

Cervantes. 1880.

A Beleaguered City, being a Narrative of Certain Recent Events in the City of Semur, A Story of the Seen and the Unseen. 1880.

Orphans: A Chapter in Life. 1880.

Harry Joscelyn (3 vols.). 1881.

The Literary History of England in the End of the Eighteenth and Beginning of the Nineteenth Century (3 vols.). 1882.

A Little Pilgrim in the Unseen. 1882.

Hester, A Story of Contemporary Life (3 vols.). 1883.

It Was a Lover and his Lass (3 vols.). 1883.

Sheridan. 1883.

The Wizard's Son (3 vols.). 1883.

The Ladies of Lindores (3 vols.). 1883.

Madam. 1884.

Sir Tom. 1884.

Two Stories of the Seen and the Unseen. 1885.

A Country Gentleman and His Family (3 vols.). 1886.

Effie Ogilvie (2 vols.). 1886.

A House Divided Against Itself (3 vols.). 1886.

A Poor Gentleman (3 vols.). 1886.

The Son and His Father (3 vols.). 1886.

The Makers of Venice: Doges, Conquerors, Painters, and Men of Letters. 1887.

Joyce (3 vols.). 1888.

Memoir of the Life of John Tulloch. 1888.

The Second Son (3 vols.). 1888.

The Land of Darkness. 1888.

Cousin Mary. 1888.

Neighbours on the Green: A Collection of Stories (3 vols.). 1889.

Lady Carr: The Sequel of a Life. 1889.

Kirsteen, A Story of a Scottish Family Seventy Years Ago (3 vols.). 1890.

Royal Edinburgh: Her Saints, Kings, Prophets, and Poets. 1890.

The Duke's Daughter and the Fugitives (3 vols.). 1890.

Sons and Daughters. 1890.

The Mystery of Mrs. Blencarrow. 1890.

Janet (3 vols.). 1891.

The Railway Man and His Children (3 vols.). 1891.

The Heir Presumptive and the Heir Apparent (3 vols.). 1891.

The Marriage of Elinor. 1891.

The Cuckoo in the Nest (3 vols.). 1892.

Diana Trelawney, The History of a Great Mistake (2 vols.). 1892.

Lady William (3 vols.). 1893.

The Sorceress (3 vols.). 1893.

Thomas Chalmers, Preacher, Philosopher, and Statesman. 1893.

A House in Bloomsbury (2 vols.). 1894.

Historical Sketches of the Reign of Queen Anne. 1894

Sir Robert's Fortune: A Story of a Scotch Moor. 1894.

Who Was Lost and Is Found. 1894.

Two Strangers. 1894.

The Prodigals and Their Inheritance (2 vols.). 1894.

A Child's History of Scotland. 1895.

The Makers of Modern Rome. 1895.

Old Mr. Tredgold. 1896.

Joan d'Arc: Her Life and Death. 1896.

The Two Marys. 1896.

The Unjust Steward; or, The Minister's Debt. 1896.

Annals of a Publishing House: William Blackwood and his Sons, their Magazine and Friends. Vols. I and II. 1897.

The Ways of Life: Two Stories. 1897.

The Lady's Work. 1897.

That Little Cutty: and Two Other Stories. 1898.

A Widow's Tale and Other Stories, with an Introductory note by J. M. Barrie. 1898.

The Autobiography and Letters of Mrs. M. O. W. Oliphant. 1898.

Stories of the Seen and the Unseen. 1902.

The Autobiography and Lettters of Mrs. M. O. W. Oliphant., with an Introduction by Q. D. Leavis. 1974.

The Autobiography and Lettters of Mrs. M. O. W. Oliphant., with an Introduction by Laurie Langbauer. 1988.

The Autobiography of Margaret Oliphant: The Complete Text. 1990.

MARY SHELLEY

1797-1851

MARY SHELLEY was born Mary Wollestonecraft Godwin on August 30, 1797, the only child of her notable parents. Her father was the philosopher William Godwin. Her mother, the radical feminist Mary Wollstonecraft, was the author of *The Vindication of the Rights of Women* (1792). Mary Wollstonecraft died ten days after Mary's birth, leaving Godwin to cope with the new infant and with Wollstonecraft's daughter, Fanny Imlay, the product of a previous liason. In 1801 Godwin married Mary Jane Clairmont, who brought her own daughter and son to the marriage. By all accounts, Mary disliked her stepmother intensely. She was educated at home, but her solitary reading was relieved by the many famous visitors—Samuel Coleridge, Charles Lamb, and William Hazlitt among them—who came to see her father.

From 1812–14, Mary lived in Dundee, Scotland. On November 11, 1812, on one of her visits home, she met the poet Percy Bysshe Shelley. Percy and Mary fell in love in 1814 and left England for Europe, leaving behind Percy's pregnant wife, Harriet, but taking Mary's stepsister, Jane (who was known as "Claire") Clairmont with them. After travelling through France, Switzerland, Italy, Germany, and Holland, Mary, Percy, and Claire returned to England, where Mary gave birth to a premature daughter who died two weeks later. Two months later, Mary was pregnant again. She gave birth to a son in January 1816. Mary and Percy returned to Switzerland in May 1816, where they lived in Byron's house on Lake Geneva. It was in that house that Byron proposed the storytelling contest that would result in the conception of *Frankenstein*, Mary Shelley's most famous work and one of the most important novels of the nineteenth century. Although Mary worked on the novel in 1816, the year brought several disruptive tragic events. In October, Mary's half sister, Fanny Imlay, committed suicide when she discovered that she was not Godwin's daughter. One month later, in November of 1816, Percy Shelley's wife, Harriet, who was pregnant by someone other than Shelley, drowned herself in the Serpentine. On December 30, Mary and Percy were married in London. William Godwin continued to disapprove of his daughter's relationship with Shelley.

In 1817 Mary published *History of a Six Weeks' Tour*, which she cowrote with Shelley. Their daughter, Clara, was born that same year. In 1818, the first edition of *Frankenstein* was published and the Shelleys left England for Italy, where their daughter Clara died in September of that year and where their son William died in 1819. Later that year, Mary Shelley finished *Matilda*, an autobiographical novel that would be published after her death, and gave birth to her only surviving child, Percy Florence.

The year 1822 brought more tragedy. On June 16 Mary almost died from complications of a miscarriage, and on July 8 Percy Shelley drowned in the Gulf of Spezia. The next year, Mary Shelley returned to England. Raising her son without any financial support from Shelley's father (who had demanded that she turn the child over to him), Mary supported herself by writing five novels in fifteen years: *Valperga* (1823), *The Last Man* (1826), *The Fortunes of Pekin Warbeck* (1830), *Lodore* (1835), and *Falkner* (1837) as well as a number of short stories and biographical sketches. She also revised *Frankenstein* for a third edition in 1831. Shelley never remarried and devoted herself to publishing Percy Shelley's *Poetical Works* (1839) and his *Essays, Letters from Abroad, Translations and Fragments* (1840). Her last work was *Rambles in Germany and Italy in 1840, 1842, and 1843* (1844). Mary Shelley died on February 1, 1851.

CRITICAL EXTRACTS

PERCY BYSSHE SHELLEY

The novel of *Frankenstein; or, The Modern Prometheus*, is undoubtedly, as a mere story, one of the most original and complete productions of the day. We debate with ourselves in wonder, as we read it, what could have been the series of thoughts—what could have been the peculiar experiences that awakened them—which conduced, in the author's mind, to the astonishing combinations of motives and incidents, and the startling catastrophe, which compose this tale. There are, perhaps, some points of subordinate importance, which prove that it is the author's first attempt. But in this judgment, which requires a very nice discrimination, we may be mistaken; for it is conducted throughout with a firm and steady hand. The interest gradually accumulates and advances towards the conclusion with the accelerated rapidity of a rock rolled down a mountain. We are led breathless with suspense and sympathy, and the heaping up of incident on incident, and the working of passion out of passion. We cry "hold, hold! enough!"—but there is yet something to come; and, like the victim whose history it relates, we think we can bear no more, and yet more is to be borne. Pelion is heaped on Ossa, and Ossa on Olympus. We climb Alp after Alp, until the horizon is seen blank, vacant, and limitless; and the head turns giddy, and the ground seems to fail under our feet.

This novel rests its claim on being a source of powerful and profound emotion. The elementary feelings of the human mind are exposed to view; and those who are accustomed to reason deeply on their origin and tendency will, perhaps, be the only persons who can sympathize, to the full extent, in the interest of the actions which are their result. But, founded on nature as they are, there is perhaps no reader, who can endure anything beside a new love-story, who will not feel a responsive string touched in his inmost soul. The sentiments are so affectionate and so innocent—the characters of the subordinate agents in this strange drama are clothed in the light of such a mild and gentle mind—the pictures of domestic manners are of the most simple and attaching character: the pathos is irresistible and deep. Nor are the crimes and malevolence of the single Being, though indeed withering and tremendous, the offspring of any unaccountable propensity to evil, but flow irresistibly from certain causes fully adequate to their production. They are the children, as it were, of Necessity and Human Nature. In this the direct moral of the book consists; and it is perhaps the most important, and of the most universal application, of any moral that can be enforced by example. Treat a person ill, and he will become wicked. Requite affection with scorn;—let one being be selected, for whatever cause, as the refuse of his kind—divide him, a social being, from society, and you impose upon him the irresistible obligations—malevolence and selfishness. It is thus that, too often in society, those who are best qualified to be its benefactors and its ornaments are branded by some accident with scorn, and changed, by neglect and solitude of heart, into a scourge and a curse.

The Being in "Frankenstein" is, no doubt, a tremendous creature. It was impossible that he should not have received among men that treatment which led to the consequences of his being a social nature. He was an abortion and an anomaly; and though his mind was such as its first impressions framed it, affectionate and full of moral sensibility, yet the circumstances of his existence are so monstrous and uncommon, that, when the consequences of them became developed in action, his original goodness was gradually turned into inextinguishable misanthropy and revenge. The scene between the Being and the blind De Lacey in the cottage is one of the most profound and extraordinary instances of pathos that we ever recollect. It is impossible to read this dialogue,—and indeed many others of a somewhat similar character,—without feeling the heart suspend its pulsations with wonder, and the "tears stream down the cheeks." The encounter and argument between Frankenstein and the Being on the sea of ice, almost approaches, in effect, to the expostulation of Caleb Williams with Falkland. It reminds us, indeed, somewhat of the style and character of that admirable writer, to whom the author has dedicated his work, and whose productions he seems to have studied.

There is only one instance, however, in which we detect the least approach to imitation; and that is the conduct of the incident of Frankenstein's landing in Ireland. The general character of the tale, indeed, resembles nothing that ever preceded it. After the death of Elizabeth, the story, like a stream which grows at once more rapid and profound as it proceeds, assumes an irresistible solemnity, and the magnificent energy and swiftness of a tempest.

The churchyard scene, in which Frankenstein visits the tombs of his family, his quitting Geneva, and his journey through Tartary to the shores of the Frozen Ocean, resemble at once the terrible reanimation of a corpse and the supernatural career of a spirit. The scene in the cabin of Walton's ship—the more than mortal enthusiasm and grandeur of the Being's speech over the dead body of his victim—is an exhibition of intellectual and imaginative power, which we think the reader will acknowledge has seldom been surpassed.

—Percy Bysshe Shelley, "On *Frankenstein*" (1818), *The Complete Works of Percy Bysshe Shelley*, ed. Roger Ingpen and Walter E. Peck (New York: Scribner's, 1926–30), Vol. 6, 263–65

MARY SHELLEY

In the summer of 1816 we visited Switzerland and became the neighbours of Lord Byron. At first we spent our pleasant hours on the lake or wandering on its shores; and Lord Byron, who was writing the third canto of *Childe Harold*, was the only one among us who put his thoughts upon paper. These, as he brought them successively to us, clothed in all the light and harmony of poetry, seemed to stamp as divine the glories of heaven and earth, whose influences we partook with him. ⟨. . .⟩

"We will each write a ghost story," said Lord Byron, and his proposition was acceded to. There were four of us. The noble author began a tale, a fragment of which he printed at the end of his poem of Mazeppa. Shelley, more apt to embody ideas and sentiments in the radiance of brilliant imagery and in the music of the most melodious verse that adorns our language than to invent the machinery of a story, commenced one founded on the experiences of his early life. Poor Polidori had some terrible idea about a skull-headed lady who was so punished for peeping through a key-hole—what to see I forget: something very shocking and wrong of course; but when she was reduced to a worse condition than the renowned Tom of Coventry, he did not know what to do with her and was obliged to dispatch her to the tomb of the Capulets, the only place for which she was fitted. The illustrious poets also, annoyed by the platitude of prose, speedily relinquished their uncongenial task.

I busied myself to *think of a story*—a story to rival those which had excited us to this task. One which would speak to the mysterious fears of our nature and awaken thrilling horror—one to make the reader dread to look round, to curdle the blood, and quicken the beatings of the heart. If I did not accomplish these things, my ghost story would be unworthy of its name. I thought and pondered—vainly. I felt that blank incapability of invention which is the greatest misery of authorship, when dull Nothing replies to our anxious invocations. "Have you thought of a story?" I was asked each morning, and each morning I was forced to reply with a mortifying negative. ⟨. . .⟩

Night waned upon this talk, and even the witching hour had gone by before we retired to rest. When I placed my head on my pillow I did not sleep, nor could I be said to think. My imagination, unbidden, possessed and guided me, gifting the successive images that arose in my mind with a vividness far beyond the usual bounds of reverie. I saw—with shut eyes, but acute mental vision—I saw the pale student of unhallowed arts kneeling beside the thing he had put together. I saw the hideous phantasm of a man stretched out, and then, on the working of some powerful engine, show signs of life and stir with an uneasy, half-vital motion. Frightful must it be, for supremely frightful would be the effect of any human endeavour to mock the stupendous mechanism of the Creator of the world. His success would terrify the artist; he would rush away from his odious handiwork, horror-stricken. He would hope that, left to itself, the slight spark of life which he had communicated would fade, that this thing which had received such imperfect animation would subside into dead matter, and he might sleep in the belief that the silence of the grave would quench forever the transient existence of the hideous corpse which he had looked upon as the cradle of life. He sleeps; but he is awakened; he opens his eyes; behold, the horrid thing stands at his bedside, opening his curtains and looking on him with yellow, watery, but speculative eyes.

I opened mine in terror. The idea so possessed my mind that a thrill of fear ran through me, and I wished to exchange the ghastly image of my fancy for the realities around. I see them still: the very room, the dark parquet, the closed shutters with the moonlight struggling through, and the sense I had that the glassy lake and white high Alps were beyond. I could not so easily get rid of my hideous phantom; still it haunted me. I must try to think of something else. I recurred to my ghost story—my tiresome, unlucky ghost story! Oh! If I could only contrive one which would frighten my reader as I myself had been frightened that night!

Swift as light and as cheering was the idea that broke in upon me. "I have found it! What terrified me will terrify others; and I need only describe the spectre which had haunted my midnight pillow." On the morrow I announced that I had *thought of a story*.

—Mary Shelley, "Author's Introduction" (1831), *Frankenstein: or, The Modern Prometheus* (New York: Modern Library 1993), xv–xx

LOWRY NELSON JR.

The gothic novel owes much to the popularity of exotic themes and to the emancipation of the novel from overt moral commitment. Perhaps it derives most from the enormous interest around the turn of the century in the solitary eccentric, the misfit, the social outcast, or, to use the handy phrase, the guilt-haunted wanderer. In the romantic transvaluation of values Cain becomes a sympathetic figure, unjustly cursed by a vengeful God and incapable of ever purging his guilt. He looks in vain for human trust and friendship; his "benevolent" impulses are thwarted; at worst he is twisted by circumstances into a monster of inhumanity—a tortured image of his tormentors. ⟨. . .⟩

Curiously enough, the fascination for the bizarre, the individual peculiarity, the monstrous seems to have led more significantly to a fictional discovery of the true depths of human nature than to a mere exploitation of the sensational and the perverse. By its insistence on singularity and exotic setting, the gothic novel seems to have freed the minds of readers from direct involvement of their superegos and allowed them to pursue daydreams and wish fulfilment in regions where inhibitions and guilt could be suspended. Those regions became thereby available to great writers who eventually demonstrated that sadism, indefinite guiltiness, mingled pleasure and pain (Maturin's "delicious agony"), and love-hate, were also deeply rooted in the minds of the supposedly normal. ⟨. . .⟩

What I should like to stress especially is that *Frankenstein* is not a mere tale of horror, but rather a significant fictional model of the mind. For the first time in gothic fiction characters take on the full symbolic resonance of inner psychological reality. To say flatly that the monster is Frankenstein's id on the rampage and that he subconsciously desires his family's extermination would be pretentious and anachronistic. Or to say that the monster uses murder as an attention-getting device would be foolishly reductive. It is quite different to argue that Frankenstein and his monster have much in common, that they are objectified parts of a single sensibility, and that they represent the intimate good and bad struggle in the human personality. Evil is within; in one's own works and creations. Good impulses are thwarted and evil ones encouraged by some inner perversity. The source of that perversity is perhaps a desire to be loved alone or an urge toward narcissism. Yet there is also the strong fascination with the gratuitous pursuit of one's evil nature. Frankenstein pursuing his monster is searching for his whole self. Human nature being what it is, total benevolence seems to create the spectre of monsters haunting the outskirts of Elysium: some sort of compromise must be made between the good and evil instincts of human nature in order to survive, since human nature deeply drives toward both good and evil; or at least some sort of modus vivendi must be found, most hopefully through full self-knowledge and self-discipline. While Ambrosio's unconscious incest was a form of unself-critical narcissism, Frankenstein's rejection of his created monster was a denial of his nether forces for which he should have accepted a fully aware responsibility.

Such mythifying interpretations of gothic novels may seem obvious and unnecessary, a case of misplaced solemnity. Still, it may not be excessive to hazard a generalization. In its earlier and cruder forms the gothic novel made irresponsible use of such claptrap as chains and dungeons and prodigies of weather. With *The Monk* and especially with *Frankenstein* we find that the claptrap has begun to take on symbolic resonance. Ambrosio's descent into the tombs is a descent into evil. His rape of Antonia in those surroundings prompts him to say, "This sepulchre seems to me Love's bower," thus reviving the old mythic and Shakespearean theme of the sepulchral marriage bed. But in Mrs. Shelley's novel much wider echoes resound. The cottage where the monster received his "upbringing" is an Eden in which he is the unwilling serpent or the reluctant Cain: his uncomprehended desire to be loved has destroyed the tranquillity of the uncomprehending others. The icy reaches in which Walton first descries the monster and his creator, and the brooding, glistening presence of Mont Blanc are ambiguous symbols of nature's innocence and also her indifference or cruelty: we are well on the way to the whiteness of the whale. Then, too, the moods of Frankenstein and his creature are often at variance with those of nature; instead of a one-to-one correspondence, often the sinister and the unnatural in men are heightened by nature's own innocent or indifferent serenity. Nature in Mrs. Shelley's novel is not the benevolently sympathetic or chastening nature of Byron and Wordsworth. In social terms we witness in *Frankenstein* a failure of "benevolence"; in personal terms, a mind incomplete without its "other" mind.

—Lowry Nelson Jr., "Night Thoughts on the Gothic Novel," *The Yale Review* 2, Vol. 52 (Winter 1963), reprinted in *Mary Shelley*, ed. Harold Bloom (New York: Chelsea House Publishers, 1985), 32–33, 40–41

HAROLD BLOOM

The antithesis between the scientist and his creature in Frankenstein is a very complex one, and to be described more fully it must be placed in the larger context of Romantic literature and its characteristic mythology. The shadow or double of the self is a constant conceptual image in Blake and Shelley, and a frequent image, more random and descriptive, in the other major Romantics, especially in Byron. In *Frankenstein*, it is the dominant and recurrent image, and accounts for much of the latent power the novel possesses. ⟨. . .⟩

Though abhorred rather than loved, the monster is the total form of Frankenstein's creative power, and is *more imaginative* than his creator. The monster is at once more intellectual *and* more emotional than his maker, indeed he excels Frankenstein as much (and in the same ways) as Milton's Adam excels Milton's God in *Paradise Lost*. The greatest paradox, and most astonishing achievement, of Mary Shelley's novel is that the monster is *more human* than his creator. This nameless being, as much a Modern Adam as his creator is a Modern Prometheus, is more lovable than his creator and more hateful, more to be pitied and more to be feared, and above all more able to give the attentive reader that shock of added consciousness which compels a heightened realization of the self. For, like Blake's Spectre and Emanation, or Shelley's Alastor and Epipsyche, Frankenstein and his monster are the solipsistic and generous halves of the one self. Frankenstein is the mind and emotions turned in upon themselves, and his creature is the mind and emotions turned imaginatively outward, seeking a greater humanization through a confrontation of other selves.

I am suggesting that what makes *Frankenstein* an important book, though it is only a strong, flawed, frequently clumsy novel is that it vividly projects a version of the Romantic mythology of the self, found among other places, in Blake's *Book of Urizen*, Shelley's *Prometheus Unbound* and Byron's *Manfred*. It lacks the sophistication and imaginative complexity of such works but precisely because of that *Frankenstein* affords a unique introduction to the archetypal world of the Romantics. ⟨. . .⟩

If we stand back from Mary Shelley's novel, in order better to view its archetypal shape, we see it as the quest of a solitary and ravaged consciousness first for consolation, then for revenge, and finally for a self-destruction that will be apocalyptic, that will bring down the creator with his creature. Though Mary Shelley may not have intended it, her novel's prime theme is a necessary counterpoise to Prometheanism, for Prometheanism exalts the increase in consciousness despite all cost. Frankenstein breaks through the barrier that separates man from God, and apparently becomes the giver of life, but all he actually can give is death-in-life. The profound dejection endemic in Mary Shelley's novel is fundamental to the Romantic mythology of the self, for all Romantic horrors are diseases of excessive consciousness, of the self unable to bear the self. Kierkegaard remarks that Satan's despair is absolute, because Satan as pure spirit is pure consciousness, and for Satan (and all men in his predicament) every increase in consciousness is an increase in despair. Frankenstein's desperate creature attains the state of pure spirit through his extraordinary situation, and is racked by a consciousness in which every thought is a fresh disease. ⟨. . .⟩

Romantic poets liked to return to the imagery of the ocean of life and immortality; in the eddying to and fro of the healing waters they could picture a hoped-for process of restoration, of a survival of consciousness despite all its agonies. Mary Shelley, with marvelous appropriateness, brings her Romantic novel to a demonic conclusion in a world of ice. The frozen sea is the inevitable emblem for both the wretched daemon and his obsessed creator, but the daemon is allowed a final image of reversed Prometheanism. There is a heroism fully earned in the being who cries farewell in a claim of sad triumph: "I shall ascend my funeral pyre triumphantly, and exult in the agony of the torturing flames." ⟨. . .⟩

Shelley's Prometheus, crucified on his icy precipice, found his ultimate torment in a Fury's taunt: "And all best things are thus confused to ill." It seems a fitting summation for all the work done by Modern Prometheanism, and might have served as an alternate epigraph for Mary Shelley's disturbing novel.

—Harold Bloom, "Frankenstein, or The New Prometheus," *Partisan Review* (Fall 1965), excerpted in *The Critical Perspective*, Vol. 7, ed. Harold Bloom (New York: Chelsea House Publishers, 1988), 4147–50

BRIAN W. ALDISS

A reading of the novel reveals how precariously it is balanced between the old age and the new. In Chapter Three, Victor Frankenstein goes to university and visits two professors. To the first, a man called Krempe who is professor of natural philosophy, he reveals how his search for knowledge took him to the works of Cornelius Agrippa, Paracelsus, and Albertus Magnus. Krempe scoffs at him. "These fancies, which you have so greedily imbibed, are a thousand years old!" This is a modern objection; antiquity is no longer the highest court to which one can appeal.

Frankenstein attends the second professor, one Waldman, who lectures on chemistry. Waldman condemns the ancient teachers who "promised impossibilities, and performed nothing." He speaks instead of the moderns, who use microscope and crucible, and converts Frankenstein to his way of thinking.

Symbolically, Frankenstein turns away from alchemy and the past towards science and the future—and is rewarded with his horrible success.

The hints in the novel as to how the "vital spark" is imparted in the composite body are elusive. In her Introduction to the 1831 edition, however, the author reveals the origins of her story. Like *The Castle of Otranto*, it began with a dream. In the dream, she saw "the hideous phantasm of a man stretched out, and then, on the working of some powerful engine, show signs of life, and stir with an uneasy, half vital motion." It was science fiction itself that stirred.

Greater events were stirring between the publication of the first and second editions of *Frankenstein*. The first volume of Lyell's *Principles of Geology* had just appeared, drastically extending the age of the Earth. Mantell and others were grubbing gigantic fossil bones out of the ground, exhuming genera from the rocks as surely as Frankenstein's creature was patched together from various corpses. Already beginning was that great extension to our imaginative lives which we call the Age of Reptiles—those defunct monsters we have summoned back to vigorous existence.

Other references in the 1831 Introduction are to galvanism and electricity. The Preface to the first edition of 1818 is also instructive. Although Mary had set herself to write a ghost story, her intentions changed; she states expressly in the Preface, "I have not considered myself as merely weaving a series of supernatural terrors." The Preface is an apologia, and Mary Shelley's chief witness for her defence, mentioned in her first sentence, is Erasmus Darwin.

The sources of *Frankenstein* are documented. As Mary Shelley explains, her dream was inspired by late-night conversations with her husband, with Byron, and with Dr. Polidori. Their talk was of vampires and the supernatural; Polidori supplied the company with some suitable reading material; and Byron and Shelley also discussed Darwin, his thought and his experiments.

Mary's dream of a hideous phantasm stirring to life carries a reminder of a nightmare recorded in her journal a year earlier. In March 1815, she had just lost her first baby, born prematurely. On the fifteenth of the month, she wrote: "Dream that my little baby came to life again; that it had only been cold, and that we had rubbed it before the fire, and it had lived." In retrospect, the words have an eerie ring.

The Outwardness of Science and society is balanced, in the novel, by an Inwardness which Mary's dream helped her to accommodate. This particular balance is perhaps one of *Frankenstein's* greatest merits: that its tale of exterior adventure and misfortune is always accompanied by a psychological depth.

—Brian W. Aldiss, *Billion Year Spree: The True History of Science Fiction* (Garden City, NY: Doubleday, 1973), 24–25

GEORGE LEVINE

Frankenstein does not look back to the sensation novel but forward to realistic books like Dostoevsky's *Crime and Punishment* or Conrad's *The Secret Sharer* which—like Coleridge's poem—explore the psychology of unorthodox aspirations and complicate traditional pieties with metaphysical mystery. ⟨. . .⟩

As many critics have noted, one of the most interesting aspects of *Frankenstein* is that, for the most part, it eschews the supernatural. Mary's originating idea for the story was developed from what was taken to be fact: "They talked," she wrote of Byron and Shelley in her introduction to the 1831 edition of the novel, "of the experiments of Dr. Darwin (I speak not of what the Doctor really did, or said that he did, but, as more to my purpose, of what was then spoken of as having been done by him), who preserved a piece of vermicelli in a glass case, till by some extraordinary means it began to move with voluntary motion. Not thus, after all, would life be given. Perhaps a corpse would be re-animated; galvanism had given token of such things: perhaps the component parts of a creature might be manufactured, brought together, and endued with vital warmth" (p. 9). In any case, beyond the fatal donnée—that it was possible to induce life into dead matter—*Frankenstein* fairly severely confines itself to the possible, if not always to the probable. It maintains a remarkable consistency and coherence of characterization and its surface details are either recognizable in ordinary experience or follow almost inevitably from the fact of the monster's existence. Given the initial idea, there is very little of the improbable in it. I don't mean to claim that it thus belongs within the traditions of realism, but rather that its effects and its power derive from its rejection of arbitrariness, indeed, from the almost austere way in which Mary Shelley insists on following out the consequences of her initial imagination. The scenery of the Alps, the mad chase across the Arctic ocean, the traditional abstract emotiveness of the language all link the novel with novels of sensation—as does the imagination of the hero himself. But by focusing so intensely on the landscape of the hero's mind, and on the product of its energies, and by eschewing any easy intervention of supernatural force, Mary Shelley sets out with astonishing clarity some of the moral implications of the heroic ideal. She writes, in fact, a brilliant psychological novel in which the psychology is the action itself, and while free to insist on the Wordsworthian, Coleridgean, and Shelleyan morals of the importance of community, domestic affections, love, and sensitivity to nature, she writes a story whose moral ambivalences of action are the real terror. ⟨. . .⟩

As a hero, Frankenstein is freed from the restraints of society usually imposed by the very texture of realism. He actually succeeds in creating what he desires, only to find that he doesn't desire it. But we can see here that the freedom is as illusory as Dorothea Brooke's or Isabel Archer's, that the pressures which, in realistic novels, seem to be imposed by a constricting society, are here imposed by the minimal condition of man—the condition, that is, of sentience and of family ties. "Alas!" says Frankenstein, "why does man boast of sensibilities superior to those apparent in the brute; it only renders them more necessary beings" (p. 97). Social pressures in fiction can frequently, if not always, be taken as objectifications of subjective states of feeling and being. In Hardy's *Jude the Obscure*, for example, it is possible to blame Jude's fate on a backward and oppressive society. But the full power of the book lies in the fact that Jude is destroyed as much by his own instincts as by society. Hardy's consistent lament at the unsuitability of man to the natural world is altogether in keeping with Frankenstein's vision here. And Lydgate's fall, we remember, though it has extraordinarily complicated social sources and implications, is as much the result of his own nature as of society's. *Frankenstein* gives us an opportunity to examine the energies of restraint and self-destruction that are built into the human condition precisely because it is not a social novel, because it does not work in the realist mode which depends so heavily on surfaces and the complexities of social relations and the multiplicity of things. In both worlds, freedom is illusory, responsibility is inevitable. ⟨. . .⟩

Thus *Frankenstein* provides us with a hero whose being, in every aspect, expresses precisely those tensions which are to preoccupy later English novelists, and Frankenstein enacts not only the role of the realist hero but the alternatives to that role which do much to explain the characteristic shape of realist fiction. The failure of Frankenstein to destroy his knowledge and to retreat to innocence foreshadows, I think, the ultimate self-destruction of realist techniques. Of course, this is a dangerously oversimple generalization, and puts rather a heavy burden on a novel which makes no such claims. But studying *Frankenstein* can help us to understand some of the powerful and inexplicit energies that lie beneath the surface of realist fiction in England and can help explain both the pervasive resistance to and distrust of ambition and energy in its heroes—their strange dullness and inadequacy—and the equally strange and subversive fascination with ambition and evil energies. Who would prefer Amelia Sedley to Becky Sharp, or Little Nell to Quilp, or Daniel Deronda to Grandcourt? The irrational is latent in every important English realist novel, and within every hero there is a Frankenstein—or his monster—waiting to get out.

—George Levine, "'Frankenstein' and the Tradition of Realism," *Novel* 1, Vol. 7 (Fall 1973), reprinted in *Mary Shelley*, ed. Harold Bloom (New York: Chelsea House Publishers, 1985), 84–85, 96–97, 99

PETER BROOKS

Mary Shelley's Monster is in many respects an Enlightenment natural man, or noble savage; his first ideas demonstrate the processes of Lockean sensationalism and Hartleyan associationism. His discovery of language implies Rousseau's argument, in the *Essai sur l'origine des langues*, that language springs from passion rather than need: need cannot form the necessary social context for voiced language, since its effect is to scatter men; and need can make do with the barest repertory of visual signs, gestures, imperatives. Passion, on the other hand, brings men together, and the relation of desire calls forth voice. It is hence no accident that what language first reveals to the Monster is human love, and that his rhetorical plea to his creator ends with the demand for a creature whom he might love.

The Monster also discovers an important corollary to Rousseau's postulate of the emotional origin of language: the radical figurality of language, its founding statute as misnaming, transference. The sign is not consubstantial with the thing it names: "the words they uttered, not having any apparent connection with visible objects, I was unable to discover any clue by which I could unravel the mystery of their reference." The Monster in this manner uncovers the larger question of the arbitrariness, or immotivation, of the linguistic sign, postulated by Ferdinand de Saussure as the foundation of modern linguistics. And the consequences of this recognition will be consonant with Saussure's: the understanding that the "godlike science" of language depends, not on simple designation, on passage from the signifier to the signified, but rather on the systematic organization of signifiers. The Monster intuitively grasps that language will be of importance to him because by its very nature it implies the "chain of existence and events" within which he seeks a place, defines the interdependency of senders and receivers of messages in that chain, and provides the possibility of emotional effect independent of any designation.

The Monster unerringly discovers language to be on the side of culture rather than nature, and to imply the structures of relation at the basis of culture. The discovery is a vital one, for the side of "nature" is irreparably marked by lack, by monsterism. Against the Monster's hearing of the cottagers' language is set his discovery of his own features mirrored in a pool—a sinister parody of Eve's discovery of her fair features in the pool of Eden, on the day of her creation, in Book IV of *Paradise Lost*. In *Frankenstein*, the reflected image convinces the beholder "that I was in reality the monster that I am." This speculary *cogito*, where the Monster witnesses his outward identity as alien to his inner desire, estranged, determined by the view and judgment of the Other, clinches the importance of language as the symbolic order that must compensate for nature. The Monster understands that he must not show himself to the cottagers until he has mastered their language, "which knowledge might enable me to make them overlook the deformity of my figure." ⟨. . .⟩

Language, and especially writing, must appear to the Monster, as it did to Rousseau, ambiguous in effect, like the Promethean gift of fire, so strange in its production of "opposite effects." Yet it remains the necessary compensation, the only hope for linkage to humankind. The Monster will try its effects first on the blind De Lacey. And here the godlike power of the science does reveal itself, as De Lacey responds: "I am blind, and cannot judge of your countenance, but there is something in your words which persuades me that you are sincere." Mutual sympathy, benefaction, protection, and relation are close to being sealed through language, when Felix, Agatha, and Safie enter and throw the situation brutally back into the speculary order: Agatha faints, Safie flees, and Felix "tore me from his father, to whose knees I clung." The result is Fall. The Monster becomes explicitly satanic—"I, like the arch-fiend, bore a hell within me," sets fire to the De Laceys' abandoned cottage, and sets forth into the world in search of his creator, the *deus absconditus* who alone now can restore, through a second creation, the Monster to the chain of living sympathies. It is during this search that the Monster commits his first murder. ⟨. . .⟩

The fact of monsterism suggests that nature in *Frankenstein* has something of the radical amorality described by Sade. For Sade, nature permits everything and authorizes nothing. Since all tastes and pleasures are in nature, no perversion can outrage and no crime alter nature; if one searches for an underlying pattern or principle in nature, what one finds is destruction itself. ⟨. . .⟩

Certainly Frankenstein's assault on and in the citadel of nature produces a monsterism that both reveals and mocks the arcane principle. The overriding fact of nature in the book—dominating Mont Blanc, the Lake of Geneva, the Hebrides, and all the other sublime natural settings—is the fact and possibility of monsterism itself. ⟨. . .⟩

It is a nature that eludes any optimistic Romanticism, and finally most resembles Freud's "uncanny": the Monster perfectly illustrates the *Unheimliche*, a monstrous potentiality so close to us—so close to home—that we have repressed its possibility, and assigned an *un* as the mark of censorship on what is indeed too *heimisch* for comfort.

The ambiguous and paradoxical nature of nature in *Frankenstein*—its seemingly equal potential as essentially good and as self-negatingly evil—cannot be resolved within the orders of the real or the imaginary, but only within the symbolic order, and only in structural terms. That is, the creations of nature will be bad or good only through the play of difference and relation, only in terms of their place in the signifying chain. This is what the Monster has understood by the time he makes his appeal to his creator for a *semblabel*, what indeed he has already grasped when he intuits the possibilities of the "godlike science." In the play of sameness and difference that founds the system of our signs for things, then in grammar and syntax, we have the basis of relation and the possibility of exchange of tokens, communication. The Monster's failure—what establishes him irremediably *as* monster—is his inability, despite his eloquence, to find relation.

—Peter Brooks, "'Godlike Science/Unhallowed Arts'': Language, Nature, and Monstrosity," *The Endurance of Frankenstein* (1979), reprinted in *Mary Shelley*, ed. Harold Bloom (New York: Chelsea House Publishers, 1985), 104–6, 111–12

JUDITH WILT

For an atheist, the palimpsest of Bible stories contrived for *Frankenstein* is suspiciously thick. Satan, Cain and Judas, Abraham, Adam and Christ, and the thousand names of the unnameable God, jostle in the figures of Victor Frankenstein and his creature like ghosts in a haunted house. Literally, their name is Legion. Shelley's protagonists wear themselves out trying to manage the spiritual archetypes laid over them by the great Christian poets—wear themselves and each other down to emaciation. ⟨. . .⟩

Still, Shelley's book derives its special force not from eccentricity but from an eerie familiarity with an astonishing variety of contexts. And one of these contexts is exactly the God-haunted English Gothic tradition. *Frankenstein* is of a piece with Matthew Lewis's *The Monk* (1796) and James Hogg's *The Private Memoirs and Confessions of a Justified Sinner* (1824), in a tradition that is painfully acting out under the nose of the Enlightenment a long line of expunged doctrines—Justification, Creation, Damnation—and unspeakable sacraments—Holy Orders, Confession, Communion. A tradition, unmistakably, from Horace Walpole's *The Castle of Otranto* (1765) to Bram Stoker's *Dracula* (1897), the Mystery Play of the Romantic mind. We thought the Gothicists were hiding something in all that incense and chapelgloom, mitres, crosses, hosts and hoods, wimples and prayers. And they hid it, Watson, where it is hardest to find, in the most obvious place: on the surface. ⟨. . .⟩

It was ⟨. . .⟩ the Trinitarian Question, the deep-structured subject of the English Gothic Mystery, the attempt to explore and explain the flight of a parental mind out of itself into what Frankenstein's Creature will gropingly call "the series" of its being. As both Frankenstein and his Creature will discover, this flight involves a double peril. If the flight is successful, each member in the series is diminished; if the flight is not successful, neither movement nor growth is possible. The struggle of Frankenstein and his Creature, the Father and the Son, is in this context powerfully arresting and inconclusive.

Nightmare waits on both sides: diminishment leads finally to non-being, yet the failure to extend brings the horrors of paralysis and inward diminu-tion. ⟨. . .⟩

Classic Gothic, the orthodox sublime, believes in correspondence, believes in love, strives against limits. It is one of the major "spines" of Romance and yet it is one of the most deeply conservative of the Romance genres, punishing first the community that declines to strive and then the striving being who preempts that function. Classic Gothic creates the Romance world of two opposite absolutes, but the special flavor of the Gothic, as Lawrence notes, is to show not the inevitability and stamina of duality, as Romance often does, but the vulnerability of it. *Pace* Lévi-Strauss, the bi-structured world is radically unstable, it seeks collapse into oneness, or else seeks to generate a third term to marshall itself into unity, not oneness. That is why in the Christian Mystery the Trinity needs the Holy Ghost, that unseen triangulation point that makes "person" possible. That is what Lawrence means by the Holy Ghost, a third dimension with no manifestation to the general world that provides space to dwell in for beings who otherwise were simply points on a line infinitely collapsing. The Gothic describes the failure of its significant people to generate that triangulation point, listen to the Holy Ghost. Romance may show the duality, the opposite absolutes, still holding apart in tension, but Gothic Romance usually shows the merge-back-together.

Frankenstein shows all these actions. At the ultimate edge of miserable hos-tile merging the creature seeks to generate a third term in the duality, a woman with whom he can triangulate sufficient mental space to deal with Frankenstein. And Frankenstein tries to do this himself with Elizabeth. Then, jealous and doomed, each destroys the other's triangulation point, the other's Holy Ghost. Instinctively Mary Shelley seeks this same thing in her artistic structure, creating the explorer Walton to raise and then to frustrate expecta-tions of greater mental space within the novel. But though she can give Walton pertinence and even some complexity, she cannot give him weight enough to make that third dimension; so the novel tightens and tautens back into its destined shape, the Gothic Romance, the duality snapping back into merge and annihilation, "borne away by the waves and lost in darkness and distance." The Trinity was never achieved. The Mystery was Poe's Mystery, Decreation.

—Judith Wilt, *"Frankenstein as Mystery Play," The Endurance of Frankenstein: Essays on Mary Shelley's Novel*, ed. George Levine and U. C. Knoepflmacher (Berkeley: University of California Press, 1979), 31–33, 47–48

KATE ELLIS

The circularity of *Frankenstein* underscores Mary Shelley's critique of the insufficiency of a family structure in which the relation between the sexes is as uneven as the relationship between parents and children. The two "outside" narrators, Walton and Frankenstein, are both benevolent men whose exile from the domestic hearth drives them deeper and deeper into isolation. Neither, however, can see that his deprivation might have been avoided through a better understanding of the limits of the institution into which he was born. Even the De Lacey family, where these limits are meaningfully transcended, is basically innocent of what Mary Wollstonecraft, in the title of chapter 9 of her *Vindication of the Rights of Woman*, had called "the pernicious effects which arise from the unnatural distinctions established in society." ⟨. . .⟩

This leaves only the Monster to articulate the experience of being denied the domestic affections of a child, sibling, husband, and parent. In his campaign of revenge, the Monster goes to the root of his father's character deformation, when he wipes out those who played a part, however unwitting, in fostering, justifying, or replicating it. If we view his violent acts as components of a horror story, the novel can be read either as a warning against uncontrolled technology and the ambition that brings it into being, or as a fantasy of the return of the repressed, a drama of man at war with alienated parts of himself, variously identified. But an additional meaning emerges if we also take the violence in the novel to constitute a language of protest, the effect of which is to expose the "wrongs" done to women and children, friends and fiancés, in the name of domestic affection. It is a language none of the characters can fully decode because they lack the perspective on bourgeois domesticity that Mary Shelley had learned, principally from her mother's writings, and which she assumed, perhaps naively, in her readers. ⟨. . .⟩

The deficiencies of Victor's family, dramatized in his inability to bring the Monster home (openly, that is), to deal with evil in the outside world, or to own the repressed impulses that others are acting out for him, stem ultimately from the concept of domestic affection on which the continuing tranquility of the family depends. The root of this evil lies in the separation of male and female spheres for purposes of maintaining the purity of the family and the sanctity of the home. The effect of domestic affection on both Victor and Walton is "an invincible repugnance to new countenances" that leads them toward the solitary pursuit of glory, which paradoxically disqualifies them for domestic affection. Once touched by the outside world, they cannot reenter the domestic circle without destroying its purity. Victor's rejection of the Monster also makes it impossible for him to embrace Elizabeth without destroying the purity that is her major attraction in his eyes.

Scholarly interest in the bourgeois family, the target of Mary Shelley's critique of domestic affection, has received a good deal of impetus in the last ten years from the feminist movement's attempts to name and trace the origins of what Betty Friedan has called "the problem that has no name." Shelley seems to suggest that, if the family is to be a viable institution for the transmission of domestic affection from one generation to the next, it must redefine that precious commodity in such a way that it can extend to "outsiders" and become hardy enough to survive in the world outside the home. It is not surprising that a woman should be making this point. Eradicating the artificial gulf between the work of the world and the work of the home is of greater concern to women than men since they experience in almost every aspect of their lives the resultant "unnatural distinctions established in society" against which Mary Wollstonecraft protested almost two hundred years ago. If we can imagine a novel in which a woman scientist creates a monster who returns to destroy her family, the relevance to women of the problem that Mary Shelley has imagined becomes more immediately apparent. ⟨. . .⟩

The kind of family that Shelley is describing shapes us still: its most distinctive feature is that of the dominant yet absent father, working outside the home to support a dependent (or underpaid), subservient wife and children, all roles circularly functioning to reinforce his dominance. *Frankenstein* is indeed a birth myth, but one in which the parent who "brought death into the world, and all our woe" is not a woman but a man who has pushed the masculine prerogative past the limits of nature, creating life not through the female body but in a laboratory.

—Kate Ellis, "Monsters in the Garden: Mary Shelley and the Bourgeois Family," *The Endurance of Frankenstein: Essays on Mary Shelley's Novel*, ed. George Levine and U. C. Knoepflmacher (Berkeley: University of California Press, 1979), 125–26, 140–42

ELLEN MOERS

Mary Shelley's *Frankenstein*, in 1818, made the Gothic novel over into what today we call science fiction. *Frankenstein* brought a new sophistication to literary terror, and it did so without a heroine, without even an important female victim. Paradoxically, however, no other Gothic work by a woman writer, perhaps no literary work of any kind by a woman, better repays examination in the light of the sex of its author. For *Frankenstein* is a birth myth, and one that was lodged in the novelist's imagination, I am convinced, by the fact that she was herself a mother.

Much in Mary Shelley's life was remarkable. She was the daughter of a brilliant mother (Mary Wollstonecraft) and father (William Godwin). She was the mistress and then wife of the poet Shelley. She read widely in five languages, including Latin and Greek. She had easy access to the writings and conversation of some of the most original minds of her age. But nothing so sets her apart from the generality of writers of her own time, and before, and for long afterward, than her early and chaotic experience, at the very time she became an author, with motherhood. Pregnant at sixteen, and almost constantly pregnant throughout the following five years; yet not a secure mother, for she lost most of her babies soon after they were born; and not a lawful mother, for she was not married—not at least when, at the age of eighteen, Mary Godwin began to write *Frankenstein*. So are monsters born.

What in fact has the experience of giving birth to do with women's literature? In the eighteenth and nineteenth centuries relatively few important women writers bore children; most of them, in England and America, were spinsters and virgins. With the coming of Naturalism late in the century, and the lifting of the Victorian taboo against writing about physical sexuality (including pregnancy and labor), the subject of birth was first brought to literature in realistic form by the male novelists, from Tolstoy and Zola to William Carlos Williams. ⟨. . .⟩

Mary Shelley was a unique case, in literature as in life. She brought birth to fiction not as realism but as Gothic fantasy, and thus contributed to Romanticism a myth of genuine originality: the mad scientist who locks himself in his laboratory and secretly, guiltily, works at creating human life, only to find that he has made a monster. ⟨. . .⟩

That is very good horror, but what follows is more horrid still: Frankenstein, the scientist, runs away and abandons the newborn Monster, who is and remains nameless. Here, I think, is where Mary Shelley's book is most interesting, most powerful, and most feminine: in the motif of revulsion against newborn life, and the drama of guilt, dread, and flight surrounding birth and its consequences. Most of the novel, roughly two of its three volumes, can be said to deal with the retribution visited upon Monster and creator for deficient infant care. *Frankenstein* seems to be distinctly a woman's mythmaking on the subject of birth precisely because its emphasis is not upon what precedes birth, not upon birth itself, but upon what follows birth: the trauma of the afterbirth. ⟨. . .⟩

The versatility of Mary Shelley's myth is due to the brilliance of her mind and the range of her learning, as well as to the influence of the circle in which she moved as a young writer. But *Frankenstein* was most original in its dramatization of dangerous oppositions through the struggle of a creator with monstrous creation. The sources of this Gothic conception, which still has power to "curdle the blood, and quicken the beatings of the heart," were surely the anxieties of a woman who, as daughter, mistress, and mother, was a bearer of death.

—Ellen Moers, "Female Gothic," *The Endurance of Frankenstein: Essays on Mary Shelley's Novel*, ed. George Levine and U. C. Knoepflmacher (Berkeley: University of California Press, 1979), 79–81, 86

SANDRA M. GILBERT AND SUSAN GUBAR

It is still undeniably true that Mary Shelley's "ghost story," growing from a Keatsian (or Coleridgean) waking dream, is a Romantic novel about—among other things—Romanticism, as well as a book about books and perhaps, too, about the writers of books. Any theorist of the novel's femaleness and of its significance as, in Moers's phrase, a "birth myth" must therefore confront this self-conscious literariness. For as was only natural in "the daughter of two persons of distinguished literary celebrity," Mary Shelley explained her sexuality to herself in the context of her reading and its powerfully felt implications. 〈. . .〉

Endlessly studying her mother's works and her father's, Mary Shelley may be said to have "read" her family and to have been related to her reading, for books appear to have functioned as her surrogate parents, pages and words standing in for flesh and blood. That much of her reading was undertaken in Shelley's company, moreover, may also help explain some of this obsessiveness, for Mary's literary inheritance was obviously involved in her very literary romance and marriage. In the years just before she wrote *Frankenstein*, for instance, and those when she was engaged in composing the novel (1816–17), she studied her parents' writings, alone or together with Shelley, like a scholarly detective seeking clues to the significance of some cryptic text.

To be sure, this investigation of the mysteries of literary genealogy was done in a larger context. In these same years, Mary Shelley recorded innumerable readings of contemporary gothic novels, as well as a program of study in English, French, and German literature that would do credit to a modern graduate student. But especially, in 1815, 1816, and 1817, she read the works of Milton: *Paradise Lost* (twice), *Paradise Regained, Comus, Areopagetica, Lycidas*. And what makes the extent of this reading particularly impressive is the fact that in these years, her seventeenth to her twenty-first, Mary Shelley was almost continuously pregnant, "confined," or nursing. At the same time, it is precisely the coincidence of all these disparate activities—her family studies, her initiation into adult sexuality, and her literary self-education—that makes her vision of *Paradise Lost* so significant. For her developing sense of herself as a literary creature and/or creator seems to have been inseparable from her emerging self-definition as daughter, mistress, wife, and mother. Thus she cast her birth myth—her myth of origins—in precisely those cosmogenic terms to which her parents, her husband, and indeed her whole literary culture continually alluded: the terms of *Paradise Lost*, which (as she indicates even on the title page of her novel), she saw as preceding, paralleling, and commenting upon the Greek cosmogeny of the Prometheus play her husband had just translated. It is as a female fantasy of sex and reading, then, a gothic psychodrama reflecting Mary Shelley's own sense of what we might call bibliogenesis, that *Frankenstein* is a version of the misogynistic story implicit in *Paradise Lost*. ⟨. . .⟩

In fact, it is his intellectual similarity to his authoress (rather than his "author") which first suggests that Victor Frankenstein's male monster may really be a female in disguise. Certainly the books which educate him—*Werter*, Plutarch's *Lives*, and *Paradise Lost*—are not only books Mary had herself read in 1815, the year before she wrote *Frankenstein*, but they also typify just the literary categories she thought it necessary to study: the contemporary novel of sensibility, the serious history of Western civilization, and the highly cultivated epic poem. As specific works, moreover, each must have seemed to her to embody lessons a female author (or monster) must learn about a male-dominated society. ⟨. . .⟩

Though *Frankenstein* itself began with a Coleridgean and Miltonic nightmare of filthy creation that reached its nadir in the monster's revelation of filthy femaleness, Mary Shelley, like Victor Frankenstein himself, evidently needed to distance such monstrous secrets. Sinful, motherless Eve and sinned-against, daughterless Maria, both paradigms of woman's helpless alienation in a male society, briefly emerge from the sea of male heroes and villains in which they have almost been lost, but the ice soon closes over their heads again, just as it closes around those two insane figure-skaters, Victor Frankenstein and his hideous offspring. Moving outward from the central "birth myth" to the icy perimeter on which the novel began, we find ourselves caught up once more in Walton's naive polar journey, where Frankenstein and his monster reappear as two embattled grotesques, distant and archetypal figures solipsistically drifting away from each other on separate icebergs. In Walton's scheme of things, they look again like God and Adam, Satanically conceived. But now, with our more nearly complete understanding of the bewildered and bewildering perspective Mary Shelley adopted as "Milton's daughter," we see that they were Eve and Eve all along.

—Sandra M. Gilbert and Susan Gubar, "Horror's Twin: Mary Shelley's Monstrous Eve," *The Madwoman in the Attic* (1979), reprinted in *Mary Shelley*, ed. Harold Bloom (New York: Chelsea House Publishers, 1985), 116–18, 128, 135–40

GIOVANNA FRANCI

The Last Man, the work which Mary Shelley wrote after the death of her husband, Perry Bysshe Shelley, and of close friends, such as Byron, is a book which is fairly complex in form and far from simple in interpretation. On one level it may be read as an autobiographical work, fruit of a desperate solitude, yet at the same time it reveals a far more insistent and intricate message which may be read as a lucid *dystopia*, an apocalyptic prophecy of the end of the world.

In *Frankenstein*, and even more so in *The Last Man*, Mary Shelley reveals herself as an "unwilling prophetess" of a human destiny of death and self-destruction. In this way she takes her place among the ranks of numerous other authors of "tales of the future" written in the first decades of the nineteenth century, a symptom of a profound uneasiness which followed the failure of great revolutions and the crisis of radical and liberal ideology which expressed a negative response to the effects of the industrial revolution.

Frankenstein and *The Last Man* may be placed between the Gothic or the literature of terror, which represents the "dark" side, the "unsaid" of bourgeois literature, even its guilty conscience, and science fiction conceived as prophetic writing or anticipation of catastrophe, as *Apocalypse* or Revelation. However, in the case of Mary Shelley definitions in terms of "genre" are not possible. Past and future, Gothic and science fiction are unified in the dream-nightmare, and the bourgeois world is presented as both self-creation and self-destruction. Reason produces monsters; the true "robot" is Man who creates a pale caricature of himself, a double, a *doppelgänger* which proves worse than the original, a monster. It is the failure of Modern Prometheus: Man is condemned to solitude, able only to create a desert around himself. It is also the negation of the doctrine of evolution and of progress. ⟨. . .⟩

Frankenstein and *The Last Man* both form part of a single imaginative trend; both represent symptoms of a critique and are cryptic carriers of a common message. The contradictory tragedy and modernness of *Frankenstein* lies in the placing of the classical hubris myth within a situation of conflictual division of Man and Nature; almost all modern art springs from and expresses such a division. It is precisely the situation of the Modern Prometheus who must move from the foolish exaltation of the individual capacities of Man in the rôle of a creator of a *new nature* (and of new life) to reach an awareness of the futility of his own exertions. ⟨. . .⟩

The problem is, fundamentally, the problem of *identity* which will form the dominant theme of almost all modern bourgeois literature, "the great puzzle," as Lewis Carroll will later define it. Mary Shelley is fully aware of this. The endless questions about his origins which the monster, creature and alter-ego of Frankenstein asks, "Who was I? What was I? Whence did I come?," are only answered when his reflected image—his specular *cogito*—brings him to the recognition that "I was in reality the monster that I am." The terrifying spectre which the mirror casts up before Lionel towards the end of his wanderings is a further manifest sign of the identity dichotomy. The reflected image in this instance is the last tattered shred of *individuality*, "the miserable object there portrayed," its final identification. Mary Shelley created an impressive myth of the present time in *The Last Man*. ⟨. . .⟩

A story of the end (of the world) is often a vehicle for fear of the end which thus succeeds in distancing death and asserting identity: *I* write about *me*. In this sense "the end is the metalinguistic utterance which appears to be capable of generating all possible texts." However, in Mary Shelley's novel the book in which Lionel Verney narrates his own story and the history of the end of the world is dedicated to the dead, to the past, and is not projected into the future. In contrast to messages which are intended to be discovered or received, cast in a bottle on the sea or hidden in some secret hiding place, this message has no intended end. It is rather a way of settling accounts with himself, of having nothing further to do with history. Here writing and myth are seen as a hieroglyphic which must be deciphered, but it is also the end of all myth because myth forms part of history. At the end of Lionel Verney's story there is only a final glance back to the "original opening scene" before the curtain drops for ever: "He is solitary; like our first parents expelled from Paradise." Separating the end from the beginning there stands "the flaming sword of plague."

> —Giovanna Franci, "A Mirror of the Future: Vision and Apocalypse in Mary Shelley's 'The Last Man'," *Mary Shelley*, ed. Harold Bloom (New York: Chelsea House Publishers, 1985), 183, 187–88, 190

BIBLIOGRAPHY

Mounseer Nongtongpaw; or, The Discoveries of John Bull in a Trip to Paris. 1808.

History of a Six Weeks' Tour through a Part of France, Switzerland, Germany and Holland (with Percy Bysshe Shelley). 1817.

Frankenstein; or, The Modern Prometheus (3 vols.). 1818.

Valperga; or, The Life and Adventures of Castruccio, Prince of Lucca (3 vols.). 1823.

Posthumous Poems by Percy Bysshe Shelley (editor). 1824.

The Last Man (3 vols.). 1826.

The Fortunes of Perkin Warbeck: A Romance (3 vols.). 1830.

Lodore (3 vols.). 1835.

Falkner (3 vols.). 1837.

Poetical Works by Percy Bysshe Shelley (editor) (4 vols.). 1839.

Essays, Letters from Abroad, Translations and Fragments by Percy Bysshe Shelley (editor)
     (2 vols.). 1840.

Rambles in Germany and Italy in 1840, 1842, and 1843 (2 vols.). 1844.

The Choice: A Poem on Shelley's Death. 1876.

Tales and Stories. 1891.

Letters, Mostly Unpublished. 1918.

Proserpine and Midas: Mythological Dramas. 1922.

*Harriet and Mary: Being the Relations between P. B., Harriet and Mary Shelley and
     T. J. Hogg as Shown in Letters between Them* (with others). 1944.

Letters (2 vols.). 1944.

Journal. 1947.

My Best Mary: Selected Letters. Ed. Muriel Spark and Derek Stanford. 1953.

Matilda. 1959.

Shelley's Posthumous Poems: Mary Shelley's Fair Copy Book (editor). 1969.

Collected Tales and Stories. 1976.

Letters (3 vols.). 1980–88.

The Journals of Mary Shelley (2 vols.). 1987.

The Mary Shelley Reader. 1990.

FRANCES TROLLOPE
1779-1863

FRANCES TROLLOPE was born on March 10, 1779, the second daughter of the Reverend William Milton, vicar of Heckfield, near Bristol. She was educated at home and then left Heckfield to go to London to keep house for her brother. In London she met Thomas Anthony Trollope, a barrister who appeared at the time to have a good career. In fact, during the Trollopes' marriage, he did not succeed as a barrister, a farmer, or a merchant. Furthermore, only two of the couple's seven children survived into adulthood. One of these was the prolific Victorian novelist Anthony Trollope. The family lived at Harrow Weald from 1813 to 1827, when there was a severe agricultural depression. In 1827, Thomas Trollope's farming failure permanently affected his personality and Mrs. Trollope took three of her children to the United States. She settled in Cincinnati, where she attempted to earn money by establishing a bazaar. The bazaar proved to be a miserable failure, but Trollope got her revenge on America by writing her first book, the infamous *Domestic Manners of the Americans* (1832). This unflattering portrait of American life generated sensational interest in England and hostility in America.

It also launched a lucrative writing career for fifty-one-year-old Frances Trollope. This was fortunate, since Trollope needed to write to support her family. Around this time, the family's house was seized by bailiffs and the family forced to flee to Belgium, where Thomas Trollope died, his spirit broken, in 1835. In addition, several of the Trollope children were suffering from tuberculosis. By temperament both energetic and cheerful, Mrs. Trollope wrote an average of two books a year. After the success of *The Domestic Manners of the Americans*, Mrs. Trollope wrote travel books about Paris and Italy. Her fiction covered a diversity of topics and genres. She wrote a number of American novels, including the antislavery work, *Jonathan Jefferson Whitlow* (1836), and her social views are also reflected in *Michael Armstrong, The Factory Boy* (1839), and *Jessie Philips* (1843). The "Widow Barnaby" trilogy, which consists of *The Widow Barnaby* (1839), *The Widow Married* (1840), and *The Barnabys in America* (1843), featured a female rogue as their main character and are today considered Trollope's best comic work. Other comedies include *Charles Chesterfield; or, The Adventures of a Youth of Genius* (1841) and *The Blue Belles of England* (1842).

Trollope spent her last years in Florence, where she settled with her son Thomas Adolphus Trollope and his wife. She established a salon, which was frequented by supporters of the Italian Revolution. She continued to write until age 76, and her rigorous work habits may have influenced her son Anthony, who, like his mother, also rose early and wrote under less-than-ideal conditions. Mrs. Trollope died in Florence on October 6, 1863.

CRITICAL EXTRACTS

HENRY T. TUCKERMAN

The truth is, that Mrs. Trollope's powers of observation are remarkable. What she sees, she describes with vivacity, and often with accurate skill. No one can read her Travels in Austria without acknowledging the vigor and brightness of her mind. Personal disappointment in a pecuniary enterprise vexes her judgment; and, like so many of her nation, she thoroughly disliked the political institutions of the United States, was on the lookout for social anomalies and personal defects, and persistent, like her "unreasoning sex," in attributing all that was offensive or undesirable in her experience to the prejudice she cherished. Moreover, her experience itself was limited and local. She entered the country more than thirty years ago, at New Orleans, and passed most of the time, during her sojourn, amid the new and thriving but crude and confident Western communities, where neither manners nor culture, economy nor character had attained any well-organized or harmonious development. The self-love of these independent but sometimes rough pioneers of civilization, was wounded by the severe comments of a stranger who had shared their hospitality, when she expatiated on their reckless use of tobacco, their too free speech and angular attitudes; but, especially, when all their shortcomings were declared the natural result of republican institutions. Hence the outcry her book occasioned, and the factitious importance attached thereto. Not a single fault is found recorded by her, which our own writers, and every candid citizen, have not often admitted and complained of. The fast eating, boastful talk, transient female beauty, inadequate domestic service, abuse of calomel as a remedy, copious and careless expectoration, free and easy manners, superficial culture, and many other traits, more or less true now as then, here or there, are or have been normal subjects of animadversion. It was not because Mrs. Trollope did not write much truth about the country and the people, that, among classes of the latter, her name was a reproach; but because she reasoned so perversely, and did not take the pains to ascertain the whole truth, and to recognize the compensatory facts of American life. ⟨. . .⟩

With more perspicacity and less prejudice, she would have acknowledged the temporary character of many of the facts of the hour, emphasized by her pen as permanent. The superficial reading she notes, for instance, was but the eager thirst for knowledge that has since expanded into so wide a habit of culture that the statistics of the book trade in the United States have become one of the intellectual marvels of the age. Her investigation as to the talent, sources of discipline, and development, were extremely incurious and slight; hence, what she says of our statesmen and men of letters is too meagre for comment. The only American author she appears to have known well was Flint; and her warm appreciation of his writings and conversation, indicates what a better knowledge of our scholars and eminent professional men would have elicited from so shrewd an observer. The redeeming feature of her book is the love of nature it exhibits. American scenery often reconciles her to the bad food and worse manners; the waterfalls, rivers, and forests are themes of perpetual admiration. "So powerful," she writes of a passage down one of the majestic streams of the West, "was the effect of this sweet scenery, that we ceased to grumble at our dinners and suppers." Strange to say, she was delighted with the city of Washington, extols the Capitol, and recognizes the peculiar merits of Philadelphia. In fact, when she writes of what she sees, apart from prejudice, there are true woman's wit and sense in her descriptions; but she does not discriminate, or patiently inquire. Her book is one of impressions—some very just, and others casual. She was provoked at being often told, in reply to some remark. "That is because you know so little of America;" and yet the observation is one continually suggested by her too hasty conclusions. With all its defects, however, few of the class of books to which it belongs are better worth reading now than this once famous record of Mrs. Trollope. It has a certain freshness and boldness about it that explain its original popularity. Its tone, also, in no small degree explains its unpopularity; for the writer, quoting a remark of Basil Hall's, to the effect that the great difference between Americans and English is the want of loyalty, declares it, in her opinion, is the want of refinement. And it is upon that that she harps continually in her strictures, while the reader is offended by the identical deficiency in herself; and herein we find the secret of the popular protest the book elicited on this side of the water; for those who felt they needed to be lectured on manners, repudiated such a female writer as authoritative, and regarded her assumption of the office as more than gratuitous.

—Henry T. Tuckerman, "British Travellers and Writers," *America and Her Commentators* (1864), excerpted in *The New Moulton's Library of Literary Criticism*, Vol. 8, ed. Harold Bloom (New York: Chelsea House Publishers, 1989), 4704–705

ANTHONY TROLLOPE

In 1827 she went to America, having been partly instigated by the social and communistic ideas of a lady whom I well remember,—a certain Miss Wright,—who was, I think, the first of the American female lecturers. Her chief desire, however, was to establish my brother Henry; and perhaps joined with that was the additional object of breaking up her English home without pleading broken fortunes to all the world. At Cincinnati, in the State of Ohio, she built a bazaar, and I fancy lost all the money which may have been embarked in that speculation. It could not have been much, and I think that others also must have suffered. But she looked about her, at her American cousins, and resolved to write a book about them. This book she brought back with her in 1831, and published it early in 1832. When she did this she was already fifty. When doing this she was aware that unless she could so succeed in making money, there was no money for any of the family. She had never before earned a shilling. She almost immediately received a considerable sum from the publishers,—if I remember rightly, amounting to two sums of £400 each within a few months; and from that moment till nearly the time of her death, at any rate for more than twenty years, she was in the receipt of a considerable income from her writings. It was a late age at which to begin such a career.

The Domestic Manners of the Americans was the first of a series of books of travels, of which it was probably the best, and was certainly the best known. It will not be too much to say of it that it had a material effect upon the manners of the Americans of the day, and that that effect has been fully appreciated by them. No observer was certainly ever less qualified to judge of the prospects or even of the happiness of a young people. No one could have been worse adapted by nature for the task of learning whether a nation was in a way to thrive. Whatever she saw she judged, as most women do, from her own standing-point. If a thing were ugly to her eyes, it ought to be ugly to all eyes,—and if ugly, it must be bad. What though people had plenty to eat and clothes to wear, if they put their feet upon the tables and did not reverence their betters? The Americans were to her rough, uncouth, and vulgar,—and she told them so. Those communistic and social ideas, which had been so pretty in a drawing-room, were scattered to the winds. Her volumes were very bitter; but they were very clever, and they saved the family from ruin.

Book followed book immediately,—first two novels, and then a book on Belgium and Western Germany. She refurnished the house which I have called Orley Farm, and surrounded us again with moderate comforts. Of the mixture of joviality and industry which formed her character, it is almost impossible to speak with exaggeration. The industry was a thing apart, kept to herself. It was not necessary that any one who lived with her should see it. She was at her table at four in the morning, and had finished her work before the world had begun to be aroused. But the joviality was all for others. She could dance with other people's legs, eat and drink with other people's palates, be proud with the lustre of other people's finery. Every mother can do that for her own daughters; but she could do it for any girl whose look, and voice, and manners pleased her. Even when she was at work, the laughter of those she loved was a pleasure to her. She had much, very much, to suffer. Work sometimes came hard to her, so much being required,—for she was extravagant, and liked to have money to spend; but of all people I have known she was the most joyous, or, at any rate, the most capable of joy.

⟨. . .⟩ She continued writing up to 1856, when she was seventy-six years old,—and had at that time produced 114 volumes, of which the first was not written till she was fifty. Her career offers great encouragement to those who have not began early in life, but are still ambitious to do something before they depart hence.

She was an unselfish, affectionate, and most industrious woman, with great capacity for enjoyment and high physical gifts. She was endowed, too, with much creative power, with considerable humour, and a genuine feeling for romance. But she was neither clear-sighted nor accurate; and in her attempts to describe morals, manners, and even facts, was unable to avoid the pitfalls of exaggeration.

—Anthony Trollope, *An Autobiography* (1883), excerpted in *The New Moulton's Library of Literary Criticism*, Vol. 8, ed. Harold Bloom (New York: Chelsea House Publishers, 1989), 4701–702

Roger P. Wallins

In creating such a character as Sir Matthew Dowling, Mrs. Trollope was appealing to a known Victorian taste for melodrama. The melodramatic element in *Michael Armstrong* is in fact one major reason that the novel has sunk into oblivion. For Sir Matthew's evilness is devoid of any redeeming qualities; he engenders in the reader no sympathetic understanding and no desire to understand. Similarly, Michael's purity and innocence are cloying in their own way: born good, raised good, he survives all the machinations of Sir Matthew and remains the good-natured, kind, and innocent youth who finally—melodramatically, of course—achieves personal happiness. But Michael's character also enabled Mrs. Trollope to convey social criticism because he had the Victorian audience's complete sympathy, evoked partly by his good nature and partly by the evil that Sir Matthew does to him. Thus the Victorian reader was agitated by the factory conditions in which such good young boys had to work, and by the poverty in which they were forced to live. When Michael is temporarily rescued from Sir Matthew's clutches, he tells his rescuer, "I should very much like never to go to work at the factory any more" (ii, 16). He thus expresses the desire held by every factory child in the book, and helps enforce the author's social message.

Mrs. Trollope thus achieves some artistic success with her characterizations. She is less fortunate in the narrative techniques she employs to convey social information to her readers. Too often she intrudes into the story in her own voice in order to comment directly on events and on the living and working conditions of the young factory workers. Her intrusions are occasionally so long that her readers can lose sight of the major plot action. At times, too, her comments are not immediately relevant to their context. ⟨. . .⟩

Mrs. Trollope often conveys necessary information by reporting discussions between characters, but such a narrative technique creates a major artistic problem: the tedium inherent in pages of dialogue asserting the author's viewpoint on a social issue. When Mary Brotherton, a member of the upper class interested in the welfare of factory workers becomes a close friend of Mr. Bell, a local champion of factory workers, Mrs. Trollope fails to integrate their long discussions effectively into the rest of her story. ⟨. . .⟩

Mrs. Trollope seems to have recognized her difficulties, although she is unable to avoid them. In Mary Brotherton's reference to Michael as "a hero of romance" (xxii, 377), Mrs. Trollope acknowledges the episodic and romantic nature of the second half of the novel. It is her way of admitting that her characters do not develop, do not change: Michael is always the pure and innocent hero, Sir Matthew the evil manufacturer. It is her means of explaining away—if not excusing—her own authorial intrusions and certainly the long question-and-answer discussions between characters. It is her acceptance too of her digressive, episodic plot, especially in the second half of the novel.

Nonetheless, we must recognize her early successful integration of her two plot strands and, just as importantly, the variation of the discussion technique which she introduces in Mary Brotherton's quest for knowledge. By Mary's insistent questioning, and more especially by the inadequate answers she receives early in the novel, we see her in the process of developing ideas about factory work and workers. As she questions the stereotyped generalizations she receives, we become as involved in the process of learning as she is. It is artistically unfortunate, to be sure, that Mrs. Trollope found it necessary to abandon this method of development in favor of the more typical—and more tedious—propagandizing, through Mr. Bell's responses in chapter xix. But it is to her credit that, at least for a time, Frances Trollope saw, recognized, and attempted to resolve the artistic difficulties inherent in the sub-genre she chose.

—Roger P. Wallins, "Mrs. Trollope's Artistic Dilemma in *Michael Armstrong*," *Ariel* 8, No. 1 (January 1977), 9–10, 13–14

HELEN HEINEMAN

After four novels peopled by lifeless aristocrats (*The Refugee, The Abbess, Tremordyn Cliff, A Romance of Vienna,*) and two serious exposés of "repulsive" subjects (*Whitlaw, The Vicar*), in December 1838, Mrs. Trollope entered the popular field of the literature of roguery with *The Widow Barnaby*. ⟨. . .⟩

But in the early Victorian period, coaching, sporting, gambling, cheating, hunting, adventuring, and living by one's wits had been the material of male writers about male characters, who used their sketches to reinforce a masculine sense of unlimited freedom and dominance. Dickens used the form, as did Borrow, Hook, Marryat, Mayhew, and Thackeray. The few women picaras were always minor characters, in most cases low types and gypsies, the best of whom usually repented at the end. Contemporary standards did not permit a woman at the center of a tale of roguery. It would be an unedifying spectacle for a female to rove the world in search of her fortunes and fair game. With the widow Barnaby, Mrs. Trollope created the feminine picaresque, a lady ready to pack her trunks of a moment's notice, one who enjoyed herself immensely while exploring and exploiting life's possibilities for a middle-aged woman.

In this, Mrs. Trollope diverged from the stereotyped heroines of the day, these "suffering angels," in Thackeray's telling phrase, "pale, pious, pulmonary, crossed in love, of course," and added a new dimension to the treatment of women in fiction. Far from being wilting or spiritual, the widow Barnaby was, in one reviewer's words, "showy, strong-willed, supple-tongued, audacious, garrulous, affected, tawdry, lynx-eyed, indomitable in her scheming, and colossal in her selfishness—*Was für cine Frau* is the widow Barnaby."

Mrs. Trollope's successful portrayal of this new kind of heroine greatly impressed her generation. Even Thackeray once confessed: "I do not care to read ladies' novels, except those of Mesdames Gore and Trollope." Some ten years after the widow's appearance, he brought out his own great version in the wily Becky Sharp. ⟨. . .⟩

Mrs. Trollope found the faults, foibles, vulgarities, and vagaries of her widow both amusing and deeply congenial to her writing talents. Her earlier fiction had drawn praise for its satiric portrayals of minor low-life characters, whom reviewers had found more in her line than noble heroes and heroines. Martha Barnaby was gossipy, vain, complacent, pretentious, and vulgar, a social-climber of epic proportions, and a compendium of all the worst middle-class vices. But in addition, Mrs. Trollope clearly gave this favorite character not only a large dose of her own ebullient personality but also some obviously autobiographical touches. The widow was always able to pick herself up after losses, dropping unsuccessful ventures without undue regrets and moving on to the next scheme. A woman whose horizons seemed endlessly expanding, she cheerfully endured a whole host of transplantings and radiated, in spite of her faults, a special brand of *joie de vivre*. In the greatest of her swindles, the widow even decided to pose as an authoress with plans to make money by writing a best-selling travel book on the United States!

Mrs. Trollope enjoyed her heroine so much that she brought her back in two sequels, which allowed ample opportunity to develop situations well suited to her talents. This willingness to repeat a well-beloved character in succeeding novels was later exploited even more successfully by her son Anthony. ⟨. . .⟩

All the Barnaby books were immensely popular. The second and third were illustrated by two of the most prominent artists of the time, R. N. Buss and John Leech. But while enjoying the books, reviewers hardly seemed to know what to do with the heroine. The *Spectator* considered the first Barnaby novel an advance "much beyond her previous fiction" and found the widow merely supplying "the broad humour," while the love-distresses of her young niece provided "the interest of the piece as a novel." Apparently the reviewer was uncomfortable with the idea that a fat, middle-aged widow with inflated hopes, calculations, and vulgar airs could constitute the true heroine of a Victorian novel. And the *Athenaeum*, while favorable toward the chief character, reassured the reader that there was nothing to be feared from this latest of Mrs. Trollope's fictions, for "Affection and Good-Fortune, and Justice . . . bring to confusion Selfishness and vulgar Pretension." Yet the widow triumphs in the end, rising above her difficulties to begin a new career. The reviewer was clearly interpreting the book according to the convention that fiction should teach and be elevating, and the widow offered no healthy example to young ladies clustering around the fireplace to hear father read aloud. Mrs. Trollope is making fun in this novel of the idea that a heroine can offer an example. No reader dared take the widow as model, but there was enjoyment to be gained in watching her exploits and adventures.

    —Helen Heineman, *Mrs. Trollope: The Triumphant Feminine in the Nineteenth Century* (Athens: Ohio University Press, 1979), 157–59, 167

Susan S. Kissel

Frances Trollope's works, printed and reprinted despite the attacks and outcries of numerous reviewers, revealed the popularity of the satirist's "moral imperative" with its insistent demand that injustices be exposed, surfaces be examined, and society's "hidden moral disorder" be set right. It was Frances Trollope who—before Dickens—not only exhibited an intense satiric concern with society's problems but also suggested, as would Dickens, that the cure for society's ills "reside[d] in some relation with the female sex." In an age where the public world was dominated by the male, and the spiritual world, through Puritanism, had taken on "the most masculine form that Christianity has yet assumed," Frances Trollope was to posit possible relief and redemption through the feminization of society. Her fiction's structural paradigm suggests that the future of civilization rests on the shoulders not of youth, nor of all woman-kind, but on the shoulders of bright, *young* women, her secular heroines. Over and over she repeats a pattern which insists on the saving power and moral influence of the youthful heroine in setting aright and balancing anew a corrupt and tottering world. In doing so, Frances Trollope displayed an acute interest in the future of humanity, significant insight into the causes and effects of human injustice, and psychological understanding foreshadowing a number of contemporary theorists. ⟨. . .⟩

Much less preoccupied with dress, with fashion, with public appearance and social convention than the women who would guide them, Frances Trollope's heroines look for truth in a world of deceit and corruption, attempting to act with intelligence, honesty, and fairness towards others. Through education and experience, Trollope insists, women can develop the knowledge of themselves and of the world that has made men too "tough" for deceitful manipulators such as Mr. Cartwright in *The Vicar of Wrexhill*. But Trollope's heroines are androgynous figures in whom a feminine feeling for others, human connectedness, love and care, remain combined with a sharp intellect and a tenacious will. For Frances Trollope, "that mixed expression of feeling and intelligence . . . makes the perfection of woman" (*RA*, 1: 271). For, as with Charles Dickens, Frances Trollope, too, portrayed the counterbalancing influence of the female in society as the cure for the maladies of the nineteenth century. Frances Trollope's heroines, however, are mature, adult women (despite their youth)—unlike Charles Dickens' "most distinctive heroines, Nell, Florence, Agnes, and Dorrit—the little mothers—and a good many others, [who] are in one degree or another children." Dickens' child-mothers, constant, nurturing, selfless angels of the home, offer succor and warmth to battered males who seek shelter there. Trollope's heroines, on the other hand, are shown to be worldly-wise and venturesome; they are the daughters, companions, or adversaries of men who can look those same men eye to eye and engage them idea for idea. Without such self-development, Frances Trollope suggests, her heroines would be virtually useless to themselves or to others. Without knowledge of the human evils and human possibilities at work in the world, Trollope implies, her heroines would become helpless victims, foolish parrots, or ignorant perpetrators of evil themselves—women who would very much resemble so many of their female elders in her fiction. In her heroines Frances Trollope celebrates women as active, achieving, altruistic adults—not symbols of child-like innocence or home-bound naivete whose only role is to provide themselves and others escape from a corrupt and troubled world.

No one knew this kind of "new" woman better than Frances Trollope. It was such a woman as this, a Scottish woman fifteen years her junior, who had changed Frances Trollope's own life so dramatically. Before setting forth to America, Frances Trollope was to describe her to her friend, Julia Garnett Pertz: "Never was there I am persuaded such a being as Fanny Wright—no never—and I am not the only one who thinks so. Some of my friends declare that if worship may be offered, it must be to her—that she is at once all that women should be—and something more than woman ever was—and I know not what beside." ⟨. . .⟩

Frances Trollope, stereotyped for more than a century as a "conservative," in reality advocated deep-seated social reform. Long after her relationship with her own young, spiritual guide, Frances Wright, had faltered and come to an end, Frances Trollope continued to imagine fictional heroines who could confront corrupt male authority figures, set out into the world to redress wrongs, and alter the future of civilization, becoming what Frances Wright had been for her, "all that women should be—and something more than woman ever was—and I know not what beside."

—Susan S. Kissel, "'What Shall Become of Us All?': Frances Trollope's Sense of the Future," *Studies in the Novel* 20, No. 2 (Summer 1988), 152–53, 160–61, 164

LINDA ABESS ELLIS

Mrs. Trollope's British audience had a vague notion that Americans were somehow rude and unsociable; she validates their prejudices by showing concrete instances of such behavior. Her American characters, in their primitive, child-like way, reveal a full range of stereotypic faults. They speak a debased form of English, are excessively proud of a dangerous form of government, are obsessed with making money (to the exclusion of more refined activities), have no sense of decorum at the dinner table, and take excessive interest in affairs that by British standards should be private. ⟨. . .⟩

Conversely, Mrs. Trollope's British characters tend to be refined and intelligent, sharing her readers' values. Most of them have reached a level of sophistication unmatched in America. In *The Refugee in America*, however, they are not necessarily more virtuous than vulgar Americans, who are merely naughty, selfish, rude, gullible children whose limited social graces make social interaction an ordeal. In this, her first attempt to fictionalize her trip to America, she modeled her American characters on the stereotypes of travel accounts. She evidently felt more comfortable with British characters—

although they are as flat and predictable as the Americans, they represent a wider range of moral traits, from the virtuous to the villainous. ⟨. . .⟩

The mildly boorish behavior of these "native" (white) Americans seems worse, however, when contrasted with the gentleness and instinctive dignity of slaves and Indians. Acknowledging the public appetite for information about exotic peoples, Mrs. Trollope details their customs. Her Indians possess an innocent and passive version of English taste and sensibility in the face of their mistreatment, while the slaves, as dignified and uncorrupted as any eighteenth century "noble savage," have primitive powers which they use to confound their oppressors. A cooperative slave in *The Refugee in America*, speaking "like an oracle from its shrine," gives Caroline Gordon information about Dally's movements and helps the Gordons rescue Lord Darcy. Old Juno of *Jonathan Jefferson Whitlaw*, the most fully developed of Mrs. Trollope's slave characters, is fully in touch with primitive emotions and uses her knowledge to exert a measure of control over Dart and Whitlaw "by playing upon the terrors which ever lie crouching in the mind of a bad man." Her tactics succeed. Although Whitlaw claims to despise her, he is intimidated by "her mockings and mysteries." He believes himself "in the power of a hateful sorceress, leagued with the devil, and in some sort his vicegerent here on earth" ⟨. . .⟩

The primitive wisdom Mrs. Trollope attributes to the slaves is matched by her portrayal of Indians as gentle, loving, wise, and noble creatures. Her narrator describes Watawanga of *The Old World and the New* as possessing "that touching look of gentleness so remarkable in the Red Indian." Most of Mrs. Trollope's English characters, repelled by boorish Americans, find the Indians fascinating. Like travel writers, however, they see the Indians more as artifacts than as persons. ⟨. . .⟩

The characteristics Mrs. Trollope ascribes to Americans convey a sense that she, like the typical travel writer, is studying an alien society. Most Americans represent types easily recognized by British readers, and they serve as a reminder of British superiority to the backwards children across the ocean. They also serve as a reminder of the dangers, for Britain, of the democratic system as practiced in the United States. Mrs. Trollope excuses lapses in propriety by placing the blame on a barbarian society which shapes the behavior of its citizens. The Americans' disorderly conduct, more apparent in the earlier novels, represents the dangers inherent in an egalitarian society where individuals have no respect for rank or position. Often, however, this disorderliness is merely annoying; only in her treatment of slavery in *Jonathan Jefferson Whitlaw* does Mrs. Trollope present it as evil. Her more gentle treatment of the Americans than that of the usual travel account reveals a less vengeful attitude towards the Americans than a superficial reading of these novels would suggest. She condemns, not the unfortunates condemned to live under democratic institutions, but the institutions themselves, which have made life unbearable, both for the visitors and for the virtuous natives. In the first three American novels, admirable American characters either die or leave the country. The slave system, or, to be precise, the Lynch Law, is literally responsible for Edward's death. Although Emily successfully challenges her Uncle Wilson's authority and exposes his murderous plot, she finds her true home in England. Lucy, Phebe, Caesar, Annie Beauchamp, and Geraldine Reynolds settle in Europe as well. The American system cannot accommodate virtue.

—Linda Abess Ellis, *Frances Trollope's America: Four Novels* (New York: Peter Lang, 1993), 78–79, 88–89, 95

MARILYN BUTTON

Trollope's influence on the Victorian English reading public was accomplished in part because of her choice of subjects. She was motivated at the beginning of her career by crushing financial and personal pressures to write gothic romances and light satire, but anger directed at religious hypocrisy, social injustices (including English factory conditions and American slavery), and the inferior status accorded to women throughout Europe and America soon directed her to the subjects for her best fiction. Mrs. Trollope's fourth novel was the first of several to address pressing social concerns. Based on experiences that Mrs. Trollope had recorded in her American travel journal, *The Life and Adventures of Jonathan Jefferson Whitlaw; or, Scenes from the Mississippi* (1836) attacks the American institution of slavery at the same time that it capitalizes both on Trollope's feminist stance and on her strident anti-American bias. Appearing fifteen years before the publication of Harriet Beecher Stowe's *Uncle Tom's Cabin* (1851) and more than six months before Richard Hildreth's fictionalized autobiography entitled *The White Slave, or Memoirs of Archy Moore* (1836), Trollope's novel was the first work of fiction published in England to address the problem of slavery in the United States. As such, it was part of an important body of antislavery propaganda which reached its peak in England between 1779–1838 and which was in large part responsible for the success of the movement in its various phases. By addressing the atrocities of American slavery, Trollope broadened her audience and the social impact of her work; by maintaining the author's personal focus on the lives of women, the novel furthered Trollope's vision of the role which women could and should play in American social and cultural life. Because of this blend of feminist and abolitionist concerns in the text, the novel marked both an important development in Trollope's literary career and a significant contribution to the history of the English novel (Heineman 143). ⟨. . .⟩

The picture which Frances Trollope gives of life in the American South is chillingly graphic, and though she may have offended the more prudish Victorian readers by her realism, she appealed to others because of her serious social intent, her empathetic characters, and the vivid evocation of suicide, murder, attempted rape, and racial prejudice. Whitlaw is assassinated by Juno for his cruelty to slaves; Edward Bligh, Lucy's brother, is murdered by a lynch mob for his abolitionist activities; and Juno's beautiful descendent Selina commits suicide rather than suffer the social ostracism that is her fate as a quadroon. Mrs. Trollope's awareness of the many social repercussions of slavery thus parallels the concerns of English antislavery propaganda. Abolishing slavery was but the first step in a long struggle to deal with the social unrest and human displacement that were the legacies of this practice.

As in her first novel, Trollope portrays American women in *Whitlaw* as both oppressed victims and triumphant manipulators of circumstance. Here, however, the source of oppression is most clearly linked to the institution of slavery rather than to other prevailing cultural norms, and the women who triumph, like Juno, Lucy, and Phoebe, are those who work to end its influence. Significantly, their success is a result of both individual and collective effort directed against a firmly entrenched racist patriarchy.

—Marilyn Button, "Reclaiming Mrs. Frances Trollope: British Abolitionist and Feminist'" *CLA Journal* 38, no. 1 (September 1994), 69–70, 84

THERESA RANSOM

The Life and Adventures of Michael Armstrong, the Factory Boy, is a powerful book which first appeared in February 1839, in one shilling monthly instalments. Few women writers had their work published in this way, but it was to ensure that the book would reach the maximum number of readers. Dickens' *Oliver Twist* had appeared in this form in the previous year, and, in the same manner that Dickens had exposed the grim corruption of children in London, Fanny Trollope exposed the exploitation and slavery of the factory children in the cotton mills of the north. ⟨. . .⟩

Fanny researched her project thoroughly. She attended meetings in the chapels and listened to the preaching of the reformers. She also visited the slums to see the degradation and filth of the wretched workers. ⟨. . .⟩

Fanny and her party managed to visit the cotton mills by pretending to be idle travellers, 'anxious to see all objects of curiosity, particularly the factories, which were, as they observed, so famous throughout all the world'.

In the story, Michael Armstrong, a nine-year-old factory boy, was adopted by the mill owner, Sir Mathew Dowling, in a sentimental gesture to impress a lady, after Michael had rescued her from the menaces of a very ancient cow.

Sir Mathew publicly announced his action throughout the district, to divert attention from the deplorable conditions in the mill. He was a boorish sadist, who quickly tired of the pretence, and then decided to get rid of the boy by apprenticing him to a remote mill run as a slave camp, and employing unwanted pauper children who were, literally, worked to death. One of Hervieu's stark illustrations showed the starving boys scrambling to steal pig-swill from a trough. A Miss Brotherton, one of Fanny Trollope's independent heroines, heard of Michael's disappearance and set off, unsuccessfully, to find him. Eventually Michael, after ten years of hard labour and many trials, escaped from his overseers and was reunited with his crippled brother and Miss Brotherton. ⟨. . .⟩

Through the telling of Michael's own experiences, and the search by Miss Brotherton, Fanny was able to paint a graphic and shocking picture of life in the textile factories and the mill villages. Her purpose was to awaken the national conscience. However, contemporary society found the facts hard to accept. They wanted to believe that this story was an exaggeration; that parents were only exploiting their children by sending them to work in the mills; children were only beaten because they were lazy; and that Christian teaching would help them to accept the hardships. ⟨. . .⟩

Once again the majority of critics were enraged. They liked their women writers to be feminine and gentle. Jane Austen and Mary Russell Mitford, both of whom wrote of village life, were lauded as good examples. Mrs. Trollope was an agitator; coarse, vulgar, unfeminine, and, potentially dangerous.

The *Athenaeum* accused her of 'scattering firebrands among the people' and asked her to remember 'that the most probable immediate effect of her pennings and pencillings will be the burning of factories'.

The *New Monthly Magazine*, however, saw the work differently:

> This striking and forcible tale improves on the reader at every step. Nothing can be more fearfully, yet touchingly true, than some of the descriptions. . . . Those will grievously mistake the design of this work who look to it for nothing beyond the mere amusement of an idle hour. It seeks at once to impress a deep moral lesson, and to work a great social change, and we are greatly mistaken if it do not ultimately effect its purpose.

The 'social change' did eventually come eight years later, in 1847, when the Factory Act was passed forbidding the employment of any child under eight in the textile mills.

—Theresa Ransom, *Fanny Trollope: A Remarkable Life* (New York: St. Martin's Press, 1995), 127–31

BIBLIOGRAPHY

Domestic Manners of the Americans (2 vols.). 1832.

The Refugee in America (3 vols.). 1832.

The Mathers Manual. 1833.

The Abess: A Romance (3 vols.). 1833.

Belgium and Western Germany in 1833 (2 vols.). 1834.

Tremordyn Cliff. 1835.

Paris and the Parisians. 1836.

Jonathan Jefferson Whitlaw. 1836.

The Refugee in America. 1836.

The Vicar of Wrexhill. 1837.

Vienna and the Austrians. 1838.

The Widow Barnaby. 1839

Michael Armstrong, The Factory Boy. 1839.

The Widow Married (3 vols.). 1840.

One Fault: A Novel (3 vols.). 1840.

Charles Chesterfield; or, The Adventures Of A Youth Of Genius. 1841.

The Blue Belles of England (3 vols.). 1842.

A Visit to Italy (3 vols.). 1842.

The Barnabys in America; or, The Adventures of the Widow Wedded. 1843.

Jessie Phillips, A Tale of the Present Day. 1843.

Hargreave; or, The Adventures of a Man of Fashion (3 vols.). 1843.

The Laurringtons; or, Superior People (3 vols.). 1844.

Young Love: A Novel (3 vols.). 1844.

The Lottery of Marriage. 1846.

The Robertses on Their Travels. 1846

Father Eustace, A Tale of the Jesuits. 1847.

The Three Cousins (3 vols.). 1847.

Town and Country: A Novel (3 vols.). 1848.

The Young Countess. 1848.

The Old World and the New: A Novel (3 vols.). 1849.

Petticoat Government: A Novel. (3 vols.). 1850.

Mrs. Mathews; or, Family Mysteries (3 vols.). 1851.

Second Love; or, Beauty and Intellect: A Novel (3 vols.). 1851.

Uncle Walter, A Novel. 1852.

The Young Heiress: A Novel (3 vols.). 1853.

The Life and Adventures of a Clever Woman. 1854.

Fashionable Life; or, Paris and London. 1856.

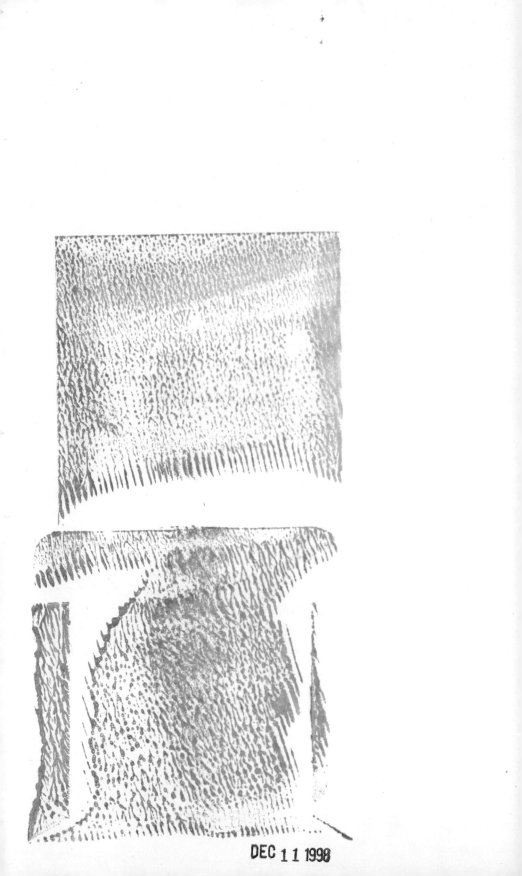

DEC 1 1 1998